Financial
Security

for
dummies®
A Wiley Brand

Financial Security

by Eric Tyson, MBA
Author of *Personal Finance For Dummies*

Financial Security For Dummies®

Published by:
John Wiley & Sons, Inc.
111 River Street
Hoboken, NJ 07030-5774
www.wiley.com

Copyright © 2022 by Eric Tyson.

Published by John Wiley & Sons, Inc., Hoboken, New Jersey

Published simultaneously in Canada

For general information on our other products and services, please contact our Customer Care Department within the U.S. at 877-762-2974, outside the U.S. at 317-572-3993, or fax 317-572-4002. For technical support, please visit https://hub.wiley.com/community/support/dummies.

Wiley publishes in a variety of print and electronic formats and by print-on-demand. Some material included with standard print versions of this book may not be included in e-books or in print-on-demand. If this book refers to media such as a CD or DVD that is not included in the version you purchased, you may download this material at http://booksupport.wiley.com. For more information about Wiley products, visit www.wiley.com.

Library of Congress Control Number: 2021946586

ISBN 978-1-119-78078-6 (pbk); ISBN 978-1-119-78079-3 (ebk); ISBN 978-1-119-78080-9 (ebk)

SKY10030131_092721

Contents at a Glance

Table of Contents

Introduction

Welcome to *Financial Security For Dummies!*

I know from my work as a personal financial counselor and educator that many Americans lack a sufficient background in the financial basics. My first book in this series, *Personal Finance For Dummies*, sought to address and help close that gap, and the feedback from that book suggests it clearly has helped.

I've seen over time, though, that folks who know many of the basics can still suffer financially at important junctures and when hit by unexpected events. So, this new book, *Financial Security For Dummies*, is like an advanced version of or a sequel to *Personal Finance For Dummies*.

About This Book

Most people value financial security and stability, of course, unless they like danger, risk, and turmoil! Living within your means, saving and investing in wise, proven investments, and securing catastrophic insurance are all keys to sound personal financial management.

Unfortunately, your financial security can be undermined by things outside of your control. Upsetting events can include macro-events like the COVID-19 pandemic (2020) or financial crisis (2008) as well as individual life changes or personal crises, such as job loss, divorce, caring for elderly parents, and so on. Part 1 addresses these two major types of crises or catalysts.

You may find that at some point, you need to access funds in the event of a crisis. It should give you peace of mind to know that there are ways to get help. Part 2 looks at all crises (economic and personal) and discusses safety nets that people can tap and emergency measures they can implement.

You may be looking to navigate the barrage of information coming at you while an economic crisis is in motion. Part 3 contains content that is central to the book and vital for you to understand as you deal with turbulent times.

To maintain financial stability, you need to keep your financial house in order. Part 4 identifies the key personal finance tasks and steps to take to maximize your future financial security and minimize problems when disruptions inevitably occur.

What does the future hold? No one knows for sure, but there are ways to be prepared. Part 5 delves into discerning what pundits may be telling you about current and future economic issues and finding out how to keep yourself and your finances on track when things look gloomy. It also touches on what future crises may be in store and how to keep your cool.

Foolish Assumptions

Whenever I approach writing a book, I consider a particular audience for that book. Because of this, I must make some assumptions about who the readers are and what those readers are looking for. Here are a few assumptions I've made about you:

>> You want the best for you and yours and would like to make the most of your money. While you understand there are no guarantees, you'd like to best prepare your financial situation to weather a wide range of adverse conditions.

>> You'd like to gain a better understanding about how the financial markets and economy work so you can intelligently process news and information that hits, especially in the midst of a crisis.

>> You'd like to be positioned to be able to invest at least some of your money when otherwise attractive investments have declined in value.

If any of these descriptions hits home for you, you've come to the right place.

Icons Used in This Book

Throughout this book, you can find friendly and useful icons to enhance your reading pleasure and to note specific types of information. Here's what each icon means:

TIP

This icon points out something that can save you time, headaches, money, or all of the above!

WARNING

With this information, I try to direct you away from blunders and mistakes that others have made when making important personal finance and related decisions.

TECHNICAL STUFF

Here I point out potentially interesting but nonessential stuff.

TRUE STORY

Look for this icon to find real-life examples to help exemplify a point.

INVESTIGATE

I use this icon to highlight when you should look into something on your own or with the assistance of a professional.

REMEMBER

This icon flags concepts and facts that I want to ensure you remember as you make personal finance decisions.

Beyond the Book

In addition to the material in the print or e-book you're reading right now, this product also comes with some access-anywhere info on the web. Go to www.dummies.com and type in "Financial Security For Dummies Cheat Sheet" in the search box to discover a list of pointers that can help you keep your finances safe.

Where to Go from Here

If you have the time and desire, I encourage you to read this book in its entirety. It provides you with a detailed picture of how to best ensure your financial security. But you may also choose to read selected portions. That's one of the great things (among many) about *For Dummies* books. You can readily pick and choose the information you read based on your individual needs. Just scan the table of contents or index for the topics that interest you the most.

1

Understanding Financial Security

Discover what financial security means.

Understand how the economy works and learn from past historical incidents and downturns.

Be prepared to navigate unexpected crises. Life is unpredictable; find ways to weather the storm.

Chapter **1**

Navigating the (Bumpy) Road to Financial Independence

Achieving financial independence and feeling financially secure are admittedly subjective assessments. A nest egg of $200,000 may seem like a lot to some people but not to a high-income earner who is accustomed to spending $100,000+ annually.

Now, for many people the feeling of financial security isn't simply a matter of how much money you have to your name. Numerous other factors may contribute to feeling secure financially, which I help you to understand.

In my work as a financial counselor and educator, I've also seen people for whom having a certain level of wealth to feel secure is a moving target. And those targets tend to keep getting bigger and bigger over time once a given lower targeted amount has been achieved.

In this overview chapter, I walk you through determining what financial security means to you, assessing where you are now, and helping you think through what you need to do to accomplish your goals. I also survey the landscape of crises, both personal and in the broader economy, which you should be prepared to handle. Finally, I discuss how to best position yourself to benefit from the inevitable opportunities that present themselves during tough economic times.

Reaching for Financial Security

A good place to begin is by defining what financial security means to you and what is and isn't important to you. Then I help you think through and understand where you are now and what you may need to do to accomplish your goals.

Defining what you value

If saving money is a good habit, the more you save, the better, right? Well, no, not really, unless your sole goal is to amass as much money in various accounts as possible. But what if you're not spending enough to eat a healthy diet? How about some time and money so that you can regularly rest and enjoy some recreation? What about some spending for the special people in your life?

Think about all the big decisions in your life: choosing and finding a job, a place to live, a spouse, and so on. For most people, there's a financial component to all of these. When thinking about personal goals, nearly all of them take money to accomplish. Money is inextricably linked to the rest of your life. Making the best financial decisions starts with the big picture and the rest of your life in mind — in other words, holistically.

Suppose like many people, you are working and earning money. You'd like to save and invest some of that and not have to continue working full-time for the rest of your life. But you probably have some other competing uses for your money. These may include things like saving to buy a home or start a business, expenses for your family, a future vacation, and so forth.

Money shares some similarities with food. If you don't have enough, you likely notice the insufficiency of your resources. Having more than enough with some reserves and extras usually provides most people with some peace of mind. Different people, though, have different views of how much extra they may want to have.

The virtue of a capitalistic economy is that within reason, if you're willing to work hard and seek to improve yourself and your work, over time you should be able to see your money grow. The progress and advancement of technology and society generally increase the purchasing power of your money over time.

Some folks lose sight of the differences between necessities and luxuries, especially in affluent and upper-middle class communities and circles. We can always find people with bigger homes and more expensive cars who have taken more exotic vacations. The bar can continually be set higher and higher in terms of how much money we "need."

The continual improvement of products and services, particularly those that incorporate a lot of technology, leads to more folks taking for granted how "luxurious" some of today's choices are compared with those of the past. Consider what's happened with personal computers and smartphones. Today, consumers buy smartphones that have many of the same functionalities and can access far more information than personal computers could a generation or two ago. And you can buy today's smartphones for less than the cost of personal computers from a generation or two ago. Today's smartphones are like a handheld personal computer, a phone (that can easily travel with you), and a quality camera all rolled into one!

Automobiles have far more features, especially safety features like air bags and anti-lock brakes, compared to those from a generation or two ago. Today's cars are dramatically more fuel efficient too.

Just walk through most homes and apartments today and you'll find all sorts of devices like microwave ovens, printers, HDTVs, washers and dryers, dishwashers, and so on, which are far better and relatively less costly than in prior generations. And in some cases, these devices didn't exist or weren't widespread not that many generations ago.

So, I urge you to step back and think about what it is that you value and to recognize how "luxurious" are so many of the choices and options that we have in modern American society. With many products and services, we get far more for our money than did folks a generation or two ago.

That said, we can all think of some expense categories like higher education, housing in some higher-demand cities (such as New York City and San Francisco) and portions of the healthcare industry where the rate of price increases (inflation) may exceed increases in typical wages and the general cost of living. These categories are the exception, not the rule, and you can take steps and actions to mitigate and blunt some or even much of the excessive price increases through the strategies I discuss in this book.

REMEMBER

Especially in our consumption-oriented society, some folks may get carried away with working and earning more and amassing more money. Life is short, and you can't take your money with you in the end. So, there's something to be said for balancing work, earning and saving money, and having sufficient time for family, friends, and your activities and hobbies.

Assessing where you are

What's your current personal financial health? There are numerous ways to measure that. When I've worked with clients as a financial counselor and as an educator, I've found the following exercises to be valuable:

>> **Net worth analysis:** Your ability to accomplish important financial goals, such as buying a home and someday retiring from full-time work, depends upon your net worth. To derive your net worth, you total up your financial assets and subtract your financial liabilities. I typically exclude a person's home in this analysis unless they plan to tap some portion of their home's equity, by trading down to a lower-priced property.

>> **Spending analysis:** You should know where your money goes in a typical month or year, especially if you'd like to save a greater portion of your employment income. Analyzing your historic spending can tell you just that.

>> **Saving analysis:** Over the past year, what portion of your work income were you able to save? Many people don't know the answer to that important question, and if you don't, you can't really know whether you're on track to accomplish your financial and personal goals.

>> **Your investment portfolio:** Can your investment portfolio be improved? Do you understand your current investments? How do your current holdings stack up in terms of costs/fees and performance within their respective peer groups? Do your current investment holdings match your risk and return preferences?

>> **Your home:** If you currently rent or own a home but are looking to sell and buy another, that takes some advance planning and analysis. Since housing costs can consume a significant portion of your income and budget, you should ensure that a change in your housing situation fits with your financial and personal goals and planning.

>> **Insurance review:** You should have insurance to protect you against losses that could be financially catastrophic to you and your loved ones. I know from my counseling work that many folks have gaps in their insurance coverage and are wasting money on overpriced or unnecessary policy features.

>> **Employee benefits review:** Plenty of employees don't bother to read and review their employee benefits, which typically include various insurance coverages and possibly a retirement savings plan. Employee benefits can actually be quite valuable and should be coordinated with your overall financial plan.

These elements form a personal financial plan. You can hire a competent and ethical financial planner to assemble such a plan for you, but you should beware that many folks sell products on commission or charge hefty ongoing money management fees. Others aren't interested or experienced enough to help you with nuts-and-bolts issues like analyzing your spending. See Part 4 for more details on getting your personal finance house in order.

Grasping financial lingo and trends

Personal financial knowledge and literacy is an enormous obstacle for too many people, including those who have invested tremendous time, energy, and money into their formal educations. Unfortunately, such education rarely includes the vital topic of personal finance.

Ubiquitous gurus are another common obstacle. Everywhere you look, especially online and in the media, there are plenty of anointed experts predicting what will supposedly happen with the economy, financial markets, and all sorts of other economic variables. Listening to all these supposed experts and their often-conflicting opinions can paralyze you or make you feel that you need to hire them (or others like them) to manage your money since it appears that they know so much more than you do.

TIP

In reality, it's important that you develop a personal financial plan of action that suits your goals, needs, and concerns and doesn't involve jumping into and out of investments based upon short-term noise or news events.

Trying not to avoid money

One big obstacle is that just about everybody avoids dealing with some aspect of money. For some, it's as simple as avoiding looking regularly at their checking account and verifying transactions and the account balance or making decisions about where to invest saved money. Others neglect needed insurance coverage, perhaps out of fear of confronting their own mortality and vulnerabilities. Some people are plagued by broader problems such as feelings of guilt and shame about money or feeling that money seems dirty and evil.

The fact that money-related issues aren't always at the top of your priority list may well be a good sign. Perhaps you spent the past weekend with friends and family or were engrossed in a captivating book or newly discovered streaming series. But continually avoiding money or some aspect of your finances can result in unnecessary long-term pain.

Some personal finance procrastinators can get away with their ways for a number of years. However, whether it's in the short term or the long term, eventually, problems do occur from avoiding dealing with money and related decisions, and sometimes the damage can be catastrophic.

Some money avoiders don't plan ahead and save toward future goals. Often, the reality hits home when they contact the Social Security Administration (SSA) or get an update from the SSA and discover what monthly retirement benefit amount they'll get at full retirement age (which is around age 66 to 67 for most people). The reality for many people means the realization that they'll have to continue working into their seventies in order to maintain the modest standard of living to which they've become accustomed.

Several issues typically cause a lack of retirement funds. Many money avoiders could save more money, but they typically aren't motivated and organized enough to do so. Generally, they haven't bothered to conduct even basic retirement analysis to understand how much they should be saving to reach their retirement goal (or even think about if and when they want to retire).

Because money avoiders dislike dealing with money, what they're able to save often gets ignored and languishes in low- or no-interest bank accounts. Avoiders also tend to fall prey to the worst salespeople, who push them into mediocre or poor investments with high fees. When avoiders choose their own investments, they often do so based on superficial research and analysis, which can lead to piling money into frothy investments when they're popular. Discomfort causes avoiders to bail out when things look bleak.

WARNING

Money avoiders, more often than not, lack wills and other legal documents that should specify to whom various assets shall pass and who is responsible for what (for example, administering the estate and raising minor children) in the event of their untimely demise. When money is to pass to heirs through an estate, the absence of documents can lead to major legal and family battles.

Making use of insurance: A necessary evil

Because insurance is an admittedly dreadful and unpalatable topic for most people, many folks avoid insurance-related issues. And while well-intentioned and commission-hungry insurance agents get some people to plug insurance gaps, these salespeople may not direct you to a policy best suited to your needs. In fact, brokers may sell you costly insurance (such as cash value life insurance) that provides them with a higher commission and you with less insurance than you need.

Insurance gaps come to light when a disability or a protracted illness occurs. Too often, we believe that these problems only happen to elderly people, but they don't. In fact, statistically, you are far more likely to miss work for an extended period of time due to a disability or lengthy illness than you are to pass away prematurely.

If others are dependent upon you financially, you likely need certain coverages that would provide for them in the event of your untimely passing. The following table shows the mortality rate for various age ranges and how the rate of course increases with age. You can see that while just 1 percent of those people between the ages of 25 and 34 pass away each decade, the portion approximately doubles with each passing decade. While 1 in 100 is a relatively small probability, it's a much greater probability than winning your local mega-millions jackpot. Nearly 1 in every 25 people passes away during the decade between the ages of 45 and 54.

Age	Percent of People Passing Away (During Decade)
25–34	1.0%
35–44	2.0%
45–54	4.3%
55–64	9.6%
65–74	23.5%
75–84	55.8%

If you're interested, you can check out the *Journal of the American Medical Association's* research that shows how older people can determine a more accurate personal risk factor based upon personal characteristics: jamanetwork.com/journals/jama/fullarticle/1660374.

Coping with Crises

Having a plan and a strategy is all well and good, until something happens that upsets that plan. And, sooner or later, something will create some, or a lot of, havoc in your life. Parts 2 and 5 go into more detail on how to deal with difficult situations.

Everyone faces challenges, obstacles, and setbacks

From the outside, it appears that some folks lead charmed lives. But trust me when I say that everyone faces challenges and problems — and I mean everyone. I know because as a financial counselor, people have shared with me intimate details of their lives.

Notwithstanding the tendency for some folks to share details of their private lives on social media, the reality is that most folks more freely broadcast their good fortunes. Negative events like job losses, divorce, a family member with an addiction, and so on, generally, not so much!

Of course, if you earn more money and have more money saved and invested, you've theoretically got more room for error. But, as you may know, those people earning more often have more expenses and commitments and can lose their money fairly quickly when their circumstances change.

Common crisis

Economies go through cycles. Good times and periods of growth and more jobs are inevitably followed by downturns and times when more people lose their jobs or face reduced salaries.

The COVID-19 pandemic and government-mandated shutdowns in 2020 quickly threw millions of people out of work, especially in the travel, retail, and restaurant businesses. Stocks cratered and suffered one of their steepest declines in modern history. The stress level was palpable.

The 2008 financial crisis was another period where lots of people lost their jobs, and stocks and real estate prices suffered large declines in most areas. Economic problems unfolded over multiple years, and the recovery was slow.

Over the generations, there have been plenty of other economic and financial crises. I discuss those and what can be learned from them in Chapter 2.

In addition to crises in the broader economy or society, plenty of people are hit with a personal or household-specific crisis. These can include things such as:

» Job loss or reduced employment income

» Medical problems

» Caring for an elderly relative

» Divorce

» Death of a spouse

I cover these in Chapter 3.

Making Decisions Based on Changing Circumstances

When broader economic and financial crises strike, for sure bad things happen. Some people lose their jobs. Stock prices and home values generally fall. This can create opportunities for those who have cash and courage to step up and buy otherwise good investments at depressed prices.

Having a good-size cash reserve for difficult times makes sense. But how large should that reserve be? If you keep too much in cash, your investment returns will suffer. Keeping too little in cash can cause your reserves to be pinched during tough times and can leave you with little, if anything, to invest when investment prices are down.

Most people with some cash find it hard to step up and make investments while the news is filled with so much gloom. And there's the natural tendency to worry about things getting even worse. In Part 3, I explain how to make sense of the economic and other data to determine when it may make sense to step in.

Chapter **2**

Understanding Capitalism and Economic Downturns

Many folks don't know about or understand the range of economic and political systems that exist around the world. That's unfortunate because if everyone better understood this, more folks would appreciate how great the capitalistic system is in the United States.

No economic system is perfect, of course, and no economic system can sustain growth forever without downturns and some problems. In this chapter, I help you to better understand our economic system and the inevitable cycles of growth and downturns, which can sometimes include more severe recessions and financial crises.

In fact, I'm going to take you on a tour of some of the worst economic periods and crises during our nation's history. Rest assured that I'm not trying to scare you or inhibit your desire to invest in stocks, real estate, or other growth assets. I'm actually taking this approach to maximize your ability and determination to stay the course during tough times and possibly even deploy available resources to buy/invest when prices are down.

Understanding Our Economic System

The United States has altered the course of human history, in a positive way, far more than would be expected considering the relatively short period of human history during which it has existed. No, it hasn't had a perfect record, but at least it has literally torn itself apart (the Civil War) and put itself back together again trying to right its own wrongs.

The post-Civil War United States has used its power to secure more freedom and prosperity for more people than ever in the history of the world, making it possible for them to pursue and achieve the fullness of their human potential. That's why people from all over the world want to come to and live in America.

In this section, I discuss the achievements and strengths of the U.S.'s capitalistic system as well as some concerns that have been raised about it.

Capitalism strengths and criticism

The original 13 American colonies are a good illustration of the origins of governments and economies. The leaders of the individual colonies elected to *federate* — to enter into a contract to coexist as one nation — in substantial part to provide for their common defense, but defense wasn't the only reason they federated. They federated also because they knew that each individual colony would be far more likely to survive and succeed if they cooperated, not only in their mutual defense, but also with regards to infrastructure, such as making it possible for their citizens, goods, and mail to travel easily between them and making it easy to transact trade using a common currency.

Since its inception, the United States of America has afforded its citizens the best environment in the history of humankind in which to achieve the fullness of their human potential. This requires high degrees of both personal and economic freedom, and the United States provides these through a democratic government, with strong protections for individuals, and through capitalism, which promotes competition between individuals and rewards the development of unique potential.

REMEMBER

There's no way for any society to guarantee that every member's every need will be met every day. Capitalism is, far and away, the best way to guarantee the highest standard of living to the greatest number of people within a society. Capitalism accomplishes this by

>> Empowering the vast majority of its members to be at least productive enough to meet their (and their dependents') subsistence needs

>> Empowering many members to be productive enough not only to meet subsistence needs but also to compassionately contribute to meeting the subsistence needs of the relatively few truly incapable members.

Consider that the United States, in just a couple of centuries, surpassed the standards of living of every other nation on Earth, including nations that had existed for hundreds, even thousands, of years prior. Capitalism did that.

Any other nation in human history that has achieved power comparable to that of the United States in today's world — a lone "superpower" — has used that power to take freedom away from people, to conquer, and thereby to stifle the development of unique human potential. For most of human history in fact, most human beings have lived in conditions wherein whoever was physically stronger (individually or collectively) largely determined how much of their potential the collectively weaker groups/societies could develop.

Comparing socialism to capitalism

Just about anyone who was raised in America doesn't know how bad it can get economically in other systems because they simply haven't experienced them. When it comes to quality of life for folks near the top, the middle, and near the bottom, capitalism is the best economic system.

That's not anywhere near the case in countries like Greece that embrace socialism. Greece has the level of government involvement, federal programs, and widespread labor unions that progressives/socialists constantly argue for, and that is precisely what drove the country into default and wrecked their economy.

As recently as 2013, Greece's unemployment rate hit a whopping 27.9 percent and was still more than 15 percent in mid-2021. Think about what a train wreck of an economy that is. And their stock market has been even uglier. From its peak in 1999, the Athens Stock Exchange General Index is still down more than 86 percent as of mid-2021.

Younger Americans, however, have come to believe that socialism is as good as or better than capitalism. According to Gallup,

> "Since 2010, young adults' positive ratings of socialism have hovered near 50 percent, while the rate has been consistently near 34 percent for Gen Xers and near 30 percent for baby boomers/traditionalists. At the same time, since 2010, young adults' overall opinion of capitalism has deteriorated to the point that capitalism and socialism are tied in popularity among this age group. This pattern was first observed in 2018 and remains the case today."

The more a person understands how the economy and financial markets work, the more likely they are to identify with and support free-market capitalism with a minimal role for government. I firmly believe, based upon many years now of observation and business world experience, that the increasing numbers of socialist-loving (and capitalist-hating) young adults in America are economically illiterate.

Understanding wealth and income inequality

Over recent years, there has been more and more discussion about the unequal distribution of income and wealth in America. Self-declared Socialist Senator Bernie Sanders (Vermont) has made income and wealth inequality a focal point of his efforts.

In a speech that Sanders delivered at Liberty University, he said:

> "In the United States of America today, there is massive injustice in terms of income and wealth inequality. Injustice is rampant. We live, and I hope all of you know this, in the wealthiest country in the history of the world. But most Americans don't know that. Because almost all of that wealth and income is going to the top 1 percent . . .

> " . . . we are living in a time where a handful of people have wealth beyond compre-hension. And I'm talking about tens of billions of dollars, enough to support their families for thousands of years. With huge yachts, and jet planes, and tens of billions. More money than they would ever know what to do with. But at that very same moment, there are millions of people in our country, let alone the rest of the world, who are struggling to feed their families. They are struggling to put a roof over their heads, and some of them are sleeping out on the streets. They are struggling to find money in order to go to a doctor when they are sick . . .

> "And while the very, very rich become much richer, millions of families have no savings at all. Nothing in the bank. And they worry every single day that if their car breaks down, they cannot get to work, and if they cannot get to work, they lose their jobs. And if they lose their jobs, they do not feed their family. In the last two years, 15 people saw a $170 billion increase in their wealth; 45 million Americans live in poverty. That in my view is not justice. That is a rigged economy, designed by the wealthiest people in this country to benefit the wealthiest people in this country at the expense of everybody else."

Senator Sanders has held such views throughout his more than four decades of being a Vermont-based politician. He is severely misguided, most likely because he doesn't fundamentally understand how the U.S. economy and the private sec-tor work. Sanders has never worked in the private sector nor done anything besides politics.

Here are my thoughts and responses to the points he makes in his speech:

» The "top" 1, 10, or 20 percent is not a fixed group of individuals. The notion that income keeps flowing and wealth is accumulating the most for a fixed group of individuals is simply wrong. Think about people you know (perhaps including yourself) who earned varying amounts of money at various points in their lives. Consider pro athletes who, if they "really make it," can earn millions per year. However, before that happens, they can endure many years of low and unremarkable wages. And the few who end up earning large sums only do so for a limited number of years. This pattern happens in other industries.

» Flawed income and wealth disparity measures don't take into account government money transfers. Income disparity measures fail to count government programs such as food stamps and Medicaid and the value of those benefits to individuals and households. The same is true for monthly Social Security benefits, pensions, and so on. Earned but not yet tapped monthly benefits can easily be worth hundreds of thousands to millions of dollars, yet these earned benefits are ignored in measures of supposed income and wealth disparity.

» Sanders fails to mention unequal distribution of taxes paid. According to the Tax Foundation, the top 1 percent of income earners earned 21 percent of all income and paid a whopping 39 percent of all individual income taxes. By contrast, the bottom 50 percent of income earners paid just 3 percent of federal income taxes. No federal income tax at all is paid by 45 percent of all Americans.

» Sanders completely omits any discussion of donations, especially those given by the super wealthy. Studies of wealth inequality ignore the fact that the wealthy, and especially the very wealthy, donate large portions of their wealth to charities. Sanders is correct that some Americans have tens of billions of dollars — far more money than they and their families could ever use. But these same super wealthy people give away large amounts of their wealth. So, much of the wealthiest folks' assets end up benefiting and helping those at the lower end of the wealth and income spectrum.

» Wealthy folks who don't give away their assets during their lifetimes get whacked with hefty estate taxes. Under current federal law, only $11.7 million can be passed to heirs free of estate tax, and amounts above this are taxed at about 40 percent. Also, the wealthy are greatly limited on how much they can give away during their lifetimes to family; they're limited to $15,000 per person per year.

» It's absurd and inaccurate to say that the economy is designed and rigged by the wealthiest to benefit themselves. In a free-market capitalist economy, small-business owners and entrepreneurs and employees at successful companies have the opportunity for upward mobility. What actually stands in the way of this economic freedom are too many laws and regulations that unequally burden small companies. Larger companies have the staff and resources to comply with such government-imposed rules more easily.

>> Calls for high minimum wages harm the very people such laws were supposedly designed to help. To redress income inequality, Sanders, among others, advocates a much higher minimum wage. Sanders has long sought a $15 minimum wage, which is about double the current level in many states and the federal minimum wage. However, local governments that have significantly increased the minimum wage have (not surprisingly) discovered that it creates more unemployment among entry-level workers. This makes sense because it gives businesses even more incentive to automate and minimize the number of workers.

On April 27, 2021, President Biden imposed a $15 minimum wage by Executive Order for federal contractors. The order requires federal agencies to incorporate a $15 minimum wage in all contract solicitations starting January 30, 2022. Agencies will have to implement the higher wage in new contracts by March 30, 2022.

Globalization increases the opportunity for companies and the wealth they can capture because of the bigger markets for their goods. So the entrepreneurs and shareholders of such companies share in the upside of these firms. The stock market allows investors of all economic means to share in the growth and upside of companies.

Fostering an environment that encourages business is the best way to create more and better-paying jobs. Competition for workers and a shortage of workers drives up wages! Misguided socialist policies would stifle and penalize creativity and investment, and corporations would flee the United States.

History of growth and downturns

Over the long term, the U.S. economy has averaged approximately 3 percent annualized real (after inflation) growth. This rate of growth has slowed to closer to 2 percent annually on average in more recent decades.

This long-term track record for growth in the U.S. economy has been great news for workers, as it has helped to keep the historic unemployment rate low. And the purchasing power of workers' wages has increased over the decades and generations. Consider for a moment how many people have smartphones today, which are more powerful and a fraction of the cost of the first generations of personal computers.

Furthermore, the long-term growth of the U.S. economy helps to explain the terrific long-term returns from U.S. stocks. Over the past two-plus centuries, U.S. stocks have averaged annualized returns of about 9 percent, or about 6 to 7 percent after inflation.

Now, the 2 to 3 percent annualized real (after inflation) growth rate of the U.S. economy should not be interpreted to mean that the U.S. economy grows every year and at a reasonably steady rate because it doesn't! That's the long-term average annual growth rate, which includes some down periods — when the economy is actually shrinking — and includes some faster growth periods, which typically happen coming out of an economic downturn. See Table 2-1 for the year-by-year growth rates of the U.S. economy since 1970.

TABLE 2-1:

Annual GDP Change for the United States

Date	GDP Growth (%)
2020	–3.5%
2019	2.2%
2018	3.0%
2017	2.3%
2016	1.7%
2015	3.1%
2014	2.5%
2013	1.8%
2012	2.2%
2011	1.6%
2010	2.6%
2009	–2.5%
2008	–0.1%
2007	1.9%
2006	2.9%
2005	3.5%
2004	3.8%
2003	2.9%

(continued)

TABLE 2-1 *(continued)*

Date	GDP Growth (%)
2002	1.7%
2001	1.0%
2000	4.1%
1999	4.8%
1998	4.5%
1997	4.4%
1996	3.8%
1995	2.7%
1994	4.0%
1993	2.8%
1992	3.5%
1991	−0.1%
1990	1.9%
1989	3.7%
1988	4.2%
1987	3.5%
1986	3.5%
1985	4.2%
1984	7.2%
1983	4.6%
1982	−1.8%
1981	2.5%
1980	−0.3%
1979	3.2%
1978	5.5%
1977	4.6%
1976	5.4%
1975	−0.2%

Date	GDP Growth (%)
1974	−0.5%
1973	5.6%
1972	5.3%
1971	3.3%
1970	0.2%

The National Bureau of Economic Research (NBER), a private nonprofit research organization which came into existence in 1920, has documented U.S. economic activity back to 1802. Through 2021, the NBER data show that the United States has experienced 48 recessions — or about one per five years.

While their definition is a bit more complicated, a *recession* is generally defined by two consecutive quarters of declining real gross domestic output. (NBER uses a more detailed definition, which looks for a decline in employment, industrial production, real personal income, real manufacturing, and trade sales.)

Touring Past Crises: What Happened and Why

When a major crisis hits — for example, the 2008 financial crisis, the 2020 COVID-19 pandemic, the 2001 terrorist attacks, and prolonged recession — unexpected things happen. And if you're one of the millions of people adversely affected, stress and emotions can add to the financial quandaries and problems you face. Each crisis is unique and impacts the economy and individuals personally in differing ways.

Past experience and the "school of hard knocks" can certainly improve how well you react to each such event. But you can prepare for and better manage through especially challenging times by examining such past episodes.

Why pilot training has relevance for your tour . . .

What I'm suggesting is a similar type of training that commercial airline pilots go through on flight simulators. Consider that you wouldn't want a pilot encountering an unusual event (for example, dual engine failure requiring a water landing) for the first time in a real flight with hundreds of passengers on board a jumbo jet! All those US Airways passengers onboard Captain Sullenberger's jet were grateful that he and his copilot had extensive training and knew what possible options to quickly consider when their plane's twin engines shut down after striking a flock of geese soon after takeoff from LaGuardia Airport in New York City.

This book aims to provide you with the training and historic perspective so that you are well prepared to deal with and navigate a wide range of personal financial challenges. When an unexpected crisis occurs, our biological wiring causes our fear reaction to kick in, which can cause more problems.

Keeping calm and keeping perspective are vital. Knowing how prior crises have unfolded and gotten resolved can help. Also, there are opportunities to benefit from lower prices on investments like stocks, real estate, and small business at such times, but many people aren't financially or emotionally positioned to do so.

When a crisis unfolds, I don't need to tell you that it's "breaking news." Nearly everyone consumes some news and media coverage, whether through traditional outlets (such as radio and television) or through newer platforms (such as social media, blogs, podcasts, and so forth). I can tell you from thousands of personal observations that the economic coverage and biases of those outlets can and will get in the way of you making the best personal financial decisions. And so too can your own biases and beliefs, especially if you follow politics and identify reasonably strongly with candidates from a particular political party or ideology.

The Panic of 1907

You probably didn't know or realize it at the time, but the 2008 financial crisis actually shared numerous parallels with the so-called Panic of 1907. And, the 1907 panic was similar to other financial panics, bank runs, and bank failures that came before it. Such episodes were reasonably common as the government-operated Federal Deposit Insurance Corporation (FDIC) insurance system for banks didn't come into existence until 1933. There was also no other federal oversight or backstop for banks, like the Federal Reserve, which didn't exist in 1907 (but came out of this crisis).

According to a Federal Reserve Bank of Boston review of the Panic of 1907 and other panics:

> "Some were more severe than others, but most followed the same general pattern. The misfortunes of a prominent speculator would undermine public confidence in the financial system. Panic-stricken investors would then scramble to cut their losses. And because it wasn't uncommon for speculators to double as bank officials, worried depositors would rush to withdraw their money from any bank

associated with a troubled speculator. If a beleaguered bank couldn't meet its depositors' demands for cash, panic would quickly spread to other banks . . . many Americans suffered sudden and dramatic reversals of fortune when a panic struck. Even in a relatively mild panic, fortunes evaporated, and lives ended in ruin."

In 1907, numerous important countries in the world's economy had a banking crisis. Problems began in the United States. and then spread to Denmark, France, Italy, Japan, Sweden, Chile, and Mexico. Some trust companies, which were quasi-banking institutions that had reserves on hand of only 5 percent of their obligations, became insolvent when their lending to copper companies led to losses when copper prices dropped.

In April 1906, the great San Francisco earthquake squeezed insurers and caused them to liquidate large portions of their financial holdings — stocks and bonds. Also in 1906, the Interstate Commerce Commission, which was the first U.S. regulatory agency (created in 1887), began price regulations on the economically important railroads. That and the resulting collapse in railroad stock prices contributed to the financial crisis.

U.S. stock prices got hammered, dropping by nearly half (49 percent) during this tumultuous economic two-year period from early 1906 to late 1907. Trust company and bank failures continued until banker John Pierpont Morgan (whose firm today is known as J.P. Morgan) put up his own money and enlisted other prominent New York bankers to do the same. The need for a banker of "last resort" led to the creation of the Federal Reserve System and their fulfilling that need (when properly engaged) during future such events. However, the Federal Reserve made some major mistakes during the Great Depression (discussed in the next section), so the Federal Reserve was very much a work in progress in the aftermath of its creation following the Panic of 1907.

Stock prices fully recovered from the 1906–1907 period decline by mid-1909. It's also worth noting that although the words "panic" and "crisis" are used to describe the economy and stock market of this period, the rate of the stock market decline was typical for a bear market. While the 49 percent stock market decline was among the larger bear markets, it played out over 22 months so there was really no "panic," and the rate of decline was about 2.2 percent a month on average over the entire period.

The Great Depression

The economic calamity that lasted a full decade (most of the 1930s) is known as the Great Depression. It was characterized by high unemployment, falling prices (deflation), collapsing stock prices, and mostly inept and wrong government responses.

The stock market crash of this period happened globally. The price declines actually began in Europe in 1928 the year before the U.S. stock market peaked in late 1929. Most European stock markets were down by about 15 percent by the time the U.S. market was peaking. From its peak in 1929 to the bottom in 1932, the U.S. stock market dropped a bone-rattling 89 percent.

The roaring '20s that preceded the Great Depression was a decade of a strong and expanding economy. U.S. stock prices advanced nearly 500 percent, marking the greatest bull market in U.S. market history, from their 1921 lows to their late 1929 peak. Over this period, the Dow Jones Industrial Average advanced from about 64 to 381.

Many factors led to the economic and financial market disaster known as the Great Depression:

>> The record run in stock prices was fueled in part by easy credit conditions for buying stock with borrowed money — known as *margin loans*. Investors were able to buy stock by putting up only 10 percent of the cost via their own money and borrowing up to 90 percent. Having just a 10 percent equity stake left little margin for a big decline in stock prices, which led to *margin calls* — forced selling of stock holdings which accelerated the decline once started.

>> The Federal Reserve raised interest rates in 1928–1929 to curb speculation in the financial markets. "This action slowed economic activity in the United States. Because the international gold standard linked interest rates and monetary policies among participating nations, the Fed's actions triggered recessions in nations around the globe," according to the St. Louis Federal Reserve. To rein in speculative buying of stocks, the Fed should have raised the stock margin purchase requirement from its low level of 10 percent (note that today it is at 50 percent).

>> The Smoot-Hawley Tariff Act passed by Congress and signed into law in 1930 led to a trade war which depressed global trade. The United States slapped 20 percent tariffs on imports to the United States, which set off retaliatory tariffs by many other countries.

>> Economic problems and falling stock prices led to depressed consumer confidence and a run on banks. The Federal Reserve failed to step in and act as the lender of last resort, and the resulting bank failures contributed to the further downward economic spiral.

>> The Federal Reserve allowed the nation's money supply to drop 30 percent, which led to an equivalent, deflationary price decline. With all of the previously mentioned economic problems, the Fed added to the misery by allowing the

nation's money supply to shrink 30 percent from 1930 to 1933, which led to an approximate 30 percent deflationary decline in prices. This deflation had the impact of increasing the burden of debt among those who owed money and further harmed the overall economy.

In addition to the stock market being crushed, the unemployment rate in the United States stayed above 10 percent for more than a decade — from 1931 through 1941. In fact, it hit a high of 25 percent in 1933 and was above 20 percent for four straight years around that time.

Over time, economists and others have come to realize how the government's response caused and greatly worsened the Great Depression. Furthermore, reforms coming out of this period led to the Federal Reserve becoming a "modern central bank" and lender of last resort.

World War II

Many folks believe that wars are bad for the financial markets and economy, but often they are not. For sure, unforeseen negative events like the attacks on Pearl Harbor (December 7, 1941) can cause a short-term decline/shock. But coming out of the Great Depression and the high unemployment rate of that period, World War II led to increased demands for various manufactures and other products needed for the wartime efforts. Hiring and output soared, and unemployment quickly declined to less than 2 percent.

Stock prices were reasonably stable during this period, rising about 30 percent over six years. After an initial modest rally following the outbreak of the war, an excess corporate profits tax enacted by Congress squashed the stock market upswing. The attack on Pearl Harbor triggered a near 10 percent decline. Stocks then resumed their rally when the Allies began to get the upper hand.

Coming out of World War II, the U.S. government had a huge debt load. This led the government and Federal Reserve to keep interest rates low in the years following the war to help service the large U.S. government debt. Keeping rates low hurt bondholders who were stuck receiving low interest rates, and when rates finally did rise, bond prices dropped, reducing bondholders' returns through declining bond market values.

Arab oil embargo and Watergate/Nixon's resignation

As a young teenager, I first began my investing experiences back in the mid-1970s when my father was laid off from his job and was handed a modest balance that he had to direct. Back then the Dow Jones Industrial Average was vacillating between 800 and 1,000 if you can believe that!

I remember 1974 well. That time period made a major impression on me. Stocks got hammered and experienced a waterfall decline as they did during the height of the 2008 financial crisis. From a peak of 1,000 in late 1973, the Dow plunged under 600 by the late summer of 1974. The country and economy had many problems. Folks were highly disillusioned with government after Vice President Agnew resigned (due to an income tax evasion scandal) and then so did President Richard Nixon (due to Watergate).

There was a war raging in the Middle East, and oil supplies were being cut off due to the Arab Oil Embargo (drivers back then remember the long lines at gas stations). Inflation was surging and broke 10 percent annually. The unemployment rate was surging to 9 percent.

The 1970s was a bad period for stocks and the economy. President Nixon instituted wage and price controls and oversaw a sagging economy with rising inflation. After Nixon resigned and his vice president, Gerald Ford, took over, he ended up losing the next presidential election to Jimmy Carter, who continued many of the same problematic economic policies of the Nixon years.

With rising and stubbornly high inflation, the Federal Reserve finally raised interest rates to double-digit levels to stop the cycle. Those actions, combined with the pro-growth economic policies of President Ronald Reagan, who was elected in 1980, finally ushered in a sustained period of lower inflation, lower interest rates, consistently strong economic growth, lower unemployment, and rising stock prices.

9/11 terrorist attacks and recession

Generally speaking, the 1990s were a good decade for the U.S. economy and financial markets. The economy grew briskly after a brief recession early in the decade, unemployment trended down, and stock prices enjoyed one of the greatest bull runs ever. And this came on the heels of the largely good 1980s.

Interest rates and inflation trended lower, and by the end of the decade, the federal government was actually enjoying a budget surplus — imagine that! A strong economy produced booming tax revenues, and believe it or not, the Congress showed restraint in their spending.

By the late 1990s, however, warning signs began accumulating. Stock prices, especially in the increasingly popular internet and technology sector, reached frothy levels. Companies with no profits and little revenue were going public and being bid up.

In the final 18 months leading up to its peak in early 2000, the tech-heavy Nasdaq index rose more than 300 percent and the price-earnings ratio of the stocks in the index exceeded 100! A book published in 1999, *Dow 36,000* by James Glassman and Kevin Hassett (published by Crown Business), said that stocks should overall be triple their then current (inflated) valuations. (These authors might finally be right about the Dow level more than two decades later!)

The rise of cheap online trading lured in novice and naïve investors and also encouraged more frequent trading. This period saw the rise of day traders who jumped in and out of particular stocks, sometimes holding a stock for mere hours. Not surprisingly, studies have found that increased trading leads to reduced returns.

As the dot-com bubble began to unravel and the collapse of internet and technology stock prices and companies began to spill over into the broader economy, a recession began to unfold. And then the 9/11 terrorist attacks happened in late 2001, and that further undermined consumer confidence and the economy. A number of high-profile corporate accounting scandals — for example, Enron and WorldCom — also hit investors and their confidence.

The bear market in the early 2000s was a big one, especially in the technology and internet space. Check out the declines of these U.S. stock market indexes:

>> Dow Jones Industrial Average: 39 percent

>> S&P 500: 49 percent

>> Nasdaq: 78 percent

>> Dot-com Index: 95 percent

2008 financial crisis

With the United States winning the war on terrorism and companies hiring again and corporate profits snapping back, stock prices rebounded and hit new highs in late 2006 and into 2007. Unfortunately, not many years into its recovery, the economy was about to hit even rougher times and a more severe crisis.

The real estate sector had continued to do well in most parts of the country through the prior recession and in the aftermath of the terror attacks. Lenders were encouraged and incentivized to make loans to increasingly risky borrowers — that is, borrowers with little to no down payment and/or mediocre credit scores and reports. These higher-risk mortgages were known as sub-prime mortgages — *sub-prime* refers to the borrowers having below prime credit reputations. Despite sub-prime mortgages' obviously higher risk during a real estate market downturn, major credit rating agencies handed out AAA ratings on these risky securities, which fostered the appetite for them among financial institutions.

Sub-prime mortgages and other real estate–related securities ended up on the balance sheets of important and often highly leveraged financial institutions, including investment banks, commercial banks, insurers, and so on. When real estate prices began falling in many parts of the United States in 2006, 2007, and into 2008, the value of these sub-prime mortgages got crushed, and that dragged down the financial institutions that owned lots of them. This led to bankruptcies (such as American Home Mortgage, IndyMac, Lehman Brothers, and New Century) and the merger of failing firms into stronger firms (for example, Countrywide Financial and Merrill Lynch were bought by Bank of America; Bear Stearns was bought by J.P. Morgan). Numerous banks and other financial institutions received emergency government loans to stay afloat.

As layoffs began to mount and home values fell, consumers increasingly felt squeezed and reduced their spending, which added to the economic slide. Lenders hit with real estate–related loan losses pulled back on other lending. Unemployment eventually reached 10 percent, the highest rate since the early 1980s recession.

From its late-2007 peak to its early-2009 bottom, stocks suffered their worst bear market since the Great Depression with the Dow Jones Industrial Average dropping 55 percent.

2020 COVID-19 Pandemic

As a student of economic and financial market history and having followed the same in real time for decades, I never thought I had seen or understood it all because while history may sometimes rhyme, it doesn't exactly repeat. So when the COVID-19 pandemic in early 2020 quickly morphed into government-mandated economic shutdowns, things began to change quickly in the economy and financial markets. This was new territory for me and just about everyone else.

DR. PHIL DECLARED A FINANCIAL 9-1-1 IN LATE 2008

At the height of the 2008 financial crisis and plunging stock prices in late 2008, television psychologist Dr. Phil ran an unprecedented show focused on the economy which was entitled "Financial 9-1-1." If that weren't enough to scare most everyone, he made numerous dire predictions backed up by various pundits who declared that the U.S. financial system as we knew it would never be the same again. Retirement as a concept would be dead, and non-wealthy folks would be unable to get a mortgage.

The great tragedy in such hype is that this scared people out of the stock market at what turned out to be one of the best buying opportunities in many, many years. U.S. stock prices are up about 790 percent since then and foreign stocks about 360 percent!

Here are the predictions and comments made on this show (after which of each are my comments):

- **"I question whether retirement as a concept is even going to exist in ten years."** This sure seems like hyperbole to me! We've gotten through challenging times before, and we will again. Most retired folks don't rely on short-term stock market gains to finance their retirement.

- **"Pension plans are in 'big trouble' and plans are going to come up short due to the poor stock market."** Pension plans are well diversified (including in bonds and other investment vehicles) and have weathered challenging stock markets before. A poor return for one year or even several years won't upset diversified pension plans managed for the long term.

- **"We've got a hurricane here, and everyone's got a hole in the roof."** For sure, some folks were weathering tough times, but many people were not.

- **"It will be 'nearly impossible' to get a mortgage unless you're very wealthy and have excellent credit."** This is utter nonsense. While it was a bit harder to get a mortgage in the aftermath of the crisis, you didn't have to be wealthy to qualify for a home mortgage.

- **"Everyone has to 'stop spending now.'"** Making a blanket statement like this without qualifications is absurd. If you lack an adequate emergency reserve (three to six months' worth of living expenses) and are burdened with consumer debt, you should examine your spending and identify ways to reduce it.

As one of America's most widely followed popular psychologists, Dr. Phil reaches millions of people and can influence how they think about important issues. Unfortunately, I found the financial advice on his "Financial 911" program highly disappointing.

What started as "15 Days to Slow the Spread" turned into a multi-months-long — and in some portions of the country, a year-long plus — shutdown, which devastated many businesses that relied upon in-person activity. Especially hard hit were smaller businesses like restaurants, retail stores, and travel-related companies that were not set up to do business digitally.

Business activity fell greatly in March 2020 when the shutdowns began and continued into the spring months. Stock prices fell at an unprecedented rate. The Dow Jones Industrial Average suffered a 38 percent drop over a six-week period after peaking (at 29,568) in early February 2020 and bottoming out (at 18,213) in late March 2020.

The economic carnage happened quickly as well. After reaching a more than 50-year low at 3.5 percent in February 2020, the unemployment rate spiked to 14.8 percent just two months later. And while millions of laid-off workers were able to return to work within a few months, more continued to be laid off as the pain inflicted by the shutdowns continued and deepened in states with long shutdowns and more restrictions.

Handling one's emotions is always a challenge during a catastrophic event, and the pandemic certainly tested large numbers of people in that regard. In addition to the perceived danger people felt from the possibility of catching the virus and possibly dying, the 24/7 media coverage focused on every last thing that could go or was going wrong. For sure, much of the media made it appear (intentionally or not) that things were worse and more dire than they really were.

Many folks expressed surprise at the stock market quickly bouncing back in the spring and summer of 2020 despite the large number of people still out of work and the many businesses hurting. This episode, like many others, highlighted that the financial markets are always forward-looking. So, while many folks were still out of work and the virus was still spreading and killing, the economy was on the mend and expected to continue to improve. The development of therapeutics to treat the virus and the rapid development and approval of effective vaccines led stocks to hit new all-time highs in late 2020, less than a year after the shutdowns began.

Hopefully, time and effort will be taken to examine what measures were and were not effective so that in a future pandemic, we won't make as many mistakes.

Mistakes Made . . . and Lessons to Carry With You

We've been on a whirlwind tour of modern American economic and financial market history. Knowing what problems have occurred in the past and how things turned out after the fact can better help you to wisely navigate future similar problems and turmoil.

Emotionally, of course, it's somewhat easy to look back in hindsight at all of the problematic events we've reviewed in this chapter. So, let's recognize that we're all human and have emotions that can get the best of us and cause us to do the wrong things at the wrong times (such as panic and sell stocks after a major decline) when we're in the midst of a storm.

TRUE STORY

Everyone makes mistakes and has reasons for why they do what they do. Consider this amazing story about a southern California woman during the 2008 financial crisis as reported in an article in the *Orange County Register*:

> "Police went to Whole Foods where managers told them an elderly customer came in a few days earlier, hysterical after she realized she had mistakenly returned the box of crackers with her life savings inside. Frightened by the government takeover of several banks, the Lake Forest woman, whose identity was not released, had decided to take her money out of the bank and hide it in her home."

For sure, plenty of folks were worried about the safety of their money with the stock and real estate markets getting pummeled during the 2008 financial crisis. But folks worrying about the safety of keeping their money in the bank reflected irrational fear. If the FDIC government system backing up our banking system failed to protect bank account depositors, holding onto paper money, also issued by the U.S. federal government, wouldn't do you any good either.

Most folks can see the silliness and danger of keeping cash in a cracker box in your home. Cash kept in your home could be stolen, forgotten, or destroyed in a fire. Hearing stories like this can lull us into thinking that well, we would never do something so ill advised, yet many people make decisions and take actions that are nearly certain to lead to suboptimal or even terrible outcomes.

Consider some other detrimental financial moves I have seen people make during economic and financial market calamities:

>> **Selling stocks at greatly reduced/depressed prices:** When stocks are falling in value fast and the daily news is filled with gloomy headlines about job losses and other economic problems, I've seen plenty of otherwise intelligent

folks dump their stocks and buy bonds or simply sit on cash in a money market or bank account. Typically, during such episodes, bonds are in high demand (and thus at elevated prices) and offering reduced yields. Now, don't get me wrong — I understand the emotions behind this. No one enjoys feeling like they're going down with a sinking ship or part of the losing team. But selling stocks low and buying bonds high is the opposite of how smart investors make money. Otherwise, sound investments that are beaten down in price offer value. That's why smart long-term investors buy, not sell, stocks after they've fallen, and you should as well.

>> **Following supposed prognosticators who claim to have predicted all these bad things that have recently happened:** Fibbing and misrepresentation are rampant on social media platforms. And the mainstream media should really do a much better job vetting people they are giving airtime to. Sure, sometimes a pundit gets something right in the short term, but what about their longer-term track record and how accurate or not that was?

>> **Heeding misinformation and uninformed people on social media platforms and blogs:** For example, in response to a 2008 news report about housing prices dropping significantly from the prior year, consider this online posting, "Even if there were mortgages to be had, people have learned a valuable lesson from this housing bubble. No one in their right mind is buying now unless they're looking at at least a 50 percent discount . . . from today's prices!" If you were already stressed about challenging economic times, reading such gibberish would just make you more anxious. The reality was that there were plenty of mortgages being done then, and real estate prices weren't going to (and didn't) fall 50 percent from those depressed levels.

>> **Immersing yourself in excessive and negative short-term news:** When a crisis is unfolding, of course you're going to want to keep up with what's happening. The problem, however, comes from the fact that news (and opinions) come at us 24/7 now and so much of it is geared toward sensationalism and raising your anxieties to keep you tuned in. The "news" almost always focuses on the very short term and fails to provide a long-term perspective. The more you consume, the more stressed and depressed you are likely to become and the more likely you are to make emotionally based moves that are detrimental to your long-term interests.

>> **Listening to politicians.** Even when there isn't a crisis or major economic problem, many politicians make things sound dire, especially when the other party is in power/control or we're coming out of an event for which they blame the other side. In the fall of 2011, more than two years into the recovery from the severe recession/financial crisis of 2008, President Obama said in a broadcast White House roundtable discussion with journalists, "Obviously we're going through the worst financial crisis and recession since the Great Depression." I had to do a double take to make sure that this was

not recorded back in 2009 early in the president's first year in office! While the economic environment in the United States in late 2011 was far from strong and robust, we had been in recovery and enjoying modest economic growth the prior two years. Millions of jobs had come back, and corporate profits and stock prices were bouncing back. Also, the recessions the United States suffered in the mid-1970s and early 1980s featured even higher unemployment rates and much, much higher inflation and interest rates (10+ percent) than the 2008 downturn.

Here are some key lessons to take away from this chapter and keep in mind as you manage your money in the years ahead:

>> Hold onto your long-term investments like stocks and real estate during downturns. It's impossible to know how long and deep a downturn will be, and history has shown that prices can bounce back quickly, so you're not going to be able to time buying back well if you try to exit and miss a part of the decline.

>> Read and review news and other sources that help you maintain balance and a long-term perspective. This likely means limiting your diet of daily news and choosing your resources carefully.

>> Consider using extra cash to take advantage of depressed investing prices to buy more at favorable prices.

>> Don't beat yourself up for past mistakes. Everyone makes mistakes. Wise people learn from and grow from their mistakes.

Chapter **3**

Coping with Personal Crises

In Chapter 2, I discuss bigger-picture crises that happen in the overall economy or country. Unfortunately, those don't represent the totality of problematic events that can upset our lives. Personal crises happen too, and that's the important subject of this chapter.

Some of life's crises come unexpectedly, like earthquakes. Others you can see coming when they're still far off, as sometimes happens with a serious illness or a big storm moving in off the horizon. Whether a life change is predictable or not, your ability to navigate successfully through its challenges and adjust to new circumstances depends largely on your degree of preparedness.

To those who have stored no emergency rations in their basement, the big storm with high winds, downed trees, and associated power outages during a hot spell that traps you in your home can lead to problems. But to the prepared person with plenty of food and water (and a good generator), that same storm may mean a break from work and some unexpected downtime.

When a Crisis Comes Calling

In my work as a personal financial counselor and now over many years interacting with many readers, I've heard and seen a lot. I can tell you with great confidence that you can get through a crisis and come out on the other side even more confident and strong with proper preparation.

In this section, I discuss some common personal crises that you should be prepared to deal with. For each, I highlight keys to your personal and financial resilience.

Losing your job or a significant source of income

During your adult life, you'll almost surely change jobs, perhaps even several times a decade. I hope that most of the time you'll be changing by your own choice. But let's face it: Job security is not what it used to be. Downsizing has impacted even the most talented workers, and more industries are subjected to global competition.

In Chapter 2, I cover many economy-wide problems that lead to more widespread job losses. The government-mandated economic shutdowns in 2020 due to the COVID-19 pandemic is a recent example. Prior to that, millions of folks lost their jobs during the 2008 financial crises.

But even when the economy overall is doing really well, as it was for example in 2019 and into early 2020 when the unemployment rate fell to a 50-year low, more than 200,000 people each week in the United States were filing their initial claims for unemployment benefits. So, bad things can happen to good people even during good economic times.

Here then are my suggestions for dealing with the inevitable loss of your job someday or perhaps an unexpected reduction in income:

TIP

>> **Always be prepared to lose your job.** As the Boy/Girl Scout motto says, be prepared! Unless you're incredibly fortunate or lucky or both, you will someday unexpectedly lose your job and/or face a significant reduction in your employment income. No matter how happy you are in your current job, knowing that your world won't fall apart if you're not working tomorrow can give you an added sense of security and encourage openness to possibility.

All companies and organizations go through tough times and layoffs are always a possibility. You may believe you're irreplaceable, but unfortunately, the senior manager making job cut decisions doesn't think the way you do. You may indeed be highly valuable and even underpaid, but let's face it, bad things happen to good people because the people making decisions in organizations sometimes don't know what they're doing or make bad or politically motivated decisions.

>> **Structure your finances to afford an income dip.** Probably the area where I've seen more people get into trouble during the good times is to overspend on their housing expense. If you're really stretched buying a home with all the associated expenses, consider what you would do and how challenged you might be on a reduced income. Now, if you lose your job and are out of work, you can generally collect unemployment benefits, but in most states and areas, those benefits typically replace a modest portion of your prior employment income. The pumped-up and inflated benefits paid during the job losses of the COVID-19 pandemic are certainly not the norm.

>> **If you lose your job, batten down the hatches.** You normally get little advance warning when you lose your job through no choice of your own. It doesn't mean, however, that you can't do anything financially. Evaluating and slashing your current level of spending may be necessary. Everything should be fair game, from how much you spend on housing to how often you eat out to where you do your grocery shopping. Avoid at all costs the temptation to maintain your level of spending by accumulating consumer debt. See Chapter 9 for more info.

>> **Arrange to continue insurance coverage.** Most importantly, that can include insurance coverages such as health insurance and possibly disability insurance and life insurance. Replacing these on your own will cost money, of course, but going without them will expose you to potentially catastrophic financial risks. Please see Chapter 11 for more details.

>> **Evaluate the total financial picture when relocating.** Sometimes when folks lose their job, they may find better opportunities out of the area that either require a move or, if a remote position, may allow you to live any number of places. Don't call the moving company or pick your new home until you understand the financial consequences of the different options. In addition to evaluating the salary and benefits of a given job, you also need to compare the cost of living of given locations. You'll want to pay attention to housing costs, commuting, state income and property taxes, food, utilities, and all the other major expenditure categories that I discuss in Chapter 9. Check online for cost-of-living information and calculators such as BestPlaces.net.

LOOKING AT LOWER TAXES OWED

When your employment income drops, the one silver lining is that your federal and state income tax owed for the year will be lower. You may actually have effectively over-paid those taxes earlier in the year when you had your full employment income and income taxes were withheld and paid on your behalf presuming you would be employed for the whole year at your full employment income.

UNDERSTANDING THE RISKS OF SMALL BUSINESS

This chapter focuses on personal crises and challenges, so you may be perplexed over why I would be talking here about starting or running your own small business, which many people aspire to do. The reason is quite simple — running a small business has many challenges, both personally and financially. And while I'm an optimistic person, I'm also realistic and know from years of observations that minor small-business problems can mushroom into big problems in short order.

Here are some tips to help get you started and increase your chances for long-term success and minimize the chances for big problems:

- **Prepare to ditch your job.** To maximize your ability to save money, live as Spartan a lifestyle as you can while you're employed; you'll develop thrifty habits that'll help you weather the reduced income and increased expenditure period that comes with most small-business start-ups. You may also want to consider easing into your small business by working at it part-time in the beginning, with or without cutting back on your normal job.

- **Develop a business plan.** If you research and think through your business idea, not only will you reduce the likelihood of your business's failing and increase its success if it thrives, but you'll also feel more comfortable taking the entrepreneurial plunge. A good business plan describes in detail the business idea, the marketplace you'll compete in, your marketing plans, and expected revenue and expenses. Small Business Development Centers (http://AmericasSBDC.org), are located in each state with branches statewide to assist with business plans and multiple aspects of small business. They offer great services that are underutilized. And most have highly educated and trained staff. You've already paid for most of their services with your tax dollars. Business plan assistance, marketing, and social media training are offered at no fee. Seminars such as QuickBooks training are the most reasonably priced around.

- **Replace your insurance coverage.** Before you finally leave your job, get proper insurance. With health insurance, COBRA regulations require many employers to allow you to continue your existing coverage (at your own expense) for at least 18 months. According to the U.S. Department of Labor: "The law generally applies to all group health plans maintained by private-sector employers with 20 or more employees, or by state or local governments . . . In addition, many states have laws similar to COBRA, including those that apply to health insurers of employers with less than 20 employees (sometimes called mini-COBRA)." You can also shop for health insurance on your own and, depending upon your household income, may qualify for a reduced price (subsidized) policy. With disability insurance, secure coverage before you leave your job, so you have income to qualify for coverage. If you have life insurance through your employer, obtain new individual coverage as soon as you know you're going to leave your job. (See Chapter 11 for more details on insurance.)

- **Stay on top of your income tax obligations.** When you run your own business, it's 100 percent on you to make your income tax payments, which you're required to do through quarterly estimated tax payments. Equally importantly is to reserve and set aside that tax money so that you have it ready to use when the payments are due. I've seen too many small-business owners dig themselves into big financial holes and in the worst cases end up in financial ruin because they failed to plan for and make their quarterly estimated income tax payments.

- **Establish a retirement savings plan.** After your business starts making a profit, consider establishing a retirement savings plan such as a SEP-IRA. Such plans allow you to shelter up to 20 percent of your business income from federal and state taxation.

Facing a medical crisis

Our personal health is often taken for granted when things are fine, which thankfully for most people is nearly all the time. But a health challenge, typically unforeseen, can turn your life and emotions upside down.

To keep your sanity and to ensure your best health, here are some important steps to take and points to keep in mind:

>> **Check your coverage.** Make sure your health insurance coverage is being paid and in force. While insurance companies can't boot you from your coverage for a medical problem, you can lose your coverage if you haven't been paying for it. If your coverage has lapsed or you simply never bothered to get coverage thinking you wouldn't need it, get signed up pronto!

>> **Take time off from your job.** We have enough stressors in our lives even when all is good with our health. Adding the uncertainty of the possible paths of a medical problem can easily cause any normal person to feel overwhelmed. If you work for an employer, they may offer sick days and/or personal days.

Currently, there are no federal legal requirements for paid sick leave except for temporary COVID-19 paid leave law. More than a dozen states mandate some sick pay beyond temporary COVID-19 requirements. At the federal level, the Family and Medical Leave Act (FMLA) allows for up to 12 weeks of unpaid sick leave for either the employee or a member of their immediate family for particular medical conditions. "Employees are eligible to take FMLA leave if they have worked for their employer for at least 12 months and have worked for at least 1,250 hours over the previous 12 months, and work at a location where at least 50 employees are employed by the employer within 75 miles," according to the U.S. Department of Labor. For more on these and other safety nets, please see Chapter 4.

>> **Enlist and embrace support.** It can be difficult to be objective and calm when your health is on the line. Having a spouse, relative, or other close friend assist you with your research and serve as a sounding board for decisions can be useful and calming. When it's your health problem, dealing with important medical decisions can feel isolating and lonely, so finding a trusted person willing and able to share some of the burden and thinking can be invaluable. Just be sure that the person you're trusting will keep your information and situation confidential and that they understand what you're hoping to get from their involvement.

>> **Seek second opinions and do some research.** There is rarely just one clear-cut course of action to deal with a particular medical problem. Be sure you ask any medical provider what treatment options exist for your problem and their opinion of the pros and cons of each. Doctors are often rushed and may make you feel that you can't ask a lot of questions. If necessary, schedule another office visit or ask a time-constrained doctor when you can follow up with them by phone. Recognize that medical providers have conflicts of interest, make mistakes, and have imperfections.

You should also do some of your own research, but please understand the dangers of unvetted things you may read online that any person with a computer can choose to publish on a website. Check and vet your sources!

Caring for elderly parents unexpectedly

As your parents age, they may need help with a variety of issues and living tasks. An illness or accident such as a fall can be a triggering event. Although you probably won't have the time or ability to perform all the help your parent(s) may need, you may end up coordinating some service providers who will. Here are key issues to consider when unexpectedly needing to care for aging parents:

>> **Get involved in their healthcare.** Your aging parents may already have a lot on their minds, or they simply may not be able to coordinate and manage all the healthcare providers who are giving them medications and advice. Try, as best as you can, to be their advocate. Speak with their primary care doctor so you can understand their current medical condition, the need for various medications, and how to help coordinate caregivers. Visit home-care providers and nursing homes and speak with prospective care providers.

>> **Get help where possible.** In most communities, a variety of nonprofit organizations offer information and counseling to families who are caring for elderly parents. Numerous for-profit agencies can help with everything from simple cleaning and cooking to health checks and medication monitoring, to assisted living and health advocacy. You may be able to find your way to such resources through your state's department of insurance, as well as through recommendations from local senior centers, doctors, and other medical providers. You'll especially want to get assistance and information if your parents need some sort of home care, nursing home care, or assisted living arrangement.

>> **Take some time off.** Caring for an aging parent, particularly one who is having health problems, can be time-consuming and emotionally draining. Do your parents and yourself a favor by using some personal or vacation time to help get things in order. Also be sure to take care of yourself and give yourself some needed downtime and a real vacation from your obligations.

>> **Understand tax breaks.** If you're financially supporting your parents, you may be eligible for a number of tax credits and deductions for elder care. Some employers' flexible benefit plans allow you to put away money on a pretax basis to pay for the care of your parents. Also explore the dependent care tax credit, which you can take on your federal income tax Form 1040. And if you provide half or more of the support costs for your parents, you may be able to claim them as dependents on your tax return.

>> **Discuss getting the estate in order.** Parents don't like thinking about their demise, and they may feel awkward discussing this issue with their adult children. But opening a dialogue between you and your folks about such issues can be healthy in many ways. Not only does discussing wills, living wills, power of attorney, living trusts, and estate planning strategies make you aware of your folks' situation, but it can also improve their plans to both their benefit and yours.

Splitting from your spouse

In most marriages that are destined to split up, both parties usually recognize early warning signs. Sometimes, however, one spouse may surprise the other with an unexpected request for divorce. Whether the divorce is planned or unexpected, here are some important considerations regarding divorce:

>> **Question the divorce.** Some say that divorcing in America is too easy, and I tend to agree. Although some couples are indeed better off parting ways, others give up too easily, thinking that the grass is greener elsewhere, only to later discover that all lawns have weeds and crabgrass. Just as with lawns that aren't watered and fertilized, relationships can wither without nurturing. Money and disagreements over money are certainly contributing factors in marital unhappiness. Try talking things over, perhaps with a marital counselor.

>> **Separate your emotions from the financial issues.** Feelings of revenge may be common in some divorces, but they'll probably only help ensure that the attorneys get rich as you and your spouse butt heads. If you really want a divorce, work at doing it efficiently and harmoniously so you can get on with your lives and have more of your money to work with. The more spent on legal fees, the less will be left for you and your soon-to-be ex-spouse.

>> **Detail resources and priorities.** Draw up a list of all the assets and liabilities that you and your spouse have. Make sure you list all the financial facts, including investment account records and statements. After you know the whole picture, begin to think about what is and isn't important to you financially and otherwise.

>> **Educate yourself about personal finance and legal issues.** Divorce sometimes forces nonfinancially-oriented spouses to get a crash course in personal finance at a difficult emotional time. This book and others I've written, such as *Personal Finance For Dummies* (also published by Wiley) can help educate you financially. Peruse a bookstore and buy a good legal guide or two about divorce.

>> **Choose advisors carefully.** Odds are that you'll retain the services of one or more specialists to assist you with the myriad issues, negotiations, and concerns of your divorce. Legal, tax, and financial advisors can help, but make sure you recognize their limitations and conflicts of interest. The more complicated things become and the more you haggle with your spouse, the more attorneys, unfortunately, benefit financially. Don't use your divorce attorney for financial or tax advice — your lawyer probably knows no more than you do in these areas. Also, realize that you don't need an attorney to get divorced. A variety of books and kits can help you. Consider divorce by mediation. Research mediators in your area. Both parties have to agree they want to reach an agreement and are willing to work together to reach that

end. The amount of money that goes back to each party and the diminished stress, particularly on children, can be substantial.

>> **Analyze your spending.** Some divorcees find themselves financially squeezed in the early years following a divorce because two people living together in the same property can generally do so less expensively than two people living separately. Analyzing your spending needs pre-divorce can help you adjust to a new budget and negotiate a fairer settlement with your spouse.

>> **Review needed changes to your insurance.** If you're covered under your spouse's employer's insurance plan, make sure you get this coverage replaced. If you or your children will still be financially dependent on your spouse post-divorce, make sure the divorce agreement mandates life insurance coverage. See Chapter 11 for more about insurance. You should also revise your will.

>> **Revamp your retirement plan.** With changes to your income, expenses, assets, liabilities, and future needs, your retirement plan will surely need a post-divorce overhaul.

Coping with the death of a spouse

Of course, everyone ultimately passes away, and we all hope to live a long, healthy life and go peacefully into the night at a ripe old age. But medical problems, accidents, and other largely unpredictable events can cause an untimely death of a spouse or other important loved one.

I've worked with numerous people and had other friends who have dealt with this situation, and the challenges are numerous. Here are some things to consider:

>> **Take some mental health time off.** With the passing of a spouse, in addition to the loss of companionship, you are thrust into a new role and unchosen lifestyle. Think about all of the things that your partner took responsibility for in your household. Allow some time and space to grieve and to adjust to your new and unplanned role.

>> **Find someone to lean on.** It could be a relative, a friend, or both who can help you to cope with your new situation and be a sounding board. Just be sure that the person you're relying upon is trustworthy and without an agenda. A counselor or psychologist may be useful as well for a period of time. Check them out and interview at least two or three and beware of those who are prone to push continual and costly sessions as far as the eye can see. If religious, some organizations offer very reasonably priced six- to eight-week group sessions for support and guidance. One example is http://mournerspath.com. Check out your faith group for offerings.

>> **Move slowly with important decisions, especially financial ones.** You might consider selling your home, moving, making changes to investments, and so on. Any of those could be a reasonable thing to do with proper time, thinking, and research. But give yourself some time to adjust and process all that has happened and changed. You also want to be sure you aren't being pushed into making a decision by a salesperson or anyone else with a financial conflict of interest or some other agenda.

>> Know where everything is. In some couples, responsibility is shared for dealing with financial matters whereas with other couples, one person deals with everything. Regardless, each of you needs to know where everything (for example investment accounts, insurance policies, wills and estate documents, car titles, and so on) is located and dealt with.

Dealing with a natural disaster

Tornados, earthquakes, floods, and hurricanes — oh my!

Yes, if you live in the United States, you're likely at risk for one (or more) of these where you live. And even if you live in an area deemed at low risk for these types of natural disasters, unusual events that rarely happen may be your unfortunate fortune. Consider the good folks living in the normally warm southern states like Texas that got clobbered in early 2021 with harsh winter conditions complete with multiple snowstorms, below freezing temperatures for a full week, power outages, and more.

It had been decades since such extreme winter conditions hit the area and combined with the power outages, led to broken pipes and displaced homeowners and renters. Coming in the aftermath of the COVID-19 pandemic, it also hurt some small businesses.

During natural disasters, I've seen some people's lives turned upside down for many months or longer. Without adequate insurance (such as business interruption insurance), the financial consequences can be devastating. Even with insurance, folks can lose big financially, especially if the disaster disrupts or devastates their small business. Supply chain issues or customers unable to buy may bring some small businesses to a halt, and many small-business owners lack contingent business interruption insurance that may cover such problems.

If you're dealing with the aftermath of a natural disaster, of course, it's too late then to do anything about the insurance you didn't have, but there are many things you can do to deal with your situation:

>> **Ensure your personal safety first.** Frontline safety responders will tell you that it's often the case that there are more fatalities in the aftermath of some natural disasters than from the disaster itself. With hurricanes, for example, numerous victims die in the flooding that follows the storm. Long power outages lead to spikes in carbon monoxide deaths as people make mistakes in rigging up generators near their home or in their garage. Downed power lines have led to some folks being electrocuted. So, please be careful in the aftermath of a natural disaster and don't rush out to do things that can wait or take unnecessary risks like trying to drive through a water-covered roadway.

>> **Think outside the box if your small business is in trouble.** To survive and thrive as a small-business owner, you need to be resilient and flexible. Conditions change, and a disruption from a natural disaster can be upsetting. So, get creative about how to find and serve your customers when the landscape changes. Maybe if your customers can't come to you, you can go to them. Perhaps you can serve them through video calls/conferencing. We're all creatures of habit, and it can be hard to change the way we are accustomed to and prefer doing things.

>> **Take a hard look at your expenses.** If you're suddenly facing a period of reduced income due to natural disaster, take a fresh look at your spending and cut non-necessities as needed. You can always restart them, and you may well find that some providers will offer you better pricing if you're set to cancel due to short-term affordability issues. Don't cut needed catastrophic insurance coverage.

Scrutinize your small-business expenses in a similar fashion. Just be careful to not cut expenditures that could cut into sales, compromise the quality of your products or services, or leave you exposed insurance-wise.

>> **If you have insurance claims, be sure to document everything and be ready to negotiate and fight for what you're due.** Some insurance companies do the right thing, but too often, they will view your claim as a business expense and do what they can to minimize your payments.

Success Plans for Personal Crises and Life Changes

I apologize for spending so much time on negative events and crises in this chapter. I hope that your life will have far more positive events and surprises than the negative things discussed here. But I can tell you that good things come out of bad events.

Following I offer some discussion points that pertain to all types of life events — not just the negative ones discussed earlier in this chapter.

Keeping your big picture in mind

First, here are some general tips that apply to all types of life changes:

>> **Stay in financial shape.** An athlete is best able to withstand physical adversities during competition by prior training and eating well. Likewise, the sounder your finances are to begin with, the better you'll be able to deal with life changes. See Part 4 for all about getting and keeping your personal finances in tip-top shape!

>> **Remember that changes require change.** Even if your financial house is in order, a major life change — starting a family, buying a home, starting a business, divorcing, retiring — should prompt you to review your personal financial strategies. Life changes affect your income, spending, insurance needs, and ability to take financial risk.

>> **Don't procrastinate.** With a major life change on the horizon, procrastination can be costly. You (and your family) may overspend and accumulate high-cost debts, lack proper insurance coverage, or take other unnecessary risks. Early preparation can save you from these pitfalls.

>> **Manage stress and your emotions.** Life changes often are accompanied by stress and other emotional upheavals. Don't make snap decisions during these changes. Take the time to become fully informed and recognize and acknowledge your feelings. Educating yourself is key. You may want to hire experts to help but don't abdicate decisions and responsibilities to advisors — the advisors may not have your best interests at heart or fully appreciate your needs.

Considering a comprehensive checklist

I close this chapter with a checklist of important items to keep in mind as you're navigating a personal crisis that is impacting your finances. We've covered all of these in one way or another in this chapter, but I provide you with this final, over-all list so you can use it to remind yourself of key things to do and consider when you've encountered tough times.

>> Be prepared for tough times. This preparation can include having an emergency reserve and flexible spending so that you can more easily reduce your spending. Try to minimize the amount of spending that you engage in that is locked in, for example, through contracts for an extended period of time.

» When trouble hits, set aside time to consider and discuss the situation with family or someone you can trust. Spend time brainstorming on your topics of concern, including ways to reduce your spending.

» Make note of benefits you lose through an employer and develop a plan to replace needed catastrophic insurance. You always need health insurance, and until you're financially independent, disability insurance. If others are dependent upon your employment income, you should also have term life insurance.

» Be flexible and keep an open mind. A crisis can lead to opportunities for change and may include things like moving or simply changing your approach to certain aspects of your life and finances.

» Be prepared to negotiate and advocate for yourself and situation. This can include things like your housing and being able to meet the terms of your mortgage repayment or rental payments for a lease or dealing with an insurance company claim. If you have a hard time doing these things, enlist the support of someone who is comfortable and adept at doing this.

» Take time for your mental health and decision making. You should always do this, but it's especially important for you to take a little time every day to do things that you enjoy and that help you to relax. For some folks, this can be exercising, reading a good book, listening to music, and so forth.

» Understand and make use of your employee benefits. In my work as a financial counselor, I often discovered valuable employee benefits that my clients had overlooked or forgotten they had access to.

» Understand the tax consequences. Many financial decisions involve tax considerations, so be sure you understand those issues and tax reduction opportunities associated with those decisions.

» Find out about safety nets. When you're facing a personal financial crisis, you may qualify for some of the numerous safety net programs at the federal, state, and local levels. Please see Chapter 4 for the details.

» Make informed decisions after doing research. When you're stressed and perhaps pressed for time with everything that's coming at you, you're more likely to make an emotionally based decision. Don't add to your difficulties by making bad decisions. Do the necessary research and consult experts or smart people who can help you to make an informed decision.

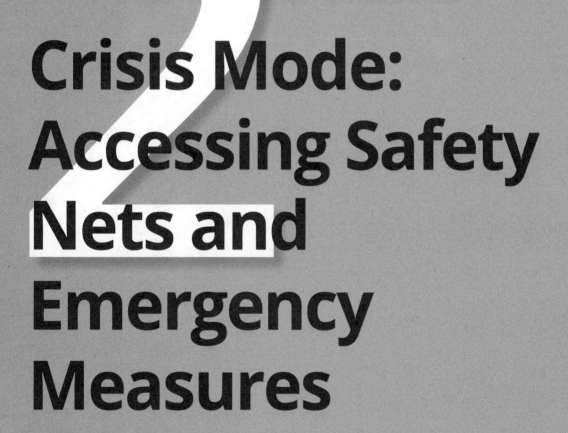

Crisis Mode: Accessing Safety Nets and Emergency Measures

Gather your resources and know how and where to find help.

Uncover ways to turn around a bad situation and find experts to help in the process.

» **Reaching out to loved ones**

» **Understanding government health insurance programs and subsidies**

» **Considering unemployment insurance, tax credits, and housing assistance programs**

Chapter **4**

Your Safety Nets

I n Chapters 2 and 3, I discuss big-picture economic problems and personal crises that can upset your financial and personal worlds. To weather such events and perhaps even thrive and capitalize on the inevitable opportunities during such times, you need resources and to be resourceful.

In this chapter, we're going to discuss how to quickly inventory and marshal your own resources when you're in the midst of a crisis and, if necessary, find someone to lean on — like a loved one you can trust — during tough times. (In Part 4, I discuss how to best position your personal finances when you have the time and space to thoughtfully plan ahead.) We'll also inventory the myriad government-administered social safety net programs for which you may be eligible.

Taking Stock of Your Resources

You've got resources — probably more than you realize. Some will be more attractive to tap than others. This section helps you recognize, inventory, and prioritize what you've got to bring to the battle.

Surveying your accessible money and spending options

First do an inventory of your available options for quickly (or reasonably quickly) available cash. Here are the common ones that you likely have access to and how I think about their attractiveness for you to consider tapping them:

>> **Accessing your emergency reserve of cash:** I've always recommended that folks have an emergency stash of cash of at least three months' worth of living expenses and perhaps as much as six to twelve months' worth for those with more uncertainty regarding their jobs and overall situations. Saving automatically through regular contributions to savings or transfers from checking can build your emergency fund.

>> **Tapping cash value life insurance balances:** Insurance agents love to sell cash value life insurance because it pays them much higher commissions than term life insurance. If you have a cash balance in your life insurance policy, you can generally tap it by borrowing against it or by cashing in the policy. If you need life insurance, please don't do the latter until you have first secured replacement term life insurance. See Chapter 11 for more about life insurance and how to best buy it.

>> **Taking out a loan.** For most people, the quickest way to borrow money (in other words, spend money you don't have) is via a credit card. If that's the only source of funding accessible to you, be sure to shop around for a credit card with good overall terms, especially for the interest rate charged on balances carried over month-to-month. While you may be able to borrow through loans tied to other specific purchases, such as a car or furniture, when times are tough, you likely won't be in a situation where you "need" to make such purchases.

>> **Borrowing from your retirement funds.** Your retirement plan may allow borrowing. I'm generally not a fan of this approach because if you borrow this money, you will miss out on the returns on that money until your loan is repaid. If the overall economy is going through a bad period, this will likely mean missing out on a good stock market rebound, since the financial markets are forward-looking (see Chapters 2 and 8) and stocks rebound well in advance of the economy actually looking better. Also, if you fail to repay a loan made against your retirement account, you will get socked with federal and state income taxes on the amount withdrawn as well as federal and state tax penalties for taking a withdrawal before age 59½.

Another option you may consider is to borrow from family, and that's the subject of the next section.

Finding assistance from family

I've seen numerous cases, including within my own family network, where lending/borrowing money can work. I'm also aware of cases, which are far fewer in number but still notable in number overall, where such borrowing has caused problems.

Here are the elements or ingredients that I think generally lead to a successful lender/borrower situation between family members:

>> **Borrow from someone financially sound.** The person doing the lending should be financially well off and not harmed in a notable way in the unlikely event that the borrower ends up not being able to repay part or even all of the loan.

>> **Get it in writing.** The terms of the loan are put in writing and signed by both parties. One page may be sufficient in most cases. This step is critical to ensure that both parties are literally on the same page! Doing such an agreement leaves no ambiguity about the fact that both sides agree that it's a loan that needs to be repaid under the terms spelled out in the short agreement.

>> **Set the loan for a reasonable (in other words, not long) period of time.** Generally speaking, the shorter the time period for the loan, the better in terms of the loan being likely to be repaid. Of course, the repayment terms need to be realistic and fit within the budget of the borrower.

>> **Charge a fair interest rate.** Loans in the real world from real-world lenders charge interest. Loans between family members can certainly be done at lower interest rates than a for-profit lender would charge.

>> **Consider "what-ifs."** Your simple loan agreement should spell out things like what happens to the loan if the borrower is unable to make payments for some period of time. The loan document should also cover things like whether it's okay to pay off the loan early and what happens to the loan if something happens to the borrower.

In many cases where I have observed or heard that a family loan didn't work out or caused a rift, no loan agreement/document was in place. It's not that the document makes everything work out, but it's the process of discussing the issues and the fact that it's a loan that is expected to be repaid that helps maximize the chances that all will be good.

WARNING

A family loan can go off the rails and cause interpersonal family problems when it leads some family member(s) to feel jealous or out of favor. Sometimes family members who see other members getting a loan may perceive that as special or favored treatment that they weren't offered or didn't get. A classic situation where such feelings may arise is if parents extend a loan to one of their adult children and the other sibling(s) feel resentment. This naturally raises the idea of discussing with other relevant family members before a loan is agreed to in order to minimize the potential for misunderstandings or hard feelings.

But the prospective borrower may not want everyone else in the family knowing their business or what precipitated the need for a loan from a family member. So, my suggestion is to begin with the prospective borrower to ask them how they feel about borrowing money and how others in the family may feel about it.

Ensuring adequate insurance coverage

Carrying and maintaining catastrophic insurance is essential to protect your personal financial situation and your family. You certainly don't want to lose or misuse such coverage when you're entering or in the midst of an economic downturn or personal crisis.

Many folks have various insurance coverages (for example, health insurance and disability insurance) through their employers. You need to stay on top of securing needed insurance so if you lose your job, you don't suffer any lapses in coverage.

WARNING

When money is tight and times are tough, you may be tempted to cut some corners and go without needed insurance for a "short time." Please don't do that! It's impossible to predict exactly when you will need to use a particular insurance policy, so you need to maintain your coverage all the time. Don't tempt fate and risk having a major insurance claim during a period when you chose to drop a particular policy in an effort to save a little money.

You need to carry the following insurance coverages:

>> **Health insurance:** This is always a must unless you are super-duper wealthy and can self-insure.

>> **Disability insurance:** You need this if you and yours are dependent upon your employment income. You likely do have some disability coverage through Social Security.

>> **Life insurance:** If your loved ones are depending upon your employment income, life insurance is a necessity.

>> **Home insurance:** Insuring your home (as well as other real estate you own) protects this asset and provides liability coverage.

>> **Auto insurance:** Maintain auto insurance for liability protection it provides and for possible financial loss in a major accident.

Please see Chapter 11 for all the details on what insurance you should and shouldn't carry and how and where to get the best value for your insurance dollars.

Surveying Societal Safety Nets

It frustrates me that a good deal of political rhetoric these days focuses on how much more income or assets some people have compared with others. For starters, the amount of money that someone else has frankly is none of anyone's business. High-income earners and those with substantial assets pay far more in taxes. Remember that the lowest 40+ percent of income earners in the United States pay no federal income tax.

What we should be discussing and debating from a policy standpoint is the adequacy of the numerous social safety net programs, which are paid for by those who pay most of the taxes — the high-income earners and those with greater wealth. For purposes of this book, all that really matters for you and your situation is whether you qualify for any of these many programs.

The requirements or thresholds to qualify vary greatly. I find that many folks are surprised at how affluent you can be and how high your income can be to qualify for some of them. The point of this section is to explain to you what's out there and get the process started for you to determine whether you may qualify for any of them.

Health insurance subsidies

When the Affordable Care Act (ACA), also known as Obamacare, was signed into law in 2010, it included subsidies for low- and moderate-income earners. The large COVID-19 relief bill known as the American Rescue Plan Act (ARP) of 2021 further expanded and increased those subsidies to include even more households that would be considered middle-class and upper-middle class. Because assets aren't an explicit factor in determining subsidies, some households that may be considered higher-income earners are also now eligible for at least partial subsidies.

Health insurance is vital insurance to continue at all times. However, as you get older and have dependents, the cost of health insurance can get quite high. Policies are also pricy due to the mandated benefits on health insurance policies under Obamacare.

Surveying the different levels of plans

If you've gone shopping for health insurance policies on your own through any of the state-based exchanges or the federal exchange, you know that the policies are categorized by the terminology of Gold, Silver and Bronze plans. As you may have guessed from these names, the Gold plans tend to be the most expensive, Silver the next most expensive, and Bronze plans the least expensive.

Gold, Silver, and Bronze plans differ from one another largely based upon the size of their cost sharing — that is, the deductibles and co-payments. Gold plans have the lowest cost sharing and therefore the highest premiums. Remember, with any insurance policies, you will pay a higher premium when you take a lower deductible, and conversely get the benefit of a lower premium when you take a policy with a higher deductible. Bronze plans have the lowest premiums because they have higher deductibles and co-payments. Silver plans are in between Gold and Bronze.

For each of these plan types, an *actuarial value* is calculated, which is the percentage of total covered medical expenses that are paid for (on average) by the insurance company for a typical group of people enrolled in that plan. The higher the actuarial value, the more financial protection the plan is likely to offer you when you get sick or need medical care. Bronze plans, which have the highest deductibles and co-payments, have an actuarial value of about 60 percent; Silver plans, 70 percent; and Gold plans, which have the lowest deductibles and co-payments, 80 percent.

Please keep in mind that these are the average percentages for the portion of covered medical benefits that are paid for by a typical plan. In all cases, if you have a relatively large amount of medical expenses in a particular year, you will have an even greater percentage of your medical expenses paid for by the insurance than you would expect from the actuarial value percentage.

Understanding how Obamacare subsidies work

Health insurance premiums with the standardized policies now required by Obamacare are expensive, but many people now qualify for at least partial or substantial subsidies. Subsidies are payments made by the federal government to health insurers to help pay part or even all of a person's costs for health insurance coverage or care. The amount of subsidized assistance you get is determined by your household income and the number of family members and dependents you have.

Two types of health insurance subsidies are available through Obamacare health insurance exchange policies: premium tax credit subsidies and cost-sharing subsidies. The premium tax credit subsidies are far more common and beneficial to a wider range of health insurance buyers than are the cost-sharing subsidies.

The *premium tax credit* is in place to ensure that your household will not pay more than 8.5 percent of its income for a Silver plan in your location. Whatever a Silver plan costs above that in your area would be paid for through a government subsidy payment to your insurance company. And you can apply that amount of subsidy to an even lower cost Bronze plan and thus lower your cost of health insurance coverage even further.

TIP

Because your health insurance subsidy is based upon your estimated income for the year, it's possible your estimate could be off by enough to materially affect the amount of subsidy you ultimately qualify for once you complete and file your federal income tax return. In the worst cases I've seen in the past, folks with incomes quite a bit higher than anticipated have had their subsidy reduced by thousands of dollars. So, if you elect to have the government pay your subsidy directly to the insurance company throughout the year your insurance is in force, you could end up having to pay far more in federal taxes when you file your federal income tax return. Alternatively, you can elect to wait and receive your health insurance subsidy as a lump-sum tax credit when you file your federal income tax return. If your subsidy is a significant portion of the cost of your health insurance and you're having cash flow issues/concerns, by all means have the subsidy paid monthly toward the cost to keep your payments to a minimum. Just be careful not to greatly underestimate your expected income for the year.

Fewer folks qualify for the second type of subsidies known as *cost-sharing subsidies,* which help reduce your out-of-pocket costs when going to the doctor or when you must get hospital care. The eligibility formulas for these subsidies require a much lower level of income (no more than 250 percent of the poverty level for the geographic area) than a person can have to qualify for the health insurance premium subsidies. Another reason fewer folks get these cost-sharing subsidies is that you must enroll in a Silver plan to get them, and please remember that Silver plans have higher premiums than Bronze plans. So these cost-sharing subsidies on Silver plans only really benefit people who use at least a moderate amount of healthcare annually.

Using a nifty online subsidy calculator

The Kaiser Family Foundation has a super-duper useful health insurance subsidy calculator that requires your entering just a handful of inputs like your state, zip code, household income, age of family members, and so on. Once entered, the calculator (www.kff.org/interactive/subsidy-calculator/) will tell you approximately what the second lowest-cost Silver plan and lowest-cost Bronze-level health insurance plan will cost you after factoring in estimated subsidies.

A discussion of several important topics is helpful to get the most accurate information from this calculator. First, how should you determine your household income to input into the calculator? Income refers to all household members (including spouse and dependents) who will be covered under your health insurance and pay taxes. Household income includes wages, investment income, Social Security, and some other income sources. For purposes of determining eligibility for health insurance premium tax credits, the calculator considers your household's Modified Adjusted Gross Income (MAGI). If you get out your most recent year's federal income tax return, you can find a line item called "Adjusted Gross Income" (AGI), which for most people is the same as or similar to their MAGI. To arrive at your MAGI, start with your AGI from your most recent federal income tax return and add to that the following other types of untaxed income:

>> Tax-exempt interest

>> Foreign earned income that was excluded from your taxable income

>> Nontaxable Social Security benefits you receive except supplemental security income

If you've been the beneficiary of an inheritance or gift, don't include that in the calculations as those are not considered income.

Here are some additional factors that determine your monthly health insurance premiums:

>> **Age:** It has always been the case that your health insurance premiums go up as you age for the simple reason that on average, older people tend to use more healthcare than do younger folks. This is still the case in 48 states — New York and Vermont do not vary premiums based upon age. There are some newer restrictions on age-based pricing, including the fact that folks age 64 and older may not be charged more than three times the amount that a 21-year-old pays. Also, covered children under the age of 21 may have somewhat lower premiums, and families will not be charged for more than three children.

>> **Where you live:** Generally speaking, the higher the cost of living and the higher the cost of healthcare in a particular area, the higher the health insurance premiums for that location. So, if you're applying for health insurance from a higher cost-of-living area, you should be eligible for a larger premium subsidy.

>> **Tobacco usage:** In 44 states, tobacco users are rightfully charged higher health insurance premiums due to the myriad documented health problems caused by tobacco usage. Six states (California, Massachusetts, New Jersey, New York, Rhode Island, and Vermont) mandate that insurers may not charge

tobacco users different health insurance rates. In those states that do charge a surcharge, it may not exceed 50 percent (and some states allow a surcharge but limit the percentage further). Also, subsidies may not cover the portion of someone's health insurance premium attributable to the tobacco surcharge. KFF's subsidy calculator, which is only providing an estimate, does not incorporate specifics on the tobacco surcharge but does offer general warnings when you may face it. The federal and state-based health insurance exchange websites can help you fine-tune those numbers and specifics.

What if your employer offers coverage?

If you work for an employer that offers you health insurance coverage, you probably won't be eligible for an exchange-based plan with subsidies. There are two exceptions:

>> Your employer's coverage isn't "affordable."

>> Your employer's plan fails to meet the "minimum value" requirement. *Minimum value* means that your employer's plan is expected to pay 60 percent or more of an average person's expected annual healthcare costs.

Your employer should have information and data that can show you whether their plan is deemed "affordable" for you and if it meets the minimum value requirement.

How Medicare eligibility affects Obamacare coverage

Medicare is the federal government–provided insurance for older Americans that kicks in for most people at age 65. If you are eligible for Medicare (and even if you're not currently enrolled in it), you may not sign up for a new Obamacare exchange-based plan.

If your household contains a mix of people, some of whom are not Medicare eligible and some who are, those who are not Medicare eligible may sign up for an exchange-based and subsidized policy.

Unemployment insurance benefits

If you lose your job, you can probably collect unemployment insurance benefits while you're seeking a new job. Employers pay into unemployment insurance funds for this very reason — so that the government has funding to pay out benefits when folks lose their jobs.

UNDERSTANDING STATE-BASED MEDICAID PROGRAMS

Medicaid is a state-based health insurance program that doesn't charge premiums for low-income people. Numerous states have elected to expand their Medicaid programs so more people are eligible for them. Why might this matter and why should you care? Well, you can't sign up for an exchange-based subsidized health insurance plan if you're eligible for Medicaid in your state.

The Kaiser Family Foundation's "Health Insurance Marketplace Calculator" factors in how each state handles Medicaid, so by using their calculator, you will be able to estimate your potential eligibility for Medicaid. For more information about Medicaid, visit www.healthcare.gov, your state's health insurance marketplace if it has one, or your state's Medicaid program office — see the list at www.medicaid.gov/state-overviews/index.html.

As a point of pride or embarrassment, some folks are reluctant to even consider filing for unemployment benefits. Please don't think that way. Think of unemployment insurance as any other insurance policy you carry such as for your car. You hope you don't need that insurance, but if you do, you should file a claim and collect.

Also, being able to collect these benefits has nothing to do with your overall financial situation and neediness or lack thereof. Your spouse could still be at their well-paying job, you may have a good deal of money saved and invested, and so forth. Unemployment benefits are for those who have lost their jobs and who meet the criteria for their state to collect benefits, which have nothing to do with your current overall personal financial situation for you and yours.

The federal government, through the Department of Labor, provides federal guidelines for the state-administered unemployment benefit programs. Each state has its own eligibility guidelines for qualifying to collect unemployment benefits. These guidelines generally are based upon needing to meet a time-worked threshold or wage amount.

To find your state's unemployment information, visit: www.careeronestop.org/LocalHelp/UnemploymentBenefits/find-unemployment-benefits.aspx.

Federal refundable tax credits

There are two separate federal income tax credits — the Earned Income Tax Credit (EITC) and the Child Tax Credit (CTC) — which are designed to assist lower-income earners. Both of these tax credits include refundable portions, which means that even if you owe no federal income tax for a particular tax year (which is the case for more than 40 percent of all households), the federal government will actually pay you for a portion of the qualifying federal income tax credit. So, rather than owing or paying any federal income tax for that year, qualifying households are paid money by the federal government.

The EITC was instituted in 1975 and has been modified numerous times since. Eligibility for this tax credit is based upon family size and the amount of earned income:

Children or Relatives Claimed	Maximum AGI (filing as Single, Head of Household, or Widowed)	Maximum AGI (filing as Married Filing Jointly)
0	$15,980	$21,920
1	$42,158	$48,108
2	$47,915	$53,865
3	$51,464	$57,414

Qualifying households must have investment income for the year of no more than $3,650.

The maximum amount of credit you can claim is as follows:

No qualifying children	$543
1 qualifying child	$3,618
2 qualifying children	$5,980
3 or more qualifying children	$6,728

To see if you qualify for the EITC, you can answer a series of questions on the "EITC Assistant" at the IRS's website: apps.irs.gov/app/eitc/general-info.

TECHNICAL STUFF

The Child Tax Credit (CTC) originated in 1997 and has been modified and increased several times since. It now provides for a credit of up to $2,000 per qualifying child under age 17. It is available to relatively high-income earners: married couples filing jointly can have adjusted gross incomes up to $400K and single taxpayers up to $200K. The refundable portion of this tax credit is $1,400 per child.

Help with housing

Federal Housing Assistance programs are administered by the Department of Housing and Urban Development (HUD). Their most well-known and utilized program is the Housing Choice Voucher Program, which is also known as Section 8 or the Tenant Based Rental Assistance program. It is run and administered by local Public Housing Agencies (PHAs), which distribute vouchers to help pay a portion of an eligible tenant's rent.

Eligible tenants have incomes that are below 50 percent of the median income for the county or metropolitan area in which they reside. The program ensures that a family's housing expense won't exceed 30 percent of that family's income.

Families may use the voucher for any housing that meets HUD's health and safety standards. HUD pays the voucher directly to the landlord. Tenants make their portion of the rental payment directly to their landlord as well.

For more information about this HUD program, please visit www.hud.gov/topics/housing_choice_voucher_program_section_8. Also, HUD's Resource Locator can be found at https://resources.hud.gov/.

For more information on safety net programs...

U.C. Davis' Center for Poverty and Inequality Research has a compilation of the major federal safety net programs in the United States. Visit: https://poverty.ucdavis.edu/article/war-poverty-and-todays-safety-net-0.

Chapter **5**

Digging Out and Forging Ahead

When you've suffered through tough times, it can be hard to think clearly and make thoughtful, informed decisions. And it's never pleasant to contemplate or face the carnage and losses, financial and otherwise.

But you and I know that the sun will rise tomorrow, and things inevitably will improve. The sooner you can grasp the reality of your situation and begin making accurate assessments, the better able you will be to make constructive decisions that will help you now and in the future.

In this chapter, I discuss overarching issues to help you make the best decisions. In addition to embracing a sound process, I also discuss how to leverage the input of useful experts and pros as well as how to keep the media's coverage of current events in proper perspective. I don't cover here how to interpret and make sense of the barrage of economic data and information in bigger-picture economic downturns and crises — that's the subject of Chapters 6 to 8.

Turning Your Eye toward Recovery

Picking up the pieces, surveying the damage, and so on are not enjoyable expressions and topics to consider. But all of us have to do so at various times in our lives.

Making a change for the sake of making a change without doing sufficient soul-searching and research may lead to poor decisions. In the midst of turmoil and difficulties, you're more likely to make hasty and not well-conceived decisions. The rest of this chapter and book helps you to maximize your chances of making sound decisions based upon factual information and your personal preferences.

Just remember: Human beings are amazingly resilient. It inspires me, and I know you're capable of being resilient too.

But I also know and have observed that stress and bad times can take their toll. So, please take your mental health seriously, and if you need help, seek it out and don't have any shame in doing so.

Knowing how long it will take to regain stable financial footing

Recovery for major problematic events is usually measured in months or years, not days or weeks. For sure, you may well see tangible signs of progress over short time periods. But it's certainly not realistic to expect a major or full recovery that quickly.

Good can and often does come out of bad situations, and I certainly encourage you to be a "glass half full" kind of person with your outlook. Take major stock market declines of more than 20 percent, which are known as *bear markets.* Owning stocks during such a slide can test your nerves and optimism.

Since World War II, it has on average taken a full year for the stock market (as measured by the S&P 500 index) to recover the losses during a typical bear market. Some recent bear markets were worse — it took four years, until 2006, to recover from the 2000–2002 bear market, and it took three years, until 2012, to recover from the 2007–2009 bear market. But recover they do.

Going through a divorce, for example, is unpleasant and raises myriad financial and other issues that require your attention. But if the relationship was filled with intractable problems that continually made you miserable, moving on and forging a new life may well be the right thing to do and lead to far greater happiness. That said, there are folks who go through a divorce and find they've still got major problems or that a new relationship sours and leads to similar problems as the previous failed marriage.

Coping with frustration and moving on

Experiencing frustration and other negative emotions is certainly not unusual. Embrace and acknowledge these feelings. If you have a loved one or close friend you can share your concerns with, that may help, but remember to be respectful of their time and concerns. Don't make repeated complaining a habit and use others as emotional dumpsters. Everyone has their own issues and problems to deal with. If you're trying someone out for the first time, ask first whether they are okay with hearing your concerns.

Check your expectations when dealing with personal or economic challenges. In addition to the amount of time required to heal problems and wounds, also recognize that forward progress is fluid. While you will enjoy progress at times, you should be prepared for inevitable setbacks.

Try not to dwell on the negative and things you can't change. It's enjoyable to invest in stocks and stock mutual funds when the economy is doing well and stocks are rising. Looking at your increasing account value feels pretty darn good! But in the aftermath of a major market decline, looking at your shrunken account values makes most people feel awful. Simple solution: Don't keep looking at things that make you feel bad!

And, remember the Serenity Prayer:

> God grant me the Serenity to accept the things I cannot change,
>
> Courage to change the things I can, and
>
> Wisdom to know the difference.

Accepting things you can't change is a necessary step to moving forward and making good decisions. For example, I've observed in numerous situations that folks sometimes have a difficult time accepting that a home or some other piece of real estate they bought is down in value. In the worst cases, rather than accepting the current market value for what it is, some people throw good money after bad and hold onto a property for more years in the hope that it will bounce back in value.

Now, I'm certainly not going to suggest that there aren't better times than others to sell a particular piece of real estate, but you should weigh the costs of holding out versus the likely possible benefits. Often, the continued carrying costs of a property outweigh the likely potential value increases (or the better returns you could earn elsewhere). Sometimes, this may even mean accepting the foreclosure of a property or simply selling a property at a loss or lower price than it was in prior years.

Thinking (and Researching) Before Making Financial Moves

At various times in your life, you'll make important financial decisions. The timing of those decisions — such as buying a home, starting or buying a small business, or contributing to a retirement savings plan — is often at your discretion. Dealing with tough times either personally or due to the broader economy can upset the timing of such decisions and how you make them.

In this section, I want to help you make sure that you're making good decisions and sidestepping commonly made bad ones.

Wise financial actions to take

Following are some examples of generally constructive things you can do during tough times:

>> **Take stock of your overall situation.** If you're like most people, it's probably been a while since you've reviewed your overall financial situation and planning.

>> **Reduce discretionary spending.** Many people have some fat and waste in their spending and cutting down on that is inevitably a good thing for your overall situation. Just be sure to discuss the issue with family members, as others will surely have different priorities in mind than you do. Be patient and explain the importance and value of everyone pulling and working together, and be open to compromise.

>> **Invest more in solid investments at depressed prices.** Good things, including otherwise sound investments, sometimes go on sale. If you've planned ahead or simply accumulated some extra cash over time, a great time to deploy it would be when pessimism is in the air and investment values are down.

Boneheaded financial actions to avoid

Whether on your own or with the encouragement of outside bad advice, most often from a salesperson or someone else with a vested financial interest in your decisions, making a poor decision can add to your misery from a personal or economic crisis. Here are some common ones to sidestep:

>> **Selling investments at depressed prices:** It's actually a normal human reaction to want to sell an investment that's getting hammered. If nothing else, it may feel like you're on board a sinking ship and better get out now while you still have something to save. But good investments inevitably rebound after downturns and that rebound in prices often happens quickly, so you don't want to miss out on it.

>> **Allowing important insurance policies to lapse:** When your cash flow is tight, it's tempting to not continue some insurance policies you haven't collected on greatly in many years. Doing so defeats the whole purpose of carrying catastrophic insurance coverage so that it's there when you may need it.

>> **Taking money out of retirement accounts before it's needed:** During tough times, folks eye money in their retirement accounts. Tapping this money before you've exhausted other options is almost always a mistake due to the federal and state income tax owed as well as penalties generally applied if you're withdrawing retirement account money before age 59½.

Leaning on an Expert for Help

Making the best personal financial decisions requires knowledge, research, and good judgment. Don't expect perfection — you can do just about everything right, but things may not work the way you hoped for reasons beyond your control. If you've invested for any length of time in the stock market, you've surely experienced that. Ditto for buying a home or investing in real estate.

That doesn't mean, however, that you should not bother working to maximize your ability and chances of making the best decisions given a reasonable input of time and energy on your part. Hiring a knowledgeable and ethical expert can help. In discussing how to make wise decisions, consider the timeless wisdom from Solomon's book of Proverbs:

> "He that walks with wise men shall become wise. But a companion of fools shall be destroyed."

All too often, people fail to hire the right expert and fail to do enough homework before making the hiring decision. This section covers who, when, and how to hire the best financial help for common financial issues and challenges.

Knowing how experts can help

If you're in the market for an advisor, of course, you should ask questions and check some references to ensure that you're engaging the services of a competent advisor who is knowledgeable, ethical, and reasonably priced. Such an advisor can help you in the following ways:

- » **Objectivity:** An advisor can be more objective than you since they are not caught up in the emotions of the situation.

- » **Interpersonal dynamics:** A good advisor can help negotiate differences and compromises with couples and broader extended family decisions.

- » **Beneficial strategies:** An advisor's technical knowledge and expertise makes them aware of strategies that can make and save you money.

Being careful in a time of need

Let's face it: You're vulnerable reaching out for help in a time of need. Here's what you can do to protect yourself and your finances.

- » Interview at least two or three possible advisors. (See the next section, "Finding financial advisors and planners," for info on interviewing). You'll learn something with each person you speak with and be able to compare their approaches and pitches.

- » Recognize and deal with your emotions. If your emotions are still raw, perhaps it's too early to engage advisors. Perhaps a good friend and/or relative can help you through this stage.

- » Run any possible plans by a good friend or family member you can trust with confidentiality and who is most likely to provide a helpful critique without a personal agenda.

Finding financial advisors and planners

There are many people who call themselves financial planners, financial advisors, and so on. And for good reason: After all, tens of millions of people have the challenge of living within their means, planning for major expenditures such as buying a car or a home; saving for retirement, paying higher education expenses, starting a small business, securing proper insurance coverage, and so on. Financial consultants and planners purport to be able to help with this far-ranging list of money challenges. And the best ones out there are able to tackle at least some of these topics competently and ethically.

MISTAKES PEOPLE MAKE WHEN OVERWHELMED

Alice Boyes, PhD, clinical psychologist and author of *The Healthy Mind Toolkit* and *The Anxiety Toolkit* (published by TarcherPerigee), has identified five common mistakes that folks make when they feel overwhelmed:

1. **You think you don't have time for actions that would help you.** Remember that there is no such thing as a perfect moment to act, so start taking the steps to do things you know will help.

2. **You don't utilize your unconscious mind enough.** Try engaging in activities — such as exercise, listening to music, running errands, bathing — that allow your mind to wander and escape from your current fears and worries.

3. **You interpret feeling overwhelmed as a weakness.** Don't procrastinate and don't feel shame in recognizing that outside assistance can help you.

4. **You default to your dominant approaches and defenses.** For example, being self-reliant can be a good trait within reason but can be an obstacle to welcoming help with a problem.

5. **You withdraw from your supports.** Seek out opportunities to fill your emotional cup and get support from those who love and care most for you.

Here are a couple overarching principles to keep in mind as you seek to make the best decisions with outside help and assistance:

» **Educate yourself first.** No matter the subject area — investing in stocks, bonds, or mutual funds; buying a home; securing life insurance — invest some time and effort into becoming familiar with the basics and lingo. Otherwise, you're much more likely to not know who may be bamboozling you and what the deal is with what you're considering. How can you possibly evaluate the competence of someone you're considering hiring if you yourself are ignorant in the area in question? Getting a crash course through a good book such as this one or a course on the topic can be a cost-effective and excellent way to start. The biggest challenges with selecting books and courses are finding those written by authors and taught by those who have sufficient expertise and high ethical standards.

» **Search hard for the best information and people you can find.** If you simply hire the first person you come across or are referred to, you're going to make more mistakes. The same holds true for selecting financial advice publications. You've got to scrutinize, ask probing questions (see the next list), check references, and prove to yourself that someone is worth listening to or hiring.

Your challenge if you desire to hire a financial planner is to do the following:

1. Define the areas you need help with.

Are you having budgeting problems and trouble with consumer debt and being able to save money? Have you got the challenge of cash languishing in low-interest accounts, and you want to know how to best invest this money for your financial future? Or is your problem that you and your spouse argue about money and can't agree on common goals?

The first step toward finding the right help and beginning to address a concern is to clearly define and acknowledge it. For example, saying, "I don't know how much I should be saving toward retirement and in what accounts and investments," states a specific problem. So does the question, "How do I prioritize among competing financial savings goals of saving for retirement, a home purchase, and my kids' college education?"

2. Identify potential experts for providing the type of help you need.

If you seek help with budgets, spending, and dealing with debt, you're obviously looking for a different type of advisor than is someone seeking an investment manager to direct a six-figure nest egg. Although you may find a firm that does both of these things well, that's unlikely given the different skill sets required. Ask people and professionals you respect for their recommendations. There's nothing wrong with calling people that you discover from your own searching as long as you ask plenty of tough questions and really do your homework before you commit to hiring them (see the next point).

3. Interview and screen potential candidates.

Once you've developed a short list of potential planners, interview them. It's amazing how uncomfortable it makes most people to ask tough questions, but you've got to do that — there's so much at stake for you! Here are the key questions you should ask:

- What is your approach to working with clients?

- What are your areas of expertise?

- What educational and professional training prepared you to be a financial advisor?

- How are you compensated — hourly or through asset management fees and/or commissions?

Presuming you are satisfied with the answers you get to the preceding questions, ask the following:

- Can I have a copy of your Form ADV? This is a form investment advisors file with the Securities and Exchange Commission (www.sec.gov/fast-answers/answersformadvhtm.html) that provides details on a firm's approach, key personnel, fees, and so on.

- Do you retain professional liability insurance?

- Can you provide references of people with whom you've worked in a similar situation to mine or who worked in a similar occupation?

TIP

After collecting all this information for several advisors, select the best one. That often comes down to personal comfort and instincts. Be careful, however, not to simply select someone with the best bedside manner, the most polished one, the most credentialed one, or the one who has (or claims to have) the most famous or highest net worth clients. The folks who select on these superficial criteria after not asking sufficient questions can end up getting burned the worst by lousy planners. Focus on evaluating the candidates on the issues important to you. By all means, consider your personal comfort with the advisor; just don't allow that to overwhelm everything else.

In the worst case, if you fail to do your homework, you can end up with more than bad advice that causes you to lose money. You may actually be defrauded out of money — think Bernie Madoff (who ran a fraudulent hedge fund that fleeced investors of billions of dollars), although there are plenty of smaller-scale scoundrels who have separated people from their money.

Being aware of budget counselors

Many organizations offering budget or credit counseling services are beholden to credit card and other consumer debt purveyors. Their goal is typically to place you on what's called a *debt management plan* if you come to them with a lot of debt and seek advice for how to deal with it.

Following are excerpts from a pitch from a credit counseling agency (interspersed with insights regarding the pitch), with the three common supposed reasons to go to them for help with your debts:

>> "We can help you pay less. Our credit counseling agency negotiates with your creditors for better repayment terms, including lower interest rates and waived late fees."

The fact of the matter is that you can do anything an agency does on your behalf. You can negotiate better payment terms. Here's a simple test to show you how easily this can be done. Suppose that you have credit card debt on which you're currently paying 18 percent interest charges. There are many credit cards to which you can transfer your debt balances, with far-lower interest rates. Once you've identified such a card, when you call your current credit card company to report that you're transferring your balance onto a low-rate card (and want to cancel your current card), you will almost be guaranteed to get an offer for as good a rate from your current company!

>> "We help to pay off your debt faster. By creating a realistic and manageable payment plan, you'll be able to pay off your debt in as few as 3 to 5 years (as compared to potentially 20 to 30 years on your own)."

What these agencies fail to disclose here — and it's a big omission — is that participating in their debt management plans can greatly tarnish your credit report.

>> "We help make it easier to pay every month. By consolidating all your credit card and other unsecured debt payments into one, you won't have to juggle multiple payments."

Well, you won't have to juggle because you are expected to make the one monthly consolidated payment. The only thing that's "easier" about that is that you're supposed to just write one check. Coming up with the money to make that monthly payment (whether it's one or many) is the hard part for people in trouble with consumer debt.

If you've had problems living within your means, managing your debt, and sticking to a regular savings and investing plan, please see Chapter 9. The key to getting out of debt is to reverse the process (spending exceeding earnings) that got you into debt. You may well have to make some significant changes and sacrifices in the ways in which you spend money.

To find the few counselors/advisors who will help with spending and debt issues, you can actually start your search by using the advice provided in the preceding section and seeking planners in your area who do this kind of work or asking them for referrals to budget counselors they know and like. You can also try searching online in your area for "Credit and Debt Counseling" or "Budget Counseling."

TIP

There is one national nonprofit that has many satellites and branches under them and has a solid reputation for doing good debt counseling work. It's the National Foundation for Credit Counseling: www.nfcc.org. Another helpful resource for debt repayment is Power Pay (https://extension.usu.edu/powerpay/). It is from Utah State University Extension. Consumers can register for a private account and enter debt information to calculate personalized repayment plans.

Investing in investment managers

If your savings and investment balances total well into the six-figures, you may be considering hiring an *investment manager* — someone who manages money for a living. By this I mean a firm that manages the money by selecting stocks, bonds, and so forth, not a financial advisor who recommends investments.

Most investment managers have investment minimums of several million dollars or more. Some managers have lower minimums. Suppose you have $500,000. That's a lot of money to most people, but to a money manager who has hundreds of millions, or more likely billions of dollars, under management, it's pocket change. Even if you could meet a manager's investment minimums, the percentage management fee you would pay would be relatively quite high. And, if you meet the minimum, then you're stuck turning over all of your assets to a single manager — not a good idea for diversification purposes.

Another reason to caution against hiring an investment manager is a lack of expertise on your part to evaluate that person. Even if you are one of those rare people who have plenty of millions to invest, how much do you know about evaluating an investment manager? Consider that investment firms such as Fidelity, T. Rowe Price, and Vanguard have entire departments devoted to the evaluation of investment managers, both before their hiring and to monitor their efforts after.

WARNING

Some money managers will offer individuals so-called separate accounts and pitch them as customized money management. However, the reality is that there will be hundreds of accounts with the same holdings and approach, and you'll pay a relatively high fee for such accounts.

The bottom line on money management firms is that the bigger and more successful firms cannot be accessed by individuals but can be through the nation's leading mutual fund companies. And, because of the purchasing power of fund companies, when you invest in mutual funds, you get access to the leading money managers for a lower cost than a wealthy individual could by directly trying to hire a money manager.

Looking into real estate agents

One type of sales agent you will surely encounter is one who works with consumers on residential real estate transactions. Real estate agents can add value to a housing transaction if they are knowledgeable and patient with their customers. The best agents are adept with marketing, customer service, and knowing how to negotiate. That said, real estate agents can also lead to problems if they cause a consumer to make a decision without performing sufficient due diligence and thought. In the final analysis, it's up to each person to be sure they have done their homework, gained sufficient knowledge, and satisfied their concerns.

WARNING

Real estate agents are salespeople who are compensated on commission. Blindly relying on such an individual in an advisory capacity with such significant money at stake is a recipe for potential disaster.

With increasing home prices over the decades, having two agents working on a transaction (one for the seller, one for the buyer) and sharing a 5 to 6 percent commission has led to larger and larger numbers. A good thing to remember when dealing with real estate money is to consider commissions. Always keep in mind that commissions are negotiable and are a cost borne by both sellers and buyers. Even though sellers "pay" the commission from the proceeds of their house sale, the cost of the commission is included in the total price paid for the home by the buyer. If you can negotiate a lower commission, the price of the home could be lowered, too.

While larger and more expensive homes typically take longer to sell, it doesn't, for example, take four times as long to sell a home worth $800,000 compared to one worth $200,000. The national median (meaning half the homes sell for more, half sell for less) home price is now well over $300,000 and of course much higher in the highest cost-of-living areas in the country. Especially if your home is in one of the higher-priced markets, you can and should negotiate for a lower commission rate when selling your home.

When listing a house to sell, be aware that when you sign a listing agreement with your agent, a determination is made as to what portion of the total commission will be advertised, typically in the multiple listing service (MLS), as the commission payable to an agent representing a buyer. For example, suppose you agree to pay the listing agency a total commission of 5 percent of the sales price of your house, but only 2 percent of the sales price goes to the agent representing a buyer. If other similarly priced houses for sale are listed in the MLS advertising greater commissions — say of 2.5 or 3 percent — some agents working with buyers may not be enthusiastic to show their buyers your house if they only get a 2 percent commission. This may not sound like a big difference, but consider that on a $300,000 sales price, a 2 percent commission comes to $6,000, but a 3 percent commission yields $9,000. To reduce your commission as a seller, have your listing agent reduce their take but don't reduce below the norm the portion of the commission paid to the agent who brings you a buyer.

When seeking the services of an agent, be sure to consider the following:

>> **Experience and expertise:** How long has the agent been working with home buyers and house sellers, and what success have they had? Be sure to ask the agent for an activity list of all their transactions over the past year.

>> **Negotiation and interpersonal skills:** An agent interacts with many people in a transaction. Does the agent know how to get along with others while advocating for your best interests?

>> **Ethics:** Can you trust the agent? Do they perform work that they promise to and within the time frame that they say they will?

These important traits and characteristics apply to other real estate–related pros you may hire such as a mortgage broker or loan officer at a bank or other lender. Others involved in real estate transactions include the escrow officer, the home inspector, and in some cases an attorney, which is required in select states.

Making note of tax preparers and advisors

Many aspects of the U.S. tax laws are complicated. Why else would there be so many accountants and tax preparers!

Several different types of tax practitioners are eager to earn your business. Preparers, enrolled agents (EAs), and certified public accountants (CPAs) do the bulk of tax return preparation for individuals in the United States. EAs and CPAs may represent you before the IRS should your tax return be audited or otherwise questioned. Tax preparation and advisory fees vary from $50 up to several hundred dollars per hour.

Hiring a competent tax advisor makes sense if you're dealing with something for the first time or are dealing with a multi-part problem that is complicated. Or perhaps you just want a second opinion.

Ideally, you should hire a tax advisor who

>> Has experience dealing with the sorts of issues you're struggling with.

>> Is focused on taxes and works at it full-time and/or has many years of experience.

>> Suits your comfort level about being aggressive or conservative in pursuing deductions and other areas. Ask about their history with tax audits and the results.

>> Provides solid references.

>> Carries errors and omission (liability) insurance.

Tax attorneys deal with more unusual tax problems with the IRS and business deals. They do not typically handle routine tax preparation.

Regardless of whom you choose to work with, organize your records as best you can before you sit down with your tax advisor. Remember, advisors charge for their time. Don't hire a tax preparer to organize receipts.

In addition to considering going the route of hiring a tax advisor, another option to consider is to instead tap tax preparation software and tax guides to help you navigate through the annual tax headache.

Dealing with insurance agents

As I discuss in Chapter 11, many folks make mistakes buying insurance, in part due to the influence of commission-compensated insurance brokers. That's why, in addition to finding ethical and competent insurance agents, you should be aware and make use of insurance that can be bought directly without agents and utilize shopping services to help you ensure that you get value for your money.

When you do deal with insurance agents, be sure you work with those who specialize in the line of insurance you seek. For example, don't buy disability insurance from an agent for whom it's a sideline.

Tuning in to attorneys

The primary reason you would seek the counsel of an attorney for financial purposes is to do estate planning, divorce, or bankruptcy (and possibly in some states for a real estate transaction). Hire an attorney with lots of experience in the specific area (such as estate planning, real estate, and so on) you need help with.

Check references for competency and ethics and be sure to comparison shop to get value for your money. Ask an attorney for a budget for a project. Because attorneys bill for their time and can profit more from conflict and dragging things out, beware of open-ended arrangements. Express your concern about managing costs, and don't hesitate to question how much something is going to cost or has been charged.

Legal book publisher Nolo Press has an excellent website (www.nolo.com) with all sorts of background information about a multitude of important legal topics. Click on the tab for "Find A Lawyer" to discover more about the best ways to hire an attorney. It also includes a lawyer directory if you'd like help with finding attorneys with specific expertise.

Minding Your Media Intake

We all want to be "informed" and know what's going on in the world around us. If you're "uninformed," you're likely to make poor choices and mistakes, right?

Well, not so fast!

Some people believe that the more they know and are informed, the better the decisions they make will be. In my work and observations with many people over time, I would say that the quality of media that you consume and keeping a proper perspective is far more important than the sheer volume of media you consume.

You will see in many places throughout this book how I highlight the downside to consuming misinformed and hyped media. In this section, I discuss through some event examples how to be selective, which requires knowing what you're actually getting and how to assess the motives and objectivity of particular media.

Example 1: The COVID-19 pandemic

Consider the COVID-19 pandemic that all of us have recently lived through. A new, seemingly strange and mysterious virus was quickly spreading around the world, and we heard early on reports of infected people becoming extremely sick, developing pneumonia, being hospitalized, and dying. It felt similar to a big-screen movie like *Contagion* except it was real and we were living it.

As case counts and death tolls rose and were being reported 24/7 by the media, stock prices began to plunge as government-mandated economic shutdowns and stay-at-home orders spread rapidly. Media ratings surged as Americans sought up-to-date and "breaking" news from television, newspapers, media websites, and social media.

Like everyone else, I wanted to know what was going on and I also follow what the media is saying and doing for my work. Sometimes, even though I'm consuming much of the media that I do to assess what others are seeing and experiencing, I find myself feeling a bit overwhelmed or influenced. This happened at times with the pandemic.

Now, I'm a mentally strong person and my nature is to question and challenge narratives, especially when they aren't supported by facts and sound analysis. For example, in March 2020 I questioned closing schools and I also questioned the hyper vigilance about cleaning surfaces, wearing gloves for protection, and wiping down groceries that were brought home. This made little sense to me since we never did, nor were we told, to do these things during prior winter flu seasons during which the flu killed tens of thousands of people annually in the United States.

TIP

One of the reasons I consume different media, particularly from outlets that have differing points of view, is to stimulate debate and challenge any assumptions that I may have. If you consume only media that agrees and comports with your view of the world, I see that as dangerous because you are far more likely to have blind spots and biases that you may not be aware of. So please try to recognize the biases of the media you do consume and to make a good faith effort to consume some media that is more likely to challenge your views.

The COVID-19 pandemic is an example of a major event that shook the economy and financial markets and had problematic reporting. With nearly any breaking news type of story that has some negative aspects to it, much of the news media went wild with hyping a never-ending stream of concerns about COVID, the financial markets, and the economy. While it's fine and normal to have some concerns and fears and to take appropriate and sensible precautions, I found early on (and over time) that those who consumed the most poorly informed media had far more extreme concerns and worries such as:

>> **Overestimating the dangers of the virus:** Many in the news media erroneously took the number of COVID deaths and simply divided it by the number of documented cases. This made it appear that the death rate was about 2+ percent for those who contracted the virus, which wasn't even close to correct. It was well known that many more people had the virus (some blood antibody tests found the number to be 10 to 20 times higher) but were never tested and documented. For children and young adults, the virus was no more dangerous — and in fact generally less dangerous — than the flu. (Older people with major medical problems and who were obese were at far greater danger and most in need of protection. Men were harder hit too.)

>> **We were entering another great depression.** With the government-mandated shutdowns and millions of people being quickly thrown out of work, this fear was an easy one for the media to play up. But pandemics don't last forever, and it was reasonably clear that the economy and most jobs would come back once the forced shutdowns were wound down. Since most of the national news media is based in New York City, one of the most heavily shutdown cities in one of the most heavily shutdown states, most of their personnel lacked a fully informed perspective on what was happening in many other parts of the country. They also engaged in a false narrative that less-shutdown states like Texas and Florida were more dangerous, which was not true — those states actually had far better overall COVID-19 fatality numbers than heavily locked-down states in the northeast, for example, and had stronger economies due to lesser shutdowns.

>> **Stocks would keep collapsing.** In March 2020 when the government-mandated economic shutdowns began and layoffs took hold, stock prices fell sharply, dropping more than 30 percent in a matter of weeks. Stock prices actually bottomed in late March 2020 and began rebounding since informed stock market investors are forward-looking and don't mindlessly respond to current news.

Example 2: The 2008 Financial Crisis

The economy was entering a recession, catalyzed in part by excessive and risky lending in the housing sector, as the calendar turned to 2008. As the year wore on, more layoffs were announced, and the financial sector was rocked by loans once thought ultra-safe that were souring. A stock market decline gathered downward momentum. For sure, there was plenty of "bad news."

But I began noticing more and more stories about a great depression, like we had in the 1930s, unfolding. Article headlines from Reuters such as these were widely circulated:

> "Merrill CEO says economic environment recalls 1929."

> "Whitehead sees slump worse than Depression."

Merrill Lynch was in the news a lot in 2008 due to the problems they'd gotten into with sub-prime mortgages, which led to the acquisition of Merrill by Bank of America. I contacted Merrill Lynch at that time to comment further on CEO Thain's extreme remarks.

My question was this: If he was stating publicly that things were as bad as during the Great Depression, was Merrill telling their retail investing clients to sell their stock holdings to avoid a further decline in stock prices? Interestingly, a Merrill spokesman stated that their analysts recommended a different asset allocation and they "don't care what Thain says" and also cited a "difference of opinion" between Thain and Merrill's investment analysts.

Most importantly, Thain's comments seemed in large part to be in reference to and motivated by Merrill's own problematic situation. Merrill took on so much toxic mortgage paper that the company had to be sold to a stronger financial institution. Reuters failed to point that out.

In the case of the comments by John Whitehead, former Chairman of Goldman Sachs, his major concern seemed to be the growing federal budget deficit and the lack of desire of either party to rein in spending or increase taxes. In his view, this would lead to the United States losing its AAA credit rating as well as increased borrowing costs.

I was unable to reach Whitehead regarding the comment attributed to him by Reuters that he supposedly thought that the current economic problems could, ". . . be worse than the Depression." The reporter told me that Whitehead made these comments in a private session at a Reuter's summit.

Rather than making comparisons to the Great Depression, how about comparing the 2008 downturn to those that had happened more recently? Consider the recession of the early 1980s when we had double-digit long-term interest rates and inflation (whereas both those readings were well under 5 percent in 2008) and the unemployment rate rose to nearly 11 percent (the unemployment rate peaked at 10 percent in early 2009). Please see Chapter 1 for what happened during the 1930s Great Depression and why it bore virtually no resemblance to the 2008 recession.

An interesting exchange got the media's economic negativity out in the open on *The O'Reilly Factor* on November 12, 2008. Bill O'Reilly discussed the weak stock market and economy with Fox business reporter Terry Keenan. O'Reilly offered some terrific common-sense advice at the outset by telling viewers not to examine their monthly investment statements, but to stand pat and not panic. Keenan unfortunately offered some terrible advice and unsubstantiated opinions in response.

Keenan said, "I think people should have been opening their statements all along and they might not have lost so much money because they bought into the buy and hold."

I've heard this countless times before. While market timing sounds good in theory, it simply doesn't work for the folks or pros over the long term. Keenan's suggestion that by following investments closely people could have minimized their losses is absurd. In fact, in my decades of experience working with clients first as a financial advisor and as a writer, more often than not, people panic during tough times and foolishly sell after a major decline — precisely the time during which they should be thinking about buying.

Next, Keenan said, "We are going into a severe downturn, the mother of all recessions. It's going to be worse than most people expect . . . Unemployment is going to go through the roof." As I said earlier, it didn't even get as high as during the early 1980s recession.

Keenan didn't seem to understand that the media had been scaring people during all of 2008 and the toll that this took was confirmed by a CNN/Opinion Research poll from October which found that an astounding 6 in 10 Americans said that they believed a depression (not just a recession) was likely!

Late 2008 turned out to be the almost exact bottom for global stock prices which came roaring back. Most countries experienced a moderate to severe recession. But don't tell that to *New York Times* columnist Paul Krugman who in June 2010, a year into the economic recovery, declared that we were in a depression.

Early in the recovery, the *Huffington Post* ran a story entitled, "Global Economic Shock Worse Than Great Depression" on May 8, 2009. And the *Daily Telegraph* ran an article entitled, "Financial Crisis Is the Worst the World Has Ever Faced" on October 7, 2011. It's a shame that such hyped and misguided columns would continue to scare people away from stocks during a time when stocks were on sale!

Example 3: Corporations not paying income taxes

The story line had been brewing for some time, and the paper of record — the *New York Times* — really ignited the concern. On March 25, 2011, the Times published an article entitled, "G.E.'s Strategies Let It Avoid Taxes Altogether." The piece said that G.E. used a maze of tax loopholes, created in part through its own lobbying efforts, to dramatically reduce the corporate income tax it paid in America.

In addition to failing to discuss what would address the corporate income tax problems (lowering the U.S. corporate income tax rate as was finally done in 2018 and eliminated the major loopholes), the Times' article failed to mention how G.E.'s tax losses during the recent severe recession enabled the company to use those losses to reduce taxable income and therefore current taxes owed.

A few weeks later, the Associated Press (AP) ran a short news article reporting that G.E. apparently had a change of heart over its selfish tax maneuvers:

> "Facing criticism over the amount of taxes it pays, General Electric announced it will repay its entire $3.2 billion tax refund to the US Treasury on April 18. GE uses a series of foreign tax havens that the company says are legal and that led to an enormous refund for the 2010 tax year. The company earned $11 billion in 2010 on revenue of $150 billion. The company, based in Fairfield, Conn., plans to phase out tax havens over 5 years and said it will create one job in the US for each new job it creates overseas."

Apparently, all the negative publicity G.E. was getting over their shirking of their U.S. tax responsibilities was having an impact. However, the impact wasn't what it first appeared to be. The G.E. bashing had so incensed reporters at outlets like AP that they were in fact duped by a totally bogus press release! The release claiming that GE was returning its $3.2 billion refund from 2010 was completely fabricated by the activist groups US Uncut and The Yes Men, who later claimed they were seeking to raise awareness of U.S. corporate tax policy.

It's bad enough that AP didn't fact-check the content of the bogus release, but they also mindlessly regurgitated key components of the fake release. The fabricated release appeared on a website with a URL that was similar to a URL used by the real GE for their real press releases. Anyone with a sense of the real business world and who took the time to read and reflect upon the fake release wouldn't have fallen for its language and tone. Another huge red flag was that the contact information for the supposed GE spokesman, "Samuel Winnacker," provided a Nashville-area phone number. GE's real corporate offices are based in Fairfield, Connecticut. If AP had taken the time to call the Nashville-area number, they would have heard a recording and associated instructions that clearly sound silly and unreal for a corporate PR department.

Lessons learned and keys to remember

The world is awash in financial reporting and opinions. Listening to and reading what's generally out there is often confusing and stressful. Unfortunately, most financial journalists are themselves financially illiterate. I know this from direct observation of their work over many years and from their own sometimes candid admissions.

The situation is especially bad at metro area newspapers and wire services such as AP and United Press International (UPI). While there are exceptions, these reporters are problematic sources of information and analysis for the financial markets and economy. They tend to have little if any business training and education and, like too many journalists of all political stripes, focus excessively on negative events.

The internet and social media have led to a mushrooming of news (and opinions). While there's a lot of misinformation and bias online, more outlets provide much needed competition to legacy media outlets like the major national television and radio outlets and major metropolitan newspapers. Those outlets make plenty of mistakes, have plenty of biases, and like to hype short-term events and noise to keep folks anxious and tuned in.

REMEMBER

Always question what you read and hear from the media — or anywhere else for that matter! Do you know the reputation of the journalist doing the reporting and their media outlet? No matter what, remember that the media's attention is generally much more on the short term and most provocative stories.

3

Being a Smart Consumer of Economic Information

» **Understanding key economic reports and which ones can be mostly ignored**

» **Seeing how the media covers the economy and its data**

Chapter **6**

So Many Numbers! Making Sense of Economic Reports

W hen you follow the financial markets and invest in securities such as stocks and bonds, you will hear, read, and see a never-ending stream of economic data. The media, of course, loves some of these reports because they are constantly changing and constitute "breaking news" when released, as they contain some surprises and unexpected information.

If you're thinking that economic reports seem kind of boring, I'm not going to disagree with you. But some of them do matter, and some contain twists and turns and sometimes negative information that get blasted all over the media landscape. So, if you're an investor, you should have some familiarity with these reports.

Consuming economic reports and data are a bit like eating. Eating too little or too much isn't optimal for your health — you should seek an optimal, reasonable amount of a healthful selection of food and economic data. So, in this chapter, I help you to understand the various economic reports that may cross your path, how to make sense of them, and which ones are the most valuable to be familiar with and possibly monitor over time. I also explain how to correctly and best use them to increase your chances of making wise investing and other personal finance decisions.

Keeping Economic Reports in Perspective

New home sales, the consumer price index, new car sales, the index of leading economic indicators, employment/private payrolls report, retail sales, the unemployment rate, the gross domestic product. These are but a few of the many economic reports and data points that are continually released.

Before we dive into the specific reports and understanding what each means, I talk a bit about some overarching concepts to keep in mind about these reports.

Reports are a (small) snapshot in time

REMEMBER

Always, always, always remember that economic reports are a short-term snapshot in time. Some cover a week (like new/initial unemployment claims), but most cover a month; yet even a month is a relatively short period of time.

A jobs report for the month of May tells you how many more or fewer jobs there were at the end of May than there were at the end of April, the month prior. It's a one-month snapshot. Gross domestic product reports, which I explain in the following section on the various economic reports, calculate overall U.S. economic activity on a quarterly (three-month) basis.

Please also keep in mind that monthly readings for some economic data can fluctuate somewhat erratically and unpredictably due to a variety of events. The data can be affected by unusual events as well as outright mistakes or errors that are corrected typically at the next release date (and sometimes even beyond that) for that specific report.

Now, I have to warn you that some folks in the financial industry, like veteran money manager Ken Fisher, have been quite outspoken about the inaccuracy of government economic reports. Consider the following that Fisher has said:

> "You shouldn't place much stock in government data. Mostly, government macroeconomic data aren't very accurate to begin with . . . They are nothing better than a blurry snapshot of reality that isn't very precise . . . coming as announced numbers that will be revised many times and materially before being finalized — and the numbers won't be very precise then."

Is economic data really that bad?

Honestly, overall, no. If it were literally and truly that awful, it would be ignored. What Fisher is implicitly saying here and warning about is not placing so much importance on any one specific report. In addition to the reason I discuss here (these reports are but a small snapshot in time), Fisher is simply pointing out that there are inaccuracies and imprecision in the measuring and reporting process. Like me, Fisher has also witnessed plenty of investors who follow these reports too closely and who are prone to making emotional, kneejerk reactions to them regarding their personal investments.

Beware annualized numbers

Some of the economic data can be even more greatly misleading for another reason — the highlighting of the percentage change in the numbers. In July 2020, the second quarter 2020 Gross Domestic Product, which reports on overall U.S. economic activity, was released. Headlines blared that the second quarter 2020 GDP plunged 33 percent!

Now, if you invested $1,000 in an investment that I told you plunged 33 percent soon after you invested, if you were fairly good at math, you could quickly determine the $1,000 investment was then worth just $670. But that's not what happened with the second quarter 2020 GDP.

The actual release of the GDP data from the government makes reasonably clear that GDP dropped at an *annualized* rate of 33 percent in the second quarter. What this means is that the economy shrank about 9 percent in the quarter (similar to your $1,000 investment dropping in value to $910), and if it continued declining at that rate for a total of one year (an additional nine months), then it would be down 33 percent over a full year.

Media outlets and their headline writers are provocative and attention seeking. So, you must always remember that they hype up the news and make things sound more extreme than what they really are in order to gain more attention, viewers, and listeners.

So, you won't generally see a headline that says that U.S. economic output declined 9 percent in the second quarter of 2020 due to government-mandated shutdowns. Instead, actual headlines were more along the lines of:

"Economy plunges 32 percent as depression concerns loom"

"US economy's worst show since Great Depression, 32.9% fall in Q2 highest since 1947"

"U.S. economy plunges at titanic 32.9% rate in 2nd quarter"

For more about how to make sense of the media's economic coverage, see the section "Interpreting Media Coverage of Economic Data," later in this chapter.

Take a long-term view of the numbers

It's fine to follow recent economic reports, but it's essential to do something that is rarely done in the coverage of those reports — putting things in a long-term perspective. I continue with the Gross Domestic Product data I was just discussing.

On the five-year graph in Figure 6-1, you can see the relatively sizeable drop in GDP in the second quarter of 2020. Notice how in the subsequent quarters, all of that decline and then some has been recovered. That's what I mean by taking a long-term view of the numbers.

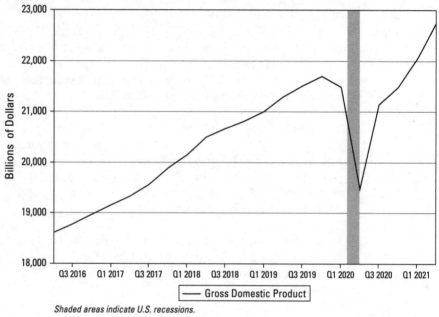

Source: St. Louis Federal Reserve

FIGURE 6-1:
A drop in GDP followed by recovery.

Shaded areas indicate U.S. recessions.

In the graph in Figure 6-2, you can see how GDP has trended since just after World War II. The shaded areas represent recessions (periods of generally declining economic activity). You will notice the near constant upward rise in GDP and that the declining periods are relatively brief and not that severe in the overall context of the decades we're viewing here.

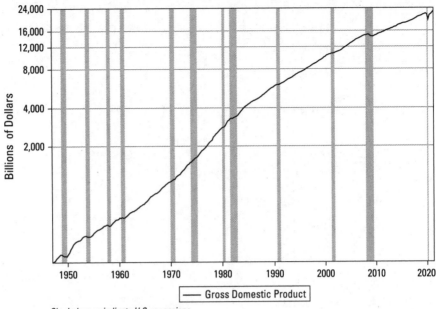

FIGURE 6-2:
GDP trend from
1948 to present.

Shaded areas indicate U.S. recessions.

Source: St. Louis Federal Reserve

Sleuthing Through Economic Reports

In this section, I walk you through economic reports that are worth understanding and how and why you should care about and use them for your financial and investing decisions. I also briefly cover the less useful reports and why they are generally not as useful even though some people may tell you otherwise.

Employment/jobs reports

The U.S. Bureau of Labor Statistics reports monthly on the number of employees on U.S. company payrolls. They don't actually survey all employers to collect this data — the survey covers nearly half of all U.S. nonfarm workers in about 400,000 businesses and government entities. This monthly report is known as the *payroll survey* or *establishment survey* (see Figure 6-3).

You can see over the decades the generally steady increase in jobs punctuated by occasional recessions (the shaded areas) during which the number of folks employed in total typically declines. The most recent recession caused by the government-mandated COVID-19 economic shutdowns led to an unusually quick and sharp drop in payrolls, which is snapping back more quickly than after a typical recession.

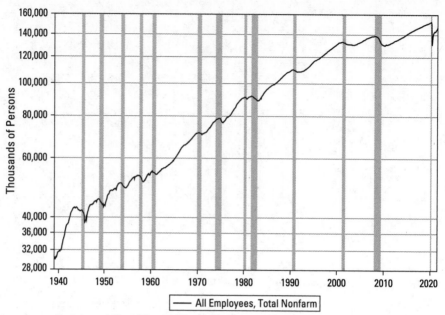

160,000
140,000
120,000
100,000
80,000
60,000
40,000
36,000
32,000
28,000

1940   1950   1960   1970   1980   1990   2000   2010   2020

Thousands of Persons

—— All Employees, Total Nonfarm

Shaded areas indicate U.S. recessions.

FIGURE 6-3:
An example of a
payroll survey.

Source: St. Louis Federal Reserve

A growing and expanding economy leads to more people being hired, and that's generally a good thing. Consider that in late 2019 and early 2020 before the COVID-19 pandemic hit, record numbers of people were employed in the United States, and the unemployment rate, which measures the percentage of people not able to find work out of the total workforce, hit 3.5 percent, the lowest in 50 years. (I talk about the unemployment rate in a moment.)

Since 2005, ADP, the payroll processing company, has published their own proprietary payroll report: the ADP National Employment Report. While their report covers fewer employers than does the BLS's payroll report, it is based upon employees counted on ADP's customers' payrolls. Since ADP's report is released two days before the BLS's payroll report, ADP's report gives some clues to the likely numbers coming out of the BLS report.

TIP

Because both of these payroll reports are based upon less than a majority of employers, they contain sampling errors and are essentially estimating what's happening with overall employment in the U.S. economy. And the month-to-month changes can be somewhat erratic, so at a minimum, you should generally be examining the past several months and not just what happened in one month.

The calculation of the unemployment rate is based upon yet another survey: the household survey, which asks questions of about 60,000 households. This BLS survey asks adult members of the surveyed households if they have been looking for work over the prior four weeks. So, from this survey the government can calculate the unemployment rate by taking the number of people who are actively looking for work but not working and dividing that by the total number of people in the U.S. labor force, which includes those who are working plus those who are unemployed (actively seeking employment but not yet employed).

Not all adults in the United States are in the "labor force." Some folks, for example, may choose to stay at home and raise children or perhaps simply not work because financially they don't need to. You can see from the long-term labor force participation rate in Figure 6-4 that that the rate increased from the mid-1960s until the 1990s (mainly due to more women entering the labor force) and reached about two-thirds. It has since declined.

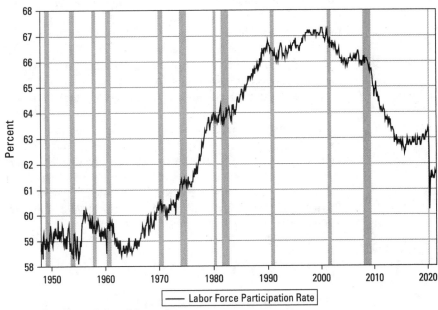

FIGURE 6-4:
Labor force
participation rate.

Shaded areas indicate U.S. recessions.

Source: St. Louis Federal Reserve

**TECHNICAL
STUFF**

Just because more jobs are created and employers are hiring doesn't necessarily translate into a direct reduction in the unemployment rate in the short term. The reason is that more people may choose to enter the workforce.

Gross Domestic Product

If you've read this chapter from the beginning, you already have some background about Gross Domestic Product (GDP) numbers, which are reported quarterly by the U.S. Bureau of Economic Analysis. GDP numbers track the value of goods and services produced by labor and property located in the United States. As such, GPD is a fairly good macro measure of whether the overall U.S. economy is growing and if so, how well (see Figure 6-2 earlier in the chapter).

Economic growth generally leads to more jobs, a higher overall standard of living, and increasing corporate profits. When the economy is contracting or shrinking, the opposite is generally happening — there are fewer jobs, a lower overall standard of living, and corporate profits that tend to be less robust. So, economic growth is a good thing.

But faster and faster economic growth overall doesn't inevitably translate into higher stock prices. Wharton Finance Professor Jeremy Siegel found from doing a long-term analysis going back to 1900 that a country's real GDP growth (that is, growth above the rate of inflation) is actually negatively correlated with stock market returns. This surprising finding means that those economies experiencing higher rates of growth relative to the rate of inflation actually tend to produce lower long-term stock market returns. (His analysis shows that this fact is even more pronounced in developing countries like China that have right rates of GDP growth and interestingly not terrific long-term stock market returns.)

In explaining how this could possibly be, Siegel points out that the primary determinants of stock prices are earnings per share and dividends per share. Economic growth does not necessarily boost earnings and dividends per share because fast overall economic growth requires higher capital expenditures and, as Siegel points out, this capital does not come freely. "The added interest costs in the case of debt financing and the dilution of earnings in the case of equity financing reduce the growth of earnings per share," says Siegel.

Consumer confidence

There are two major surveys, done by the University of Michigan and the Conference Board, of consumer confidence or sentiment. For each of these, a number of people are asked to rate and evaluate their current financial situation and expectations for the future.

In Figure 6-5 you can see the University of Michigan Consumer Sentiment survey going back to 1952. You can see from the graphic that during periods of economic recession (shaded areas), consumer sentiment is generally quite low and depressed. During periods of economic expansion (non-shaded areas), consumer sentiment is elevated and tends to rise when a recovery is improving and aging.

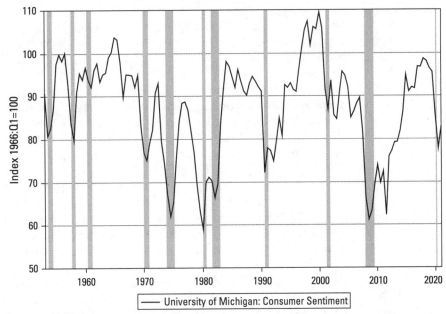

FIGURE 6-5:
University of
Michigan
Consumer
Sentiment.

Shaded areas indicate U.S. recessions.

Source: St. Louis Federal Reserve

TIP

Now, here's an interesting way to use this economic data as a "contrarian indicator." When consumer confidence and sentiment are quite low and depressed, that historically has proven to be a great time to find otherwise worthy investments at attractive low prices. This makes sense when you stop and think about the fact that this indicator is mostly measuring how folks feel about the time in which they are being asked.

So, in late 2008 in the midst of that year's financial crisis and spring 2020 when millions of workers were thrown out of work and the stock market was crushed due to the government-mandated COVID-19 economic shutdowns, it makes sense that most people would have a negative view of what was happening at those times. But, just as the sun will shine again after a big storm, the economy inevitably rebounds after a downturn.

Corporate profits

The thing that matters most to financial markets and stock market investors is corporate profits. When you invest in stocks, which simply are shares of ownership of a company, the long-term value of those stocks will vary greatly depending mostly upon the profits those companies are able to achieve.

REMEMBER

The financial markets are always forward-looking, so they won't just react to today's earnings announcements but will also weigh what is called *guidance* — that is, what companies say they see coming in the near future.

Many investors and numerous professional money managers were somewhat surprised by how powerful the stock market rebound was after the severe decline in March 2020 due to the government-mandated COVID-19 economic shutdowns. Most major stock indexes hit new all-time highs in late 2020 and then continued rising into 2021.

Savvy investors were looking ahead, and by early 2021, many companies, including those that had to lay off some workers in 2020, were posting record profits. In fact, in the first quarter of 2021, a large portion of companies beat analysts' profit expectations by a wide margin and increased their guidance for the year ahead. That's a recipe for rising stock prices.

REMEMBER

Stock prices are ultimately driven by corporate profits. After an economic downturn during which companies have laid off some employees and cut other costs, when business picks back up, companies are usually set up for a strong increase in profits.

HIGH-FREQUENCY ECONOMIC DATA

This type of economic data got more exposure and discussion during the COVID-19 pandemic. *High-frequency data* simply means economic data that comes out or is measured frequently — typically daily, instead of the more common monthly or weekly economic reports that I discuss in this chapter.

With the rapidly changing conditions during the COVID-19 pandemic, high-frequency data was appealing to economists and financial market participants to monitor because it would give some earlier insights into how the economy was changing. Take the example of the number of daily airplane travelers who were passing through the TSA's airport screening at the many U.S. airports around the country. This daily data told us how the number of airplane travelers compared with the same period of prior and recent years and allowed for closer monitoring of the healing and return to normalcy taking place within that industry.

Other examples of high-frequency data included daily hotel occupancy and average room rate data and mobility data as tracked by big tech companies through our cellphones. The regional Federal Reserve districts, which you can find at www. federalreserve.gov/aboutthefed/federal-reserve-system.htm, have all sorts of high-frequency data for the geographical territory covered by their districts.

Consumer prices (also known as inflation)

The most widely followed inflation gauge is the Consumer Price Index (CPI). It gets plenty of attention from some financial market participants. There are always some who are predicting a new round of high inflation, and often these folks are suggesting or pitching holdings such as gold (or now some cryptocurrencies) that supposedly will benefit from high inflation and pressure on traditional government-backed currencies like the U.S. dollar.

Monthly, the U.S. Bureau of Labor Statistics releases two versions of the CPI: one overall number, the so-called headline inflation number; and the core CPI, which is inflation excluding changes in energy and food prices. Take a look at Figure 6-6 where you can see the overall (more volatile) inflation rate (blue line) compared with the core (less volatile) inflation rate (red line). Food and energy prices generally fluctuate more than other types of prices, so examining inflation without those components (core inflation) gives us a more accurate read on what's really happening with inflation.

The CPI historically has been about 3 percent per year but has been closer to 2 percent in more recent years. Note that back in the late 1960s, it began trending higher and continued rising and falling until it breached 10 percent per year in the mid-1970s and late-1970s/early-1980s. This period had double-digit interest rates, poor economic growth, and a terrible stock market.

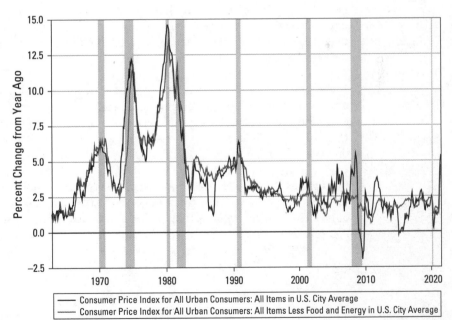

FIGURE 6-6:
Overall versus core CPI.

Consumer Price Index for All Urban Consumers: All Items in U.S. City Average
Consumer Price Index for All Urban Consumers: All Items Less Food and Energy in U.S. City Average

Shaded areas indicate U.S. recessions.

Source: St. Louis Federal Reserve

The Federal Reserve keeps a close eye on inflation and hopefully has learned from past mistakes, including those made in the 1970s.

The reports you can mostly ignore

For sure, there are lots of economic reports, far more than you're going to have the time and interest to track and understand. In this section, I briefly discuss some of the less important economic reports that you may hear about and perhaps have some interest in.

This section isn't meant to be exhaustive of all the remaining economic data out there. And it's possible that because of your professional work you may have a greater interest in certain economic data. For example, perhaps you like to follow more real estate–related economic data because your job is directly or indirectly impacted by that sector or you have notable investments in that sector.

Initial claims for unemployment benefits

Every Thursday, the government announces *initial claims* for unemployment benefits. What this number tells us is how many people over the prior week just applied for unemployment benefits.

Given that this number is reported weekly, some financial market participants like watching it for important changes in layoffs because the jobs reports and unemployment reports come out less frequently — monthly. Beware, however, that these weekly reports have some volatility and inaccuracies and are often revised after their initial release.

Sometimes, economic watchers may point to a multi-week increase in initial claims as a concerning sign for the overall economy that it may be slowing down or heading into a downturn (recession). While this may happen, more often than not, it doesn't. Thus, you may say that in the short term, following this data can produce some false alarms.

During the COVID-19 government-mandated economic shutdowns, these weekly unemployment claim filings got more attention than usual during the initial wave of layoffs in the spring of 2020 and then continuing through the rest of the year and into 2021. Rather than having to wait and see what was happening in the monthly employment reports, these weekly reports gave investors more to chew on.

Other economic data sometimes in the news

Sorry to say but there are yet more economic data sets that are tracked and reported. Here's a short list of other common ones you'll hear about and the basics on what you should know about each. I don't think you need to track or follow any of these lesser important data.

>> **Durable goods orders:** This includes both consumer and business durable goods. Consumer durables, which are goods bought by individuals and households, include things like autos, electronics, furniture, luggage, sports equipment, and so forth. Business durable goods are used by businesses and include airplanes, boats, buses, trucks, property, plant and equipment, and industrial equipment such as machinery.

>> **Industrial production:** This economic statistic is comprised of the output, capacity, and capacity utilization in the U.S. industrial sector. The Federal Reserve defines that sector to include companies in the following industries: manufacturing, mining, and electric and gas utilities.

>> **ISM Manufacturing and Non-Manufacturing (Services):** The Institute for Supply Management reports Manufacturing and Services sector data based upon data compiled from a national survey of purchasing and supply executives.

>> **New and existing home sales:** Monthly reports show how many new homes were sold by builders and a separate report presents how many existing (for example, used) homes were sold (changed hands from sellers to buyers). Since new homes sold actually represent new buildings and demand for those, that index is slightly more relevant to the health of the real estate sector.

>> **Producer price index:** The Producer Price Index (PPI) reports the average change in the selling prices received by domestic producers for their output. The prices included in the PPI are from the first commercial transaction for many products and some services. This index does not measure the ultimate price changes that consumers face when they purchase goods and services.

>> **Vehicle sales:** This simply measures the total number of new vehicles, which includes autos, light trucks, and heavy trucks, sold monthly.

Interpreting Media Coverage of Economic Data

In Chapter 5, I discuss some general concepts to keep in mind as you consume the many varieties of news and media out there. If you haven't done so, please be sure to read that material to make more sense of the media you choose to read, watch, and listen to.

In this section, I discuss how to intelligently use media reports on the economy. First, I cover the media's overall tendencies on these types of reports and then discuss some recent periods of turmoil to highlight what types of things to watch out for.

Understanding the short-term and provocative focus

If there are five recent economic reports floating around and the media have time to cover just one or two of them, guess how they choose? They are almost always going to pick the one that appears to be the most jarring, concerning, and provocative. Think of it this way: They don't report on the millions of auto drivers who arrive safely back at home; they report on the big accidents of the day.

With the economy, there are rarely any reports that are the equivalent of an auto accident, but some can more easily garner attention. Companies laying people off, product shortages, rising prices, and so on are the kinds of things that get lots of media coverage. Negative events almost always crowd out positive events.

Consider that when the stock market makes larger moves, its coverage gets more visibility and promotion in various media outlets. Large point drops in the Dow Jones Industrial Average are plastered on the front pages of newspapers, lead stories on the television evening news, trend on social media (thanks to all the posts there from media outlets), and so forth.

Keeping an eye out for biases

It shouldn't be news to you that many media outlets have a political bias, and that can and often does color how they cover various news, including economic news. For example, left-leaning media outlets (such as CNN, MSNBC, and most legacy media outlets) are happy to report negative economic news if doing so reflects poorly on conservative politicians. The same can of course be said the other way — that right-leaning outlets (such as Fox News and conservative talk radio programs) enjoy skewering liberal politicians by covering economic data that can make them look bad.

Now, please make it a habit to try to note the difference between opinion shows and actual news programs. Granted, there are fewer and fewer of the latter as more and more journalists are actually opinion people with a political agenda and bias. (In Chapter 7, I discuss further how to best manage the influence of your own political point of view.)

Without any further ado, following are some recent examples of the media's coverage of two recent major economic downturns: the COVID-19 pandemic and the 2008 financial crisis.

Example 1: The COVID-19 pandemic

During the COVID-19 pandemic, especially during the early stages of the government-mandated economic shutdowns, I wanted to shout from the rooftops to all who would listen that the media was making many things, especially those related to the economy and financial markets, sound far worse than reality. And the result of this was that it was causing good people to make bad decisions with their investments and the rest of their personal finances.

There are many examples of misleading and extremely negative media coverage of economic reports, especially in the early weeks and months of the pandemic economic shutdowns. What follows are some that highlight the problem and how good people were misled.

Greatly overstating the number of unemployed

Every week, the government releases the number of initial claims, which tells us approximately the number of people who have just applied for unemployment benefits. For sure, in the early weeks of the government-mandated economic shutdowns, millions of people filed weekly for unemployment claims. As those weeks turned into months, many media outlets began mindlessly adding up the total number of initial claims filed — and the number soon broached tens of millions of people out of work — since the onslaught began.

Most of the media failed to point out the fact that significant numbers of people laid off early on began getting hired back, and that was actually reflected in the *continuing claims* data, which reports on the number of people who are still receiving unemployment benefits. Take, for example, the provocatively titled article from July 30, 2020, "We Are Experiencing Economic Devastation on A Scale That America Has Never Seen Before." Within that piece was the statement, "Overall, a grand total of more than 54 million Americans have filed new claims for unemployment benefits during the last 19 weeks."

Yes, that statement was technically true but was hugely misleading since most of those people had returned to their jobs. In fact, at that same time, continuing claims, which represented folks then collecting unemployment, stood at 17 million, a far cry from the 54 million cited in the article. This would suggest that about 37 million people had returned back to their jobs of the 54 million total who lost their jobs.

Most such articles also failed to point out that those out of work were receiving greatly bolstered benefits which in most cases for lower- and moderate-income earners led to them being paid as much (or even more) while on unemployment than they were earning in their recent job. Also, most non-high-income earners ended up receiving three sizeable government stimulus payments (spring 2020, winter 2020, and spring 2021).

Focusing on industries getting hit hard

Especially in the early months of the pandemic, the news media coverage of the economy also focused quite a bit on hard-hit industries. We regularly saw pictures and video segments of near-empty airports and hotel lobbies, and shuttered restaurants, sports arenas, and other entertainment venues.

This was real and important news and should have indeed been covered. However, this should not have been done to the exclusion of talking about the reality that some companies and sectors (such as big technology companies) were actually benefiting from the lockdowns and doing greater business.

I personally found this a bit hard to take, especially since the media continued to give megaphones to those who harped on the supposed dangers of going out to a restaurant, the local gym, and so on and then failed to discuss and show how crowded stores like Home Depot, Target, and Walmart were, for example. I remember being dumbfounded and shocked when I made a trip to a local Home Depot and had a hard time finding parking because the store was so flooded with customers. Inside the store, there were long lines and people weren't exactly keeping their distance from one another, especially in the front part of the store.

So, as I watched big company stocks like Home Depot and many in the technology sector rapidly rebound after the March 2020 sharp selloff and then push through to new highs later in 2020, it wasn't surprising to me at all.

Presenting annualized GDP and other data

As I discuss early on in this chapter in the section entitled "Beware annualized numbers," the media frequently and often presents annualized data without disclosing, let alone explaining, that the data cited cover a far shorter period of time than one year. They did this with GDP data in the second quarter of 2020 as I explain in that section.

This was done with plenty of other economic data in the months of March, April, and May 2020 when other economic measures, such as prices, dropped sharply, but the media made some of those numbers sound worse by annualizing them. Annualizing sharply falling prices made the period sound like what happened during the 1930s Great Depression, when prices tumbled for an extended period of time.

Example 2: The 2008 financial crisis

During the financial crisis of 2008, there was certainly plenty of bad news as folks, especially in the financial and affiliated sectors including real estate, were thrown out of work. The media, however, as they almost always do, made things sound worse than what they really were. (In Chapter 5, I explain how they erroneously compared this period to the 1930s Great Depression.)

Here, I talk through how they misled people regarding the actual situation and the extent of the downturn in corporate profits as well as how they used anecdotes rather than facts and common sense to make it sound as if this recession was permanently and negatively altering the U.S. economy.

Corporate profits plunged 85 percent in 2008?

Every year, *Fortune* magazine publishes its Fortune 500 list of the 500 largest U.S. companies (ranked by revenue). When the 2008 list was published in early 2009, the big news was that the companies on that list had reported profits that were down 85 percent. That headline and lots of negative commentary associated with it was everywhere in the media landscape.

One good example was when *Fortune* top brass appeared on NBC's popular *Meet the Press* to discuss. Here in a nutshell is what transpired. NBC's then program host David Gregory opined, ". . . even if there is some return to profitability, the economy's not coming back to where we were before, because where we were before was simply not sustainable."

Gregory, who has no background in economics, has been a journalist his entire professional career. No matter — he was proffering highly negative economic forecasts. Gregory failed to understand that many companies were still profitable and in every economic downturn in our nation's history, including the Great Depression, the economy has always exceeded its prior peak, usually within a few years.

Nina Easton, Washington Editor for *Fortune* then referenced her publication's recent release of their Fortune 500 issue and said, "We've been doing this for 55 years. The earnings drop among the Fortune 500 was 85 percent last year," to which *Time* magazine's Managing Editor Rick Stengel said, "Wow!"

Easton then said, "That is the largest drop, the steepest drop in the history since we've been releasing this issue." And just to make sure that the audience didn't miss these points, Gregory said, "Last year the worst economic performance in the 55-year history of the Fortune 500 list . . . companies' earnings dropped 84.7 percent, as you just said, from the previous year, from $645 billion to $99 billion. It's the largest ever one-year decline."

There's a big problem here, however. Losses are netted against profits, and one in four (126 of the Fortune 500) companies reported losses in 2008. In fact, *Fortune* calculated for me that the companies posting a loss for the year posted losses totaling $514 billion. (The 10 biggest money losers that year alone reported losses totaling $351 billion led by AIG, which posted a whopping $99 billion loss.) The 374 Fortune 500 companies posting a profit in 2008 produced profits totaling $613 billion. This only represents a 19.5 percent profit decline from the 443 companies posting a profit the prior year (2007).

Consumers have a "new frugality?"

Rick Stengel appeared on *Meet the Press* in early 2009 to discuss *Time* magazine's recent cover story entitled, "The New Frugality." Stengel said, "The recession has changed more than just how we live. It's changed what we value, what we expect even after the economy recovers."

Program host David Gregory asked Stengel what the story reveals about how the recession is changing people's lives. Stengel said, "People are recalibrating their lives . . . They're thinking about how they consume, they're thinking about how they live. They're thinking that those endless horizons that we were always told we'd have are not there anymore . . . They're cutting back on things like bottled water. They're growing their own gardens . . . they're exercising more but going to health clubs less."

REMEMBER

I had been thinking about that issue a lot and always talking to people I ran into and corresponded with regarding what they were doing. A recession, no doubt, serves as a wake-up call to some of those hit hardest by it. But we've had recessions before, and it should be remembered that even during good economic times, some folks are hit hard. Conversely, some companies and people do well (and even better) in a recession (more on that in moment).

Consumers hadn't been cutting back on bottled water. And we didn't see more folks exercising outside more and going to the gym less. In fact, I remember noting that past winter the robustness of gym membership and usage at some local gyms, which made sense the more people I spoke with about it. During stressful times, the release and relief that comes from exercise and personal contact is refreshing to most people. (Is running on a hard asphalt road on your own and dodging SUV drivers yapping on their cellphones a risk worth taking?)

As for planting more home vegetable gardens, that prediction really shows how off base and out of touch *Time* is. The folks I spoke with at that time who still had jobs were generally working harder and longer hours. Planting a vegetable garden for the first time wasn't on folks' to-do list.

Of course, in an economic downturn, more folks are suffering, and I'm not trying in any way to minimize that. But it's important to remember that the media exaggerates the negative and uses anecdotes without supporting data to push particular narratives.

Chapter **7**

Says Who? Weighing "Experts'" Advice

The media can serve an important function. In addition to covering the news of the day, the media serve as gatekeepers of sorts in whom they choose to interview and present as experts.

As I've long discussed in my writings and presentations, it's challenging to select experts in a field in which you yourself are not an expert. You should always keep that in mind while consuming various media because the gatekeepers you're relying upon may not know any more than you do about the financial and economic topics they're covering. Even worse, they may well know less than you and/or have a conflict of interest that isn't apparent to you.

In this chapter, I help you to understand how and why various pundits are getting the media's attention. I also explain how to evaluate individual gurus and experts to determine whether you should consider their advice and predictions.

Understanding Why Particular Pundits Get Attention

In this section, I take you "behind the scenes" to show you how and why the media pick particular pundits to interview and feature. As a writer myself for various outlets and as a best-selling author, I've observed and participated from both sides of the media, so I'm uniquely qualified to share with you how things work.

Important things to know about the "news" media

The media often tests my patience, but I found myself more exasperated than usual with their coverage of the COVID-19 pandemic. Ditto for their coverage of what's going on in the economy and financial markets.

I've had an inside view of the media for many years and gotten to know many people in the media. Years ago, I had a regular column in the *San Francisco Chronicle* and the *San Francisco Examiner*. I also wrote for numerous other local and national publications. After writing some books, I appeared on and was interviewed by many media outlets. As my years of experience have morphed into decades, my observations, insights, and opinions have become clearer.

WARNING

Some of what you are about to read may seem pointed and critical! And it includes some discussion of politics, which I know is taboo for some. But it's an 800-pound elephant in the room that can't be ignored, especially if you want to make the most of your money.

As a media consumer, here's what I think you need to keep in mind and remember:

>> Some people are attracted to go into the media because they see it as a way to improve the world and make it a better place. An exceptional few people in the news media do indeed do that — I've met and worked with some decent people over the years.

>> Too many media outlets today are filled with opinions rather than actual journalism. This is especially true among political reporters who as a group have corrupted and polluted vast swaths of the media landscape. Opinion people who call themselves reporters and journalists aren't, and they're ruining the profession of journalism. Such commentary under the guise of news reporting can negatively impact your perceptions about what's going on in the economy and financial markets.

>> Most mainstream media outlets tilt left politically. This is true of most daily newspapers, legacy television outlets (CBS, NBC, ABC) and cable outlets like CNN and MSNBC. Conservative media is significant among talk radio and on opinion shows on Fox News. The internet is more balanced; although social media outlets also skew left, they have some balance since the content is somewhat user and more democratically generated.

>> Media outlets focus on the short term — the very short term — and this trend is worsening thanks to the ubiquitous social media platforms (Facebook, Instagram, Twitter, and so on). It's all a big contest to get the most eyeballs and clicks, so speed and appeal conquer quality and thoughtfulness. The media's hyper-focus on the noise of the day and the very short term can have the same impact on you when you regularly consume what they're serving!

>> Most reporters who report on the economy, financial markets, investing, and personal finance know little about the subject area. I noticed this many years ago, which became a big source of motivation for me to write about these areas given my background in the financial services industry and work as a financial advisor.

>> Editors and reporters often and more typically begin to write a piece with a particular point of view or narrative and bring in evidence, opinions, and information to support that point of view. In fact, articles are typically assigned by managing editors in this fashion, or a reporter proposes a specific angle and gets approval to write that article.

>> Headlines may be somewhat disconnected or not perfectly aligned with the pieces they are attached to. The reason for this is that the headline writer is rarely the person who wrote or produced the bulk of the article or segment.

>> When the media has experts on, those experts should never be assumed to be the best or brightest in their field or even to have sensible insights that could help you. Some may and do, but many do not. Think about something you know a lot about and then evaluate the supposed experts you see quoted and cited by the media and you'll know exactly what I mean.

"Journalists have opinions and look for people to fit a narrative. That skews the expertise that you get to hear," says psychologist Dr. Brian Russell who has appeared on numerous media outlets himself. He adds that television producers, for example, do "pre-interviews" where they ask you many more questions than you will be asked on-air so they know what you are likely to say and can sidestep asking you a question that might lead to your saying something that doesn't fit with their narrative.

>> Specific publications and media outlets often have an overarching narrative or point of view. Only exposing yourself to outlets that reinforce your partisan political point of view can be hazardous to your wealth. I saw this happen to

some conservatives when Barack Obama was elected in 2008, and it happened again in 2016 and the following years with President Trump in office. The stock market did quite well during both of these presidencies but those who opposed them politically sometimes missed out on the gains because they were convinced the economy and stock market would do poorly due to misguided policies.

Getting media attention is a competitive business

Many people are seeking attention for their business. Media folks are often inundated with contacts from those who want to be interviewed and quoted and featured.

For sure, it's a competition among those who want some attention. Here are some key factors that determine who gets attention and who doesn't:

>> **Merit matters, somewhat.** The media does ferret out and discover some of the best and most talented people in a particular field, but merit does not matter as much as some would like to think.

>> **Some publicists are better than others.** Whether a pundit is promoting themselves or has hired someone else to promote them, the fact is that some folks are better salespeople and promoters than others.

>> **Networking and contacts matter.** Some experts and pundits get airtime and coverage because of who they know. Of course, that's not to say that just because you know people in media you will get coverage, but it does help to have a foot in the door.

>> **Controversy (and negativity) often sell.** While the media does some feel-good stories and good-news stories, the reality is that most of what's covered is either controversial or negative. This happens so often in fact, it's the subject matter of the rest of this section.

Controversial points of view often attract

The business media interviews lots and lots of economists. They are inevitably asked to tell us mere mortals what the economy is likely to do in the road ahead.

Economists predict, but what's their actual track record? Some economists bask in the news media spotlight and make boastful claims about the accuracy of their prior forecasts.

Examining economists' forecasts is difficult. Most economists make their living through working with a modest number of corporate and institutional clients. Their predictions and publications are not a matter of public record, and they generally refuse to provide copies of their published predictions to an independent entity that may attempt to track their accuracy. (That should tell you something!)

Over the years, I have seen some studies that examine economists' predictions, and those analyses have routinely found that economists don't have such a swell track record, especially when it comes to calling turning points in the economy. Later in this chapter, I highlight and document economists who were or are popular with the media and whose predictions have largely been wrong.

Michael Bryan and Linsey Molloy of the Federal Reserve Bank of Cleveland analyzed dozens of economists' predictions going back to 1983. They found a reason why certain economists are popular with the media, and it has nothing to do with the quality of their forecasts:

> "In virtually every way, the work we present here has been confirmed by many before us. In the 1980s, Stephen McNees documented the superiority of consensus forecasts relative to most individual forecasts, a result that has been upheld time and again. Further, many others have failed to find evidence that some forecasters possess a special insight into the economy that allows them to predict its course better than others.

> "One major assumption of these analyses is that an economist's primary goal is, in fact, to make an accurate forecast. However, it may be the case that a forecaster has an objective other than accuracy . . . some forecasters appear to seek publicity by being outliers, and that this publicity is of greater value than the relative accuracy of their predictions (David Laster, Paul Bennett, and In Sun Geoum). These ideas have been reworked more recently by Jordi Pons-Novell, who shows that forecasters from different institutional backgrounds appear to be motivated by different incentives, such that investment bankers may be trying to maximize publicity or other similar criteria, while forecasters who work at nonfinancial corporations seem to mimic more closely the consensus prediction.

> "Regardless of what motivates the forecaster, our investigation suggests that over the past 23 years, economists have had trouble producing forecasts that were superior to naïve predictions, and only a small proportion of forecasters were more accurate than the median forecast—and none statistically so . . ."

Some economists, like Nouriel Roubini (discussed in the next section), have made extensive efforts to gain exposure through the media. Roubini's track record has been awful, and I have also documented his misrepresentation and selective recall of his past predictions. Roubini has also made the mistake of attempting to forecast movements in the financial and commodities markets, which is clearly way beyond whatever economic expertise he actually does have. Not surprisingly, his forecasts of these markets, which individual investors are more likely to follow, have been quite terrible.

TIP

For academic economists, there is a tracking of who publishes the most research, the so-called "Top 10% Authors" (ideas.repec.org/top/top.person.all.html). While this doesn't tell us who is a top forecaster or which economists even make forecasts, the ranking at least shows you who is doing research of sufficient quality to get published.

TIP

You can examine the same data by economic institution to get a sense of which universities and organizations have the most economic academic publishing (ideas.repec.org/top/top.inst.all.html).

Political partisans can be hazardous to your wealth

As you listen to various economists and other pundits, especially those frequently cited in the media, be aware that some of them have strong political ideologies, which color their view of the world, politicians, and economic policies. Following their advice can and often is hazardous to your wealth. But media love controversy, and few things stir up more controversy quickly than political partisans!

My regular readers know that I call them as I see them, and I give more than equal criticism to liberals and conservatives when they offer poor or biased financial advice. In the following sections, I lay out some examples of when a few particular analysts made commentary on topics they were not well informed on and how that can skew the viewer's thinking.

Misleading economic predictions

The only thing worse than your typical economist whose predictions are no better than an extrapolation of recent trends is an ideologically driven economist like Nouriel Roubini or Paul Krugman. Roubini is the economist who claims, falsely I might add, to have predicted the 2008 financial crisis. Since that time, he has made scores of erroneous predictions, yet he continues to be quoted and interviewed all over the media.

Krugman has a horrible track record when it comes to his economic predictions. Like Nouriel Roubini, year after year beginning in 2002, Krugman said that we were still mired in a recession or about to reenter one. He wrote so many columns attacking the Bush administration's economic policies that he won the title, based upon a statistical analysis of his positive and negative references to various politicians, as the most partisan liberal columnist for seven consecutive years from 2002 through 2008. (Lying in Ponds, the website behind this analysis, has since ceased performing this important but time-consuming task.)

In a July 14, 2008, column just as the economy and stock market began a terrible slide, Krugman predicted that concerns about a possible collapse of the government-sponsored lending agencies Fannie Mae and Freddie Mac were "overblown." Months later, both Fannie and Freddie required a massive government bailout that ballooned to more than $100 billion. Besides that huge blown call, Krugman also erroneously stated in that same column that Fannie and Freddie were not involved with risky sub-prime loans.

Knowing what causes economic growth

Krugman was a major proponent of the federal government stimulus to create jobs lost in the 2008 recession. Economists Christina Romer and Jared Bernstein, who were hired by the Obama administration, authored a paper including the now infamous graph in which they claimed that unemployment would rise to no higher than 8 percent if the stimulus package ("recovery plan") were passed. In fact, the massive government stimulus package did pass, and yet unemployment surpassed 10 percent and stayed elevated above 8 percent for quite some time.

Despite these facts, Krugman continued calling for even more federal government stimulus (spending) programs despite the first program's near complete failure to generate jobs. In fact, he ramped up his rhetoric over government actions in a June 27, 2010, column:

> ". . . you might have expected policy makers to realize that they haven't yet done enough to promote recovery. But no: over the last few months there has been a stunning resurgence of hard-money and balanced-budget orthodoxy. As far as rhetoric is concerned, the revival of the old-time religion is most evident in Europe . . ."

I'm not sure where Krugman is getting his news, but I don't see most governments, and certainly not those in Europe, having anywhere near balanced budgets!

With all due respect, Krugman doesn't fundamentally understand what leads to job creation and economic growth. This doesn't come from excessive government spending programs but from creating the right environment to foster business and capital formation and growth. During strong economic times in any country, private companies, especially small businesses, not the government, are the economic engine that drives the economy.

Watching for economic experience

And then there are pundits like Fareed Zakaria, who writes for *Newsweek* and has a show on CNN. Zakaria pontificates on economic issues (with a strong liberal bent) yet has no training or work experience in the field.

This is a problem, albeit less so, among some pundits on the right. But I do have some examples for you. In the spring of 2009 (April 30, 2009, to be exact), conservative commentator Glenn Beck on Fox TV said that he would not invest in stocks or muni bonds at all and recommended other investments, including gold and Treasuries. I was queried by multiple viewers about his advice.

Beck made these comments on *The O'Reilly Factor* television show. In that segment, Beck first admitted that as recently as the year 2000, he had been "broke" and had only in recent years come into money from his syndicated radio show and then his nationally televised cable television show on Fox (previously on CNN). During the segment, O'Reilly pointed out that Beck was currently negative on the economy and "warning people," and so O'Reilly asked him how he was investing his own money.

Beck said that some of his money was in cash and some of it was in Treasuries. "I was in bonds . . . municipal bonds . . . but these cities are spending money like water too . . . so we sold those . . ." Beck said. I disagree with his logic for dumping municipal bonds, which are issued by state and local governments, and buying Treasuries. If you're worried about the widespread failure of state and local governments, then you should also be worried about investing in Treasuries, which are backed by the federal government. The federal government would not allow the failure of states, and if they couldn't stop that from happening, then Treasuries were going to be in trouble too.

During the height of the financial crisis in 2008, municipal bond prices dipped (for example, Vanguard's Long-Term Tax-Exempt muni bond fund dropped about 7 percent) but quickly recovered in early 2009. A 7 percent drop may not seem like much (compared to the stock market's 50 percent bear market drop around that same time), but 7 percent is a rather substantial drop for muni bonds over a couple of months. That decline was largely due to panic selling from folks worried about the same issue that caused Beck to sell his muni bonds. Folks who sold during the decline in 2008 shouldn't have because they missed out on the rebound in muni bond prices late in 2008 and into 2009.

Beck also recommended investing in gold. Host Bill O'Reilly chimed in saying, "It's a hedge against disaster to buy gold and everybody should." Gold has been a poor long-term investment — just barely producing a small return (about 0.5 percent) above the rate of inflation. (See Chapter 10 for more on returns on various investment options.)

When asked about investing in stocks, Beck said, "Are you kidding me?" He went on to say he would not invest in stocks at all until he believed that ". . . the government is done meddling and we actually have entrepreneurs wanting things again."

When I interviewed Beck in early March 2009 (which is when stocks bottomed and the Dow was around 7,000), he told me that a few months prior, he had predicted that the Dow would slump to around 3,000 to 5,000, but now he was thinking it was going to drop to 3,000. Those who listened to Beck missed out on one of the greatest buying opportunities for stocks in many years.

With all due respect to his media success and talents as a political commentator, I would not take investing advice from Glenn Beck. As best I can tell, he has no relevant background to be offering sound investing or financial advice.

I would also like to note that Goldline, the gold coin dealer Beck was a pitch man for, was investigated and penalized in California due to dozens of consumer complaints for misrepresentation among other alleged misdeeds. Beck and his staff should do more homework so that he doesn't lead his large viewing audience astray in the future.

Looking at a party rather than facts

Ann Coulter, another popular, conservative political pundit, has also dispensed terrible financial advice. She actually has something in common with Mr. Krugman. According to an analysis of her columns (by Lying In Ponds, which no longer performs such analysis), she has repeatedly made the top ten lists of the most partisan columnists (for conservatives; Krugman, of course, for liberals).

Despite her enormous success, for some reason Coulter has chosen to be a pitch woman for Mark Skousen's investment newsletter *Forecasts & Strategies.*

In the mass mailing ("My #1 Way to Profit as Obama Destroys Capitalism"), which I got a copy of, Coulter gushes about Skousen and says the following about him:

> ". . . I've got just the man to help you take control of your own investments and put your mind at ease about your financial future.

> "His name is Dr. Mark Skousen, a free-market economist and editor of the investment newsletter *Forecasts & Strategies* — and he just might be the smartest financial advisor working today."

Apparently, Coulter didn't do any homework or due diligence on Skousen because if she had, she would have run in the other direction.

Mark Hulbert, who has independently tracked investment newsletters' recommendations and performance for decades, has plenty of helpful data on Skousen's newsletter. And the record is not kind to Skousen. Over the 17 years prior to Coulter's pitch, Skousen's recommendations generated average annual returns of just 3.8 percent per year versus 7.0 percent per year for the Wilshire 5000 Index. So, he underperformed by more than 3 percent per year.

Also, contrary to Coulter's claim that Skousen not only predicted the 2008 financial crisis but also told his subscribers how to protect themselves, Hulbert's analysis of Skousen's recommendations during that period show that Skousen's portfolio slid 53 percent versus a 43 percent loss for Wilshire 5000.

Another troubling insight regarding Skousen from Hulbert is the sheer number of model portfolios which Skousen has discontinued over the years. Just as some mutual fund companies shutter underperforming funds (and often merge them into others with better records), disreputable investment newsletters engage in a similar practice. Fortunately, Hulbert holds newsletters accountable for all their recommendations in his composite rankings.

REMEMBER

Beware taking financial and investing advice from pundits who are recognized as experts in other fields. Just as liberals who agree with Paul Krugman's and Nouriel Roubini's political views are at risk of following his poor financial advice, conservatives who adore Ann Coulter and Glenn Beck are at risk of being duped into following their investing advice and endorsements.

Uncovering Gurus' Agendas

I know, of course, that you're going to be exposed to and listen to many gurus and supposed experts, especially through any media you consume. So, in this section, I explain a process to help you separate out the few who are worth listening to over time from the morass of pundits who are unlikely to aid your future decision making.

Figuring out what they're really selling

Everyone's got something to sell. You should understand first what it is that they are selling or hoping to sell. That may not be clear and apparent when you hear from them.

It's actually not hard to uncover in most cases how a person or their firm makes money. It's something I always consider the first time I encounter someone in the media, and I encourage you to investigate *first* before you follow anyone's advice and commentary.

I find that many people make the mistake of not considering this issue when they're on the internet perusing "free" websites, blogs, and content. Before consuming anywhere you've not previously done such investigative work, find out who is behind the content, what they are selling, and how they make money.

For example, suppose you find a website that has short write-ups on stocks they like and bashes mutual funds and exchange-traded funds, tarring them all as costly and not tax-friendly. Upon probing further, you find out that the proprietors of said website are money managers who will take investors' money and create a portfolio for them for an ongoing fee of about one percent per year. You can often find such information by looking around a website, reading the "About" tab contents, looking up what services and products they are selling, and doing some simple Google searches about its proprietors.

This is revealing because it explains why this firm puts out the content that they do, bashing funds (which they see as competition) with broad sweeping generalizations and making it sound as if stock picking solves the problem. Everyone's entitled to their own beliefs and philosophy, of course, but you should understand, as I said, what someone is selling, why, and how they make their money.

Take another example: I noticed a steady parade of talking heads on CNBC talking up investing in specific cryptocurrencies. Often, these people had large stakes in what they were promoting and operated some sort of investment fund with a large stake in them as well. These facts were often neither clearly disclosed nor obvious.

Checking out their qualifications and track records

Once you figure out how someone or their company is making money and what they're selling, your investigative work isn't complete. Next, you should spend some time checking out their qualifications and track record if applicable.

TRUE STORY

Here's a real example of someone I came across on social media (a guru whose name rhymes with guru) who claimed to be a retired/former money manager and who was dispensing his stock picks gratis. He also posted all sorts of charts claiming to show how extraordinary his social media–posted stock picks had performed over recent years, and it sure looked amazing.

I was unable to unearth any real investment management history with actual notable money management firms for this individual. I was able to find a few dated articles online that didn't speak to any remarkable investment prowess or process.

I then began examining his past online postings to see what he had been recommending and how that turned out. With the few older articles I found, his suggestions didn't turn out well at all. And for some mysterious reason, his older social media posts were all gone. He claimed that they were deleted due to his account being hacked, but there was zero proof that had happened, and it sure looked as if he himself had deleted his older social media posts. Others online had posted some screenshots of those older and now deleted posts, and they weren't flattering to the guru. As with his older online articles, his missing and older social media posts suggested his advice should be ignored and not followed.

REMEMBER

Never blindly accept as truthful anything a person promoting themselves is telling you. Do your own investigative work and due diligence before listening to or following any supposed expert's advice.

Deciding Whether Hiring an Advisor Is the Right Choice

If you've been with me from the beginning of this chapter, you understand my concerns about following any supposed guru or expert's opinions and recommendations. In addition to the myriad concerns I discuss in this chapter, there's also the fact that those in the media are making general comments and recommendations, and they don't know your situation and personal profile and preferences.

For all of these reasons, I strongly encourage you to educate yourself first on important financial and related topics and then and only then consider hiring specific advisors who can help you with solving specific problems. Your choosing to read this book is an excellent step toward accumulating the necessary knowledge to make the best decisions.

In Chapter 5, I discuss a range of advisors for hire and how to find competent, ethical, and affordable advisors.

Chapter **8**

Following Financial Markets

N ever before has so much financial news, information, and advice been at our fingertips and available for near instant access including through our computers. Unfortunately, for many people, this is not a good thing.

We're doing more trading and less investing. We're being brainwashed by websites hosted by wannabe pundits and money managers with an agenda to scare you and undermine your confidence in the economy, financial markets, and your ability to invest. Their message: Investing is too hard and fraught with peril to do without turning your money over to them.

Many free financial websites are designed to be addictive and gamified/entertaining, encouraging visitors to return multiple times daily to see ever-changing content. Other financial advice sites are operated by active money managers who seek to convince investors to turn over money to them to invest. The best managers prove their investing chops by presenting their audited track record along with information about their experience and backgrounds. Unfortunately, plenty of charlatans misrepresent their track record and prey on people's fears about investing and the world at large.

In this chapter, I help you understand the financial markets, develop insights about the financial markets, keep your mind clear, and better control your destiny.

Understanding Stocks and Bonds

All businesses start small — whether they begin in a garage, a spare bedroom, or a rented office. As companies begin to grow, they often need more money (also known as *capital*) to expand and afford their growing needs, such as hiring more employees, buying technology, and so forth.

REMEMBER

Many smaller companies rely on banks to lend them money, but growing and successful firms have other options, too, in the financial markets. Companies can choose between two major money-raising options when they go into the financial markets: issuing stocks and issuing bonds.

A world of difference exists between the two major types of securities, both from the perspective of the investor and from that of the issuing company:

>> **Bonds:** *Bonds* are loans that a company pays back. Instead of borrowing money from a bank, many companies elect to sell bonds, which are IOUs to investors. The primary disadvantage of issuing bonds compared with issuing stock, from a company's perspective, is that the company must repay this money with interest. On the other hand, the business founders/owners don't reduce or relinquish ownership when they borrow money. Companies are also more likely to issue bonds when interest rates are relatively low and/or if the stock market is depressed, meaning that companies can't fetch as much for their stock. For investors, bonds hold the promise of paying interest regularly and hopefully repaying the investor's principal at a pre-set future date so long as the company can afford to. Bonds don't offer an "upside" to investors in the event that the issuing company is growing and making greater profits.

>> **Stocks:** *Stocks* are shares of ownership in a company. Some companies choose to issue stock to raise money. Unlike bonds, the money that the company raises through a stock offering isn't paid back because it's not a loan. When the investing public buys stock, these outside investors continue to hold and trade it. When a company is growing and increasing their profits, their stock price tends to rise. (Although companies occasionally buy their own stock back, usually because they think it's a good investment, they're under no obligation to do so.) Issuing stock allows a company's founders and owners to sell some of their relatively illiquid private stock and reap the rewards of their successful company. Many growing companies also favor stock offerings because they don't want the cash drain that comes from paying loans (bonds) back.

TECHNICAL STUFF

Although many company owners like to take their companies public (issuing stock) to cash in on their stake of the company, not all owners want to go public, and not all who do go public are happy that they did. One of the numerous drawbacks of establishing your company as public is the burdensome financial reporting requirements, such as publishing quarterly earnings statements and annual reports. Not only do these documents take lots of time and money to produce, but they can also reveal competitive secrets. Some companies also harm their long-term planning ability because of the pressure and focus on short-term corporate performance that comes with being a public company.

Ultimately, companies seek to raise capital in the lowest-cost way they can, so they elect to sell stocks or bonds based on what the finance folks and investment bankers tell them is the best option. For example, if the stock market is booming and new stock can sell at a premium price, companies opt to sell more stock. Also, some companies prefer to avoid debt because they don't like carrying it.

TIP

A stock's price per share by itself is meaningless in evaluating whether to buy a stock. Ultimately, the amount that investors will pay for a company's stock should depend greatly on the company's growth and profitability prospects. To determine the price-earnings ratio of a particular company's stock, you take the price per share of the company's stock and divide it by the company's earnings per share.

From your perspective as a potential investor, as I discuss in Chapter 10, you can usually make more money in stocks than bonds, but stocks are generally more volatile in the short term.

Making Informed Investing Decisions

Who wouldn't like to know how the economy and stock market will perform in the weeks, months, and years immediately ahead? And for good measure, many folks would also like to know what's going to happen with interest rates.

Truthfully, these things can't consistently and accurately be predicted. But take heart, because you can succeed in managing your personal finances and investment portfolio without knowing these things in advance. In the following sections, I explain what you need to know about how the factors that influence the financial markets and economy work so you can make more informed investing decisions.

Connecting corporate profits to stock prices

The goal of for-profit companies is typically to make money, or earnings (also known as *profits*). *Earnings* result from the difference between what a company takes in sales (revenue) and what it spends (expenses). Companies that trade publicly on the various stock exchanges seek to maximize their profit — that's what their shareholders want. Higher profits generally make stock prices rise. Most private companies seek to maximize their profits as well, but they typically have more latitude to pursue other goals.

Among the major ways that successful public companies increase profits are by doing the following:

>> **Developing new and better products and services:** Some companies develop or promote an invention or innovation that better meets customer needs. We have smartphones, 3D-printers, electric cars, online investing through low-cost mutual funds, casual restaurants that can serve up healthy food at a decent price in just minutes — the list goes on and on.

>> **Opening new markets to their products:** Many successful U.S.-based companies, for example, have been expanding outside our borders to sell their products. Although some product adaptation is usually required to sell overseas, selling an already proven and developed product or service to new markets generally increases a company's chances for success.

>> **Expanding into related businesses:** Consider the hugely successful Walt Disney Company, which was started in the 1920s as a small studio that made cartoons. Over the years, it expanded into many new but related businesses, such as theme parks and resorts, movie studios, radio and television programs, Disney streaming service, toys and children's books, and video games.

>> **Building a brand name:** In blind taste tests, popular sodas and many well-known beers rate comparably to many generic colas and beers that are far cheaper. Yet some consumers fork over more of their hard-earned money because of the name and packaging. Companies build brand names largely through advertising and other promotions.

>> **Managing costs and prices:** Smart companies control costs. Lowering the cost of manufacturing their products or providing their services allows companies to offer their products and services more cheaply. Managing costs may help fatten the bottom line (profit). Sometimes, though, companies try to cut too many corners, and their cost-cutting ways come back to haunt them in the form of dissatisfied customers — or even lawsuits based on a faulty or dangerous product.

>> **Watching the competition:** Successful companies usually don't follow the herd, but they do keep an eye on what the competition is up to. If lots of competitors target one part of the market, some companies target a less-pursued segment that, if they can capture it, may produce higher profits thanks to reduced competition.

Looking at financial market efficiency

Companies generally seek to maximize profits and maintain a healthy financial condition. Ultimately, the financial markets judge the worth of a company's stock or bond. Trying to predict what happens to the stock and bond markets and to individual securities consumes many a market prognosticator.

In the 1960s, to the chagrin of some market soothsayers, academic scholars developed a theory called the *efficient market hypothesis.* This theory basically maintains the following logic: Lots of investors collect and analyze all sorts of information about companies and their securities.

If investors think that a security, such as a stock, is overpriced, they sell it or don't buy it. Conversely, if many investors believe that a security is underpriced, they buy it or hold what they already own. Because of the competition among all these investors, the price that a security trades at generally reflects what many (supposedly informed) people think it's worth.

Therefore, the efficient market theory implies that trading in and out of securities and the overall market in an attempt to be in the right stocks at the right time is (largely) a futile endeavor. Buying or selling a security because of "new" news is also often fruitless because the stock price generally adjusts so quickly to this news that investors can't profit by acting on it.

As Burton Malkiel so eloquently said in his classic book *A Random Walk Down Wall Street* (W. W. Norton & Company), this theory, "taken to its logical extreme. . . means that a blindfolded monkey throwing darts at a newspaper's financial pages could select a portfolio that would do just as well as one carefully selected by the experts." Malkiel added, "Financial analysts in pin-striped suits don't like being compared with bare-assed apes." Ouch!

Some money managers have beaten the market averages. In fact, beating the market over a year or three years isn't difficult, but few can beat the market over a decade or more. Efficient market supporters argue that some of those who beat the markets, even over a ten-year period, do so because of luck. Consider that if you flip a coin five times, on some occasions you get five consecutive heads. This coincidence actually happens, on average, once every 32 times you do five coin-flip sequences because of random luck, not skill. Consistently identifying in advance which coin flipper will get five consecutive heads isn't possible.

Strict believers in the efficient market hypothesis say that it's equally impossible to identify the best money managers in advance. Consistently identifying in advance which professional investment manager will get returns that beat the market averages isn't possible. Some money managers, such as those who manage mutual and exchange-traded funds, possess publicly available track records. Inspecting those track records (and understanding the level of risk taken for the achieved returns) and doing other common-sense things, such as investing in funds that have lower expenses, improve your odds of performing a bit better than the market.

REMEMBER

Various investment markets differ in how efficient they are. *Efficiency* means that the current price of an investment accurately reflects its true value. The stock market is reasonably efficient. The real estate market is less efficient because properties are unique, and sometimes less competition and access to information exist. If you can locate a seller who really needs to sell, you may be able to buy property at a sizeable discount from what it's really worth. Small business is also less efficient. Entrepreneurs with innovative ideas and approaches can sometimes earn enormous returns.

Focusing on interest rates, inflation, and the Federal Reserve

For decades, economists, investment managers, and other often self-anointed gurus have attempted to understand the course of interest rates, inflation, and the monetary policies set forth by the Federal Reserve. Millions of investors follow these economic factors. Why? Because interest rates, inflation, and the Federal Reserve's monetary policies seem to move the financial markets and the economy.

Realizing that (much) higher interest rates are generally bad

Many businesses borrow money to expand. People like you and me, who are affectionately referred to as *consumers*, also borrow money to finance a home and auto purchases and education.

Larger interest rate increases tend to slow the economy. Businesses scale back on expansion plans, and some debt-laden businesses can't afford high interest rates and go under. Most individuals possess limited budgets as well and have to scale back some purchases because of higher interest rates. For example, higher interest rates translate into higher mortgage payments for home buyers.

If high interest rates choke business expansion and consumer spending, economic growth slows, or the economy shrinks — and possibly ends up in a recession. The most common definition of a *recession* is two consecutive quarters (six months) of contracting economic activity.

The stock market usually develops a case of queasiness as corporate profits shrink. High interest rates may depress investors' appetites for stocks as the yields increase on certificates of deposit (CDs), Treasury bills, and other bonds.

Higher interest rates actually make some people happy. If you locked in a fixed-rate mortgage on your home or on a business loan, your loan looks much better than if you had a variable-rate mortgage. Some retirees and others who live off the interest income on their investments may be happier with interest rate increases as well. But are higher interest rates better if you're living off your investment income? Not necessarily (see the next section for more info on this).

Seeing the inflation and interest rate connection

Consider what happened to interest rates in the late 1970s and early 1980s. After the United States successfully emerged from a terrible recession in the mid-1970s, the economy seemed to be on the right track. But within just a few years, the economy was in turmoil again. The annual increase in the cost of living (known as the rate of inflation) burst through 10 percent on its way to 14 percent. Interest rates, which are what bondholders receive when they lend their money to corporations and governments, followed inflation skyward.

REMEMBER

Inflation and interest rates usually move in tandem. The primary driver of interest rates is the rate of inflation. Interest rates were much higher in the 1980s because the United States had double-digit inflation. If the cost of living increases at the rate of 10 percent per year, why would you, as an investor, lend your money (which is what you do when you purchase a bond or CD) at 5 percent? Interest rates were so much higher in the early 1980s because you or I would never do such a thing.

In recent years, interest rates have been very low. Therefore, the rate of interest that investors can earn lending their money has dropped accordingly. Although low interest rates reduce the interest income that comes in, the corresponding low rate of inflation doesn't devour the purchasing power of your principal balance. That's why lower interest rates aren't necessarily worse and higher interest rates aren't necessarily better as you try to live off your investment income.

TIP

So what's an investor to do when he's living off the income he receives from his investments but doesn't receive enough because of low interest rates? Some retirees have woken up to the risk of keeping all or too much of their money in short-term CD and bond investments. A simple but psychologically difficult solution is to use some of your principal to supplement your interest and dividend income.

Using your principal to supplement your income is what effectively happens anyway when inflation is higher — the purchasing power of your principal erodes more quickly. You may also find that you haven't saved enough money to meet your desired standard of living — that's why you should consider your retirement goals well before retiring.

Exploring the role of the Federal Reserve

When the chairman of the Federal Reserve Board speaks, an extraordinary number of people listen. Most financial market watchers and the media want to know what the Federal Reserve has decided to do about monetary policy. The Federal Reserve is the central bank of the United States. The Federal Reserve Board comprises the 12 presidents from the respective Federal Reserve district banks and the 7 Federal Reserve governors, including the chairman who conducts the Federal Open Market Committee meetings behind closed doors eight times a year.

REMEMBER

What exactly is the Fed (as it's known), and what does it do? The Federal Reserve sets monetary policy. In other words, the Fed influences interest-rate levels and the amount of money or currency in circulation, known as the money supply, in an attempt to maintain a stable rate of inflation and growth in the U.S. economy.

Buying money is no different from buying lettuce, computers, or sneakers. All these products and goods cost you dollars when you buy them. The cost of money is the interest rate that you must pay to borrow it. And the cost or interest rate of money is determined by many factors that ultimately influence the supply of and demand for money.

The Fed, from time to time and in different ways, attempts to influence the supply of and demand for money and the cost of money. To this end, the Fed raises or lowers short-term interest rates, primarily by buying and selling U.S. Treasury bills on the open market. Through this trading activity, known as *open market operations*, the Fed is able to target the federal funds rate — the rate at which banks borrow from one another overnight.

The senior officials at the Fed readily admit that the economy is quite complex and affected by many things, so it's difficult to predict where the economy is heading. If forecasting and influencing markets are such difficult undertakings, why does the Fed exist? Well, the Fed officials believe that they can have a positive influence in creating a healthy overall economic environment — one in which inflation is low and growth proceeds at a modest pace.

Over the years, the Fed has come under attack for various reasons. Various pundits accused former Fed Chairman Alan Greenspan of causing speculative bubbles (see Chapter 2), such as the boom in technology stock prices in the late 1990s or in housing in the early 2000s. Some economists have argued that the Federal Reserve has, at times, goosed the economy by loosening up on the money supply, which leads to a growth spurt in the economy and a booming stock market, just in time to make the president look good prior to an election. Conveniently, the consequences of inflation take longer to show up — they're not evident until after the election. In recent years, others have questioned the Fed's ability to largely do what it wants without accountability.

REMEMBER

Many factors influence the course of stock prices. Never, ever make a trade or investment based on what someone at the Federal Reserve says or what someone in the media or some market pundit reads into the Fed chairman's comments. You need to make your investment plans based on your needs and goals, not what the Fed does or doesn't do.

Challenging Financial Markets During Changing Times

Our tendencies can lead us astray and cause us to do the opposite of what we should be doing. This happens to many of us, especially with investing decisions. And, to make a bad situation worse, advice purveyors online and in the media often unwittingly add fuel to this fire. Here's a recent example to illustrate what I'm talking about.

In the fall of 2008, during the height of the financial crisis and global stock market slide, I was speaking with a lawyer I know — Wes. He was a partner in a fairly large firm, well-educated, and earning a robust income. In speaking with Wes, I really wanted to hear his observations and opinions given his clients and vantage point. Wes worked with some financial companies in New York City, the epicenter of the financial crisis, so it didn't surprise me that Wes was quite negative not only about what had transpired but also about what lay ahead. Wes saw it being years until the economy would get turned around. As a result, he had been selling his stock holdings during the worst of the market slide. "I'll wait until things look better to invest again," he told me.

In the course of talking with lots of people, including friends, business acquaintances, and so on, I lost track of how many people in late 2008 and 2009 told me that they were selling stocks and other investments and sitting on the sidelines until things "got better." These worriers had plenty of help from the negative news and hype that was all around them — proof that misery really does love company.

The many folks like Wes who panicked and sold stocks during the height of the late 2000s market slide missed out on the huge global stock market rally that ensued. After stock prices generally bottomed in late 2008/early 2009, global stock prices approximately doubled in a few years and went on to much greater gains. History clearly shows us that the rebound that stocks enjoy after a major market slide is usually substantial — and quick. Over the past eight decades since the Great Depression, stocks have roared ahead an average of 30 percent in the first six months of a new bull market. And the second six months, which have averaged returns of 17 percent, have never produced negative returns, even if gains during the first six months were huge. The bull markets with the strongest initial returns have sometimes had the strongest returns in the following six months as well.

One of the reasons that uninformed investors often miss the biggest part of a rally coming out of a recession is that the financial markets are looking ahead and care most about corporate profits, not employment. Hiring, which leads to a reduced unemployment rate, often greatly lags a stock market rebound. In fact, if you look back over the decades, you'll find conclusive data showing that stocks produce higher returns during periods of high unemployment — the opposite of what most of us would expect!

The bottom line: Smart stock market investors look years into the future, which is why those who wait until it's obvious that conditions are improving miss out on big stock market gains.

What really moves financial markets (in the short term)

Next, I discuss some real-world examples that quickly show what moves the financial markets in the near term. I'm sticking with the U.S. stock market since that is familiar to more folks and more interesting than, say, the bond market, but you could draw similar conclusions from looking at bonds and selected other important financial instruments.

On the morning of September 11, 2001, terrorists highjacked four U.S. commercial airplanes and crashed three of them into landmark buildings in New York City and Washington. The fourth plane crashed in rural Pennsylvania thanks to the heroic actions of passengers on board that plane who thwarted the terrorists' actions.

All air traffic was immediately grounded for days in the United States, and worried Americans wondered what had happened and was happening to their country. The major stock exchanges were closed for several days, and when they reopened, stock prices got hammered.

In March of 2020, as news of the COVID-19 pandemic took hold, government-mandated economic shutdowns were announced. Stock prices plummeted as millions of workers were quickly laid off. Then in the fall of that year, stock prices were rebounding, and the initial vaccine trials showed that the COVID-19 vaccines had very high levels of effectiveness, and that spurred a greater rally in stock prices as faster economic reopenings were anticipated.

Financial markets are pretty darn efficient at pricing all currently known information into today's prices. That said, as you can see from these examples, surprises can move the markets, especially in the short term. These surprises are not things you're going to be able to predict; even thinking, "Gee, we could have a pandemic," fails to pin down the exact timing of such an event if and when it happens.

Please keep in mind this awesome and insightful quote from veteran money manager Ken Fisher:

> "If you try to outguess where the market will go or what sectors will lead and lag or what stock to buy based on what you read . . . or chatter about with your friends and peers — it doesn't matter how smart or well-trained you are — you will sometimes be right or lucky or both, but more often wrong or unlucky or both, and overall do worse than if you didn't make such bets at all."

As discussed earlier in this chapter, over time, stock prices are largely driven by corporate profits. For more on this and other important investing topics, please see Chapter 10.

Why market timing is so hard to do

In 2015, six years into a bull market in stocks, some folks were questioning whether they should sell their stocks. Stocks had been on a roll the prior six years. In fact, the rally in U.S. stock prices over that period was among one of the longest and strongest bull markets of the past century. So it's only natural for folks to be wondering at such a time whether they should sell stocks and get out while prices are still so elevated. After all, it wouldn't be fun and would hurt financially if stocks took a tumble as they did in 2008 or just after the turn of the new century.

So, why not sell half or even all of your stocks before they are clobbered in the next bear market? Well, consider that with market timing, you need to decide when to sell and then when to buy back in. So, you have multiple opportunities to get it wrong.

For example, suppose you thought back in 2015 that stocks were destined to fall so you sold your stock holdings. Suppose they didn't fall for another two years after rising 25 percent further in the meantime. Suppose that they then fell 30 percent.

What are the odds you would have been adept and smart and lucky enough to buy in at that bottom? And even if you were, you would only have "saved" yourself about 12 percent since you missed out on the 25 percent rise as well as the 30 percent decline.

Besides the stress of trying to time the financial markets, the reality is that something is bound to go wrong even if you get some of your decisions mostly correct. A number of revealing stock market studies show statistically how often you have to be right in your market timing to outperform a buy-and-hold strategy.

Even if you were smart and lucky enough to be out of stocks all the time during bear markets and were in for 50 percent of the bull markets, your annualized returns would still fall short of what you'd get by simply buying and holding. Just to equal the buy-and-hold returns, you'd have to be right about the direction of the markets 71 percent of the time. And that doesn't even factor in transaction costs and taxes! By definition, market timing requires more trading, and more trading jacks up your brokerage costs and taxes.

So, you'd have to be right at least 80 percent of the time with market timing when you consider the added drag from transaction costs and taxes. In other words, you'd have to correct about four times as often as you were wrong. Good luck with that!

TIP

As I have recommended over many years and decades, come up with an overall asset allocation that makes sense for your situation and be well diversified. Periodically rebalance (perhaps every five years or so) if your allocation strays from your chosen allocation and remember to slowly reduce your risk as you approach and eventually enter retirement. See Chapter 10 for more details.

4
Keeping Your Personal Finance House in Order

IN THIS PART . . .

Know how to control your spending and saving during tough times.

Make the most of your financial portfolio and improve your investing habits.

Combat risk and obtain the right kind of insurance.

Chapter **9**

Getting on the Right Road with Spending and Saving

Taking charge of your spending and saving habits will get you into good financial health and help you be ready should any issue or unforeseen problem arise that could otherwise take you off track. You are in the driver's seat, you have the power to keep your financials on the secure path, and I can help show the way.

When the going gets tough, you should pay extra close attention to your cash flow and spending, especially if you weren't well on top of it during good times. While you can't change the past, there are plenty of actions you can take to improve the difference between your income and outgo.

Please keep in mind throughout this chapter that I am presenting you with suggestions to consider. Some will not float your boat; others may be acceptable and dare I say even welcomed!

Please try to keep an open mind and be sure to include your family members and loved ones in discussions about making important personal financial changes. Think collaboration and cooperation, not manipulation and bullying.

Getting a Handle on Your Spending

The vast majority of people in America have some "unnecessary" (in other words, luxury) spending in their budget. Even if you believe that all the money you spend is for necessities, there are probably some ways for you to reduce your spending on the various goods and services you purchase. If you can reduce your spending by just 5 percent, you can make enormous progress towards accomplishing your longer-term personal and financial goals.

In this section, I present you with a smorgasbord of ways to reduce your spending. I also explain some useful ways for you to budget going forward.

Differentiating necessities from luxuries

One silver lining to an economic or personal crisis that upsets your finances is that it can provide greater clarity on your non-necessity spending. For example, cars and televisions, including multiple ones, are considered necessities. In some households, there's almost one car and one television per person! Are cars and televisions necessities? I would say definitely not for the televisions and probably not for most people in terms of cars.

Besides the money you could save on the purchase and upkeep of these devices, some would argue that not having these trappings of modern life can improve the quality of your life. Consider the benefits of not having a car: No more insurance premiums, no more parking hassles, and increased exercise and sunshine from walking.

You may not be willing or easily able to give up your car. If you're part of a two-income household with kids, your commutes and other commitments may require a car. That's fine. However, you should question all the things you spend your money on to prioritize what's most important and reduce spending on those items that are not. These are personal choices, but all choices come down to making trade-offs. This includes where you live, where you shop, as well as what you buy. Although some people will tell you how they think you should be spending your money, ultimately, only you can decide.

Is the second car more or less important than a vacation abroad? Are you willing to give up regular clothing purchases, or would you rather quit your gym membership and start exercising in other ways? And what about those new smartphones you've been buying for $600, $800, or perhaps even more?

TIP

Try brainstorming a list of five luxuries that you currently spend some money on that you might consider doing without. Your list might include things like morning Starbucks latte, salon hair products, or Friday night at the movies. Pick one or two items from the list that you would be most comfortable going without and then see how you feel about that change before possibly considering eliminating other spending.

Reducing your expenditures

It's one thing to want to reduce your spending and quite another to actually do it. Sloppiness in our spending more typically happens when times are good and money is more plentiful.

Whenever you make a purchase (of a product or service), it pays to shop around and make sure that you're getting value for your money. Remember that you don't always get what you pay for. Sometimes less-costly items are better.

Also, don't assume that reducing your spending has to entail great sacrifices. Often, simple changes in behavior can go a long way toward reducing your spending. For example, buying things in bulk typically reduces the cost per item purchased.

Other ways to reduce spending are more challenging. Keep in mind that what you're willing and able to reduce will be different from what your neighbor is able to do. The following sections highlight proven ways to trim spending and boost your savings. You can cherry-pick those that you are more interested in trying.

Housing expenses

For most people, the money that they spend on shelter is their single largest expenditure (or second biggest behind taxes). Everyone needs to have a roof over their heads. A common mistake is making housing decisions in a financial vacuum and not considering how these decisions affect your ability to achieve important financial goals. Some people spend too much on a home, which then hampers their ability, for example, to enjoy a particular lifestyle (such as more vacations or scaling back on work) or to comfortably accomplish important goals, such as saving sufficiently toward retirement.

In addition to your monthly mortgage payment, property taxes, and homeowner's insurance, other home-related expenses include maintenance of the home, commuting costs, and educational and other expenses for your children given the amenities and services of the community.

There are various strategies to reduce your home ownership expenses:

>> **Spend less on a home.** What do you do if you already own a home that is stretching your finances thin? Many people think of their housing expenses as fixed. It's not true in the vast majority of cases. After weighing the costs of selling and buying, you may want to consider a move to a less-expensive area or residence.

>> **Keep an eye on interest rates.** If they fall at least 1 percent from the level at which you bought, consider the costs and benefits of refinancing.

>> **Check on property value.** If property prices in your area have been falling, you may be able to appeal to lower your property's assessed value and reduce your property taxes.

>> **Consider a renter.** In the spirit of brainstorming ideas, perhaps you could stay in your current home but find ways to bring in some rental income to help offset some of your costs. You could take in a longer-term renter, for example. This may be more palatable if your home can have a self-contained area/unit for the renter.

REMEMBER

If you are currently a renter, you might move to a less-expensive rental or move into a shared rental. Living alone certainly has its advantages, but it is expensive. Also, consider eventually buying a property. It may seem counterintuitive but being a renter can be quite expensive. Think long-term: As a property owner, someday your mortgage will eventually be paid off. In the meantime, a fixed-rate mortgage payment doesn't increase over the years. Your rent, on the other hand, does generally increase with the cost of living or inflation.

Taxes

Do you pay a lot in taxes? (For most people, taxes are typically their second largest expense category after housing.) If so, you can do something about it if you get your finances organized and take advantage of the legally allowed tax breaks in our tax laws.

Reducing your taxes generally requires some advance planning. Making sound financial decisions involves considering tax and other financial ramifications. Don't wait until you're ready to file your tax return to find out how to reduce your tax burden. Please see the complete section on taxes ("Lowering Your Tax Bill") later in this chapter.

Retirement account contributions

Readers of my books and those who have taken my courses know that I've long been an advocate of funding retirement savings accounts as a way to reduce taxes and build a future nest egg. That said, it may make sense that when you're going through unusually tough times and need to find ways to improve your cash flow, you may consider cutting back on these contributions if necessary.

I far prefer finding other ways to reduce real "spending" and only reducing retirement account contributions as a last resort. This is especially the case during a general economic downturn because history has strongly shown that continually investing in stocks during such periods ends up being a rewarding move as it often leads to making purchases at attractive reduced prices.

If you do weigh reducing these contributions, consider the immediate tax impact if you were funding accounts that provided an up-front tax break. In other words, recognize the fact that you won't "save" the full amount of the reduced contributions. You'll just see an increased cash flow equal to the after-tax value of the reduced contributions. Also, I highly recommend trying to contribute enough to employer plans to gain the matching dollars for which you're eligible.

Food and dining

Eating in restaurants is costly, particularly if you're not careful about where and what you eat. If you are busy, eating out may be a time-saver, and if you can afford it, certainly do so. Some people eat out a lot because they don't know how to cook, so why not give it a try? Cooking is a valuable and fun lifelong skill and can pay big dividends.

TIP

When you do eat out, to keep costs down, minimize the alcohol and desserts, which can greatly increase the cost of a meal and undermine its nutritional value. Also try going out more for lunch rather than dinner, which is usually more expensive.

Regarding groceries, try to keep a decent inventory of things at home (but don't go overboard with perishables, which you may end up tossing out if you don't use them in time). This will minimize trips to the store and the need to dine out for lack of options at home. Try to do most of your shopping through discount warehouse-type stores, which offer low prices for buying in bulk, or grocery stores that offer bulk purchases or discount prices. If you live alone, don't be deterred — find a friend to share the large purchases with you.

Eating healthier, fresher, unprocessed, and more organic foods can seem to cost more. But it really doesn't when you factor in the more nutritious value you get and the potential long-term health benefits and reduced health problems.

Cars and transportation

Cars can be major money pits. While you probably want a car that is safe and comfortable, you need to buy a car within your financial means.

When you buy a car, research what the car is worth. The dealer markup, especially on new cars, can be substantial. Numerous publications and services such as Consumer Reports (www.consumerreports.org), Kelley Blue Book (www.kbb.com) and Edmunds (www.edmunds.com) provide this information. Before you purchase, also consider insurance costs of the different makes and models you're considering. Before committing to buy a particular make and model, call auto insurers to shop for insurance quotes, as rates vary greatly and should factor into your purchase decision.

Avoid taking an auto loan or lease. The seemingly reasonable monthly payment amount of loans and leases deludes people into spending more on a car than they can really afford. In the long term, paying with cash is less costly.

TIP

If you owe on an auto loan, consider selling that car if you can manage without it. Getting out of an auto lease before its official end is more challenging. Two websites — www.swapalease.com and www.leasetrader.com — help match folks looking to exit a lease early with people interested in taking over a lease. You can also contact local dealers to see if they'd be interested in buying the car from you.

TIP

Also take a hard look at whether you need a car. Although living in a particular community may appear to save you money, it may not if it requires you to have a car because of the lack of other transportation options such as public transit or the distance from work.

Recreation and entertainment

Often, spending money is equated with having fun. Many ads and sales pitches (even game shows) imply this. Please consider shedding this mindset. Spending a lot of money isn't fun if it leads you into debt or prevents you from saving toward your desired goals.

Think of ways to substitute activities to reduce spending without reducing your enjoyment. Exchange invitations with friends to cook dinner at home rather than going out to restaurants. Don't be shy about using coupons or special offers at restaurants you normally frequent. Find friends to visit when you travel. Attend a matinee movie instead of one during the high-priced evening hours.

Many of the most enjoyable things in life — time spent with family and friends, outdoor activities, and so on — don't have to cost much or even any money at all. Be creative and take advantage of these.

Clothing

Avoid the temptation to buy new clothes for a new season or to use shopping as a hobby. If you enjoy the visual stimulation, go window shopping and leave all forms of payment at home. (Carrying a small amount of cash is fine!) Avoid fashions that are trendy and that you won't wear after the trend moves on. Minimize clothing that requires dry cleaning, which is costly and exposes your body to unnecessary and unhealthy chemicals.

TIP

If you have recently purchased costly new clothing for which you now have buyer's remorse, consider returning it for a refund. Seek a cash refund, not a future credit/gift certificate to be used only at that merchant.

If you have old clothing that you absolutely refuse to wear anymore, donate it to a charity such as Goodwill or the Salvation Army. Ask for a receipt and take a write-off on your tax return if you itemize. (See the section on taxes later in this chapter.) Alternatively, consider listing for sale some of your valuable and lesser-worn clothing at a consignment store or at an online resale site.

Utility bills

Check out opportunities to make your home more energy efficient. Adding insulation and weather-stripping, installing water-saving devices, and reducing use of electrical appliances can pay for themselves in short order. Many utility companies will even do a free energy review or audit of your home and suggest money-saving ideas.

You may qualify for Residential Energy Credits, which reduce your tax bill (see IRS Form 5695). For the latest on federally approved energy tax breaks, visit the website `www.energystar.gov/about/federal_tax_credits`. Also check out the state-specific energy tax credits you may be eligible for by visiting the website "Database of State Incentives for Renewables & Efficiency" at `www.dsireusa.org`.

Insurance

Insurance fills a vital and useful role. You don't want to be in the position of absorbing a financial catastrophe. That's why, for example, you want adequate homeowner's and health insurance. If your home burns down or you have a major illness or accident, it could ruin you financially if you don't have proper insurance.

If you're dependent on your employment income, long-term disability protection is a must. Purchase term life insurance if others are financially dependent on your employment income. This is critical during your working years when you may have significant financial obligations, such as a mortgage and young children to raise.

In the event that you have any money in cash value life policies and/or are actively funding such policies, you should strongly consider ending them and getting the current cash value out of them. If you need life insurance, term is far cheaper, and you can find much better investment options than through a cash value life policy. Before making changes to such policies, however, you should first determine whether you still need life insurance and if so, be sure to replace that first. (See Chapter 11 for more details.)

There's no need to waste money on insurance. Many people overspend on insurance by purchasing coverage that's unnecessary or that covers small potential losses. Coverage of small losses, such as $100 or $200, is not useful for most people since such a loss wouldn't be a financial catastrophe. Examples would be buying insurance when shipping a package or for the possible loss or damage of your $200 smartphone.

Take high deductibles on your insurance policies — as much as you can afford in the event of a loss. If you are no longer dependent on your employment income and have sufficient financial resources to retire, there's no need to continue paying for disability insurance.

Also, be sure to shop around. Rates vary significantly among insurers. Of course, an insurer's quality of service and financial stability are important as well. (See Chapter 11, which is all about insurance, for more details.)

Kid-related expenses

Children don't come cheaply, but they also need not break the bank. Childcare is often a major expense for parents of young kids. For some people, this is a necessity; for others, this is a choice. While there are certainly many reasons to work, check that your analysis of what you earn and what you spend on childcare makes sense. How much of that extra income do you keep after factoring in taxes, commuting, and the other "costs" of that extra income?

Another challenge for parents is distinguishing between necessities and luxuries for the kids, who inevitably think everything they want is a necessity. More toys are not necessarily better. Ditto for more activities, sports teams, and so forth. Share with your children the realities of your family's finances and set limits — this will help them to find out about financial responsibility and obligations and why you can't purchase every item advertised on TV.

Charitable contributions

Many worthy charities and nonprofits provide important and vital services that otherwise would not be available. Deciding how much and to which organizations you would like to contribute are personal decisions.

Your charitable contributions are part of your budget, and as such, should be reviewed. Did you know that Americans are among the most giving people on Earth? Can you afford the amount that you are contributing? Perhaps you're at a stage of life where you should give less. Again, the decision is yours — just give it some extra consideration!

Setting and following a budget

In the midst of a challenge or a crisis, it's fine to look for specific immediate areas where you can make spending cutbacks. In addition to doing that, I encourage you to plan ahead with (in other words, budget) your spending.

Some people budget for the same reason that businesses do — so that the difference between the amount of money coming in and going out is not left to chance. Suppose that you analyze your past six months' worth of spending and realize that you're saving just 5 percent of your income. Perhaps you set as a goal saving 10 percent of your income. How do you accomplish that? You can go through the various spending categories and set targets that cut your spending enough so that your rate of savings increases to 10 percent. That's what budgeting is all about.

WARNING

Budgeting is not perfect, and it offers no guarantees. All a budget represents is a plan or set of targets. You may plan to cut your spending on streaming services and delivered food in half, but whether or not you do in actuality is another matter. Don't let temptation get the better of you!

There are two common ways to develop a budget. The first method involves examining each of your spending categories that I discuss in the "Reducing your expenditures" section earlier in this chapter and developing your best estimate for how much to reduce in each. Most people will cut more in some categories than others. You must decide which expenditures provide you with the most value. It involves trade-offs, and it is rarely easy.

The other method of budgeting is to start from scratch. Rather than looking at changes to your existing spending, you figure out how much you would like to be spending in the different categories. You start with a clean slate so to speak — you're not constrained by starting with or examining what you're currently spending. The advantage of this approach is that it allows for a more significant change. The disadvantage is that the estimates can be unrealistic and harder for you to achieve.

Almost everything is fair game for change in the long haul. In the short term, some expenses are easier to reduce than others. People who have difficulty saving money tend to think of everything in their budget as a necessity. The reality is that there are opportunities to spend less on many items that seem like necessities or are things we spend money on mostly out of habit.

Develop a plan and check back periodically to see how you're doing. You may go over a little in one category, but you may be able to make up for it by staying under budget in another.

Part of smart spending and budgeting involves keeping an emergency cushion for unexpected expenses. What if you lose your job or your roof springs a leak? What if both of these unfortunate events happen soon? How would you stay afloat?

Ideally, you should have an emergency reserve of at least three months' worth of living expenses in an account that is liquid and accessible without penalty. The riskier and more volatile your employment income is, the greater the reserve you should have. If your job is unstable and you have no other family members to turn to for financial help, you may want to keep as much as a year's worth of money in your emergency reserve.

Some final spending reminders . . .

Of course, it's generally easier to save more when you're earning more. Regardless of your income though, you can make the most of the money passing through your hands and accounts. Here are the common traits among those who are able to consistently save a healthy portion of their income. Successful savers

>> **Understand needs versus wants.** Don't define necessities by what those around you have. A new $30,000 car is not a necessity, although some people try to argue that it is by saying, "I need a way to get to work." Transportation, in this case for work, is a necessity, not a new $30,000 car! What about a good-quality used car? What about carpooling, public transportation, or living close enough to work to be able to walk or bike most days? I'm not going to tell anyone exactly how they should spend their money. But I will tell you that if you take out an auto loan to buy a car that you really can't afford, and you take a similar approach with other consumer items you don't truly need, you're going to have great difficulty saving money and accomplishing your goals and will probably feel stressed.

>> **Routinely question spending and value research.** Prior to going shopping for necessities that aren't everyday purchases, make a list of the items you're looking for and do some research first. (Consumer Reports is a useful resource.) After you're sure that you want an item; your research has helped you identify brands, models, and so on that are good values; and you've checked in with your bank or money market account to ensure that you can afford it; check in with various retailers and compare prices. When you set out to make a purchase, only buy what's on your list.

The internet can be a time-efficient tool for performing research and price comparisons but be careful of common online problems. The first is advertising that masquerades as informative articles. The second problem is small online retailers who may be here today and gone tomorrow or who may be unresponsive after the purchase. Finally, internet retailers are adept at pushing additional items that they have good reason to believe will appeal to you given your other purchases.

>> **Always look for the best values for products purchased.** Value means the level of quality given the price paid for the item. Don't assume that a more expensive product is better, because you often don't get what you pay for. That said, you can sometimes get a significantly better-quality product by paying a modest amount more. Don't waste money on brand names. If you're like most folks, you've bought products for the status you thought they conveyed or because you simply assumed that a given brand-name product was superior to the alternative choices — without thoroughly researching the issue before making the purchase. But thanks to advertising costs, brand-name products are frequently more expensive than less well-known brands of comparable quality.

>> **Reduce time spent on earning and spending money.** The saddest part about being on the work and consumption treadmill is how much of your time and life you may occupy earning and then spending money. Consider in a typical week how many hours you spend working and shopping. In addition to the time actually spent at work, consider commute time and time spent getting dressed and prepared for work. Now add in all the time you spent shopping and buying things. Compare the grand total of time spent on work- and shopping-related activities to time spent on the things you really enjoy in life.

>> **Make saving money a habit.** Just as with changing what you eat or your exercise routine (or lack thereof), modifying your spending and savings habits is easier said than done. The information that follows can help motivate you and get you on the path to consistently saving and then investing your money wisely to achieve your desired goals.

Saving: Necessary Rocket Fuel

In order to make your money grow and work harder for you, you need to save money to invest. You don't need large sums of money, for example, to invest and do well in the stock market. And you don't need to be a market genius or to understand what's going to happen to the economy next week, next month, or next year. To participate, you simply need to regularly save money and invest it wisely.

Understanding compounded returns

One of the most magical and powerful mathematical concepts to understand relating to your personal finances is the concept of compound investment returns. Simply put, for every dollar you save and invest, you keep earning returns on the original amount invested plus returns on the recent and historic investment returns.

Here's a quick example to illustrate the power of compounded investment returns over time. The following table shows you how $1,000 grows at different rates of return and over various lengths of time:

	5 years	10 years	20 years	30 years	40 years
1%	1051	1105	1220	1348	1489
3%	1159	1344	1806	2427	3262
5%	1276	1629	2653	4322	7040
7%	1403	1967	3870	7612	14974
9%	1539	2367	5604	13268	31409

Considering your short- and long-term personal and financial goals

In my work as a personal financial counselor and in the personal finance course that I teach, I ask people to think about and develop a list of their personal and financial goals. Such a list will greatly influence developing specific goals. It's also helpful to include price tags (the savings you'll need) to accomplish those goals.

Money, when put in its proper perspective, is a means to an end. And having money and financial security can provide people with freedom, choices, and options. So, while someone may have the goal of saving for their future, that future may include changing careers, for example. Sometimes, people stay in well-paying jobs longer than they might prefer in order to achieve a certain level of financial security.

The next sections discuss the common goals toward which people often want to save money.

Major purchase planning

Unfortunately, many of the things that you purchase over the course of your life cost a hefty chunk of money. In some cases, you're not going to have sufficient cash on hand to buy what you want when you want. So, what should you do?

The answer really depends on what it is you're buying. If, for example, you're buying a home, the purchase price will likely preclude a cash purchase unless you live in a low-cost area or you are fortunate in having flush finances and relatively simple wants. Financing most of a home purchase via a mortgage can make good financial sense in the long run. Why? First, mortgage interest rates are quite competitive, and the interest on your home loan is generally tax-deductible subject to IRS limits (typically on up to $750,000 of indebtedness). Second, because homes are assets, they usually appreciate in value over the long haul. This doesn't mean that they go up in value every year.

Borrowing for purchases such as a car or vacations, for example, can be financially dangerous. The difference here is that you're buying items that lack "investment" value. In other words, these are consumption purchases.

Although vacations, a new wardrobe, or living-room furniture may enhance the quality of your life and make you feel good, these aren't investments. You can live without these purchases, and they won't enhance your long-term financial health.

What's more, borrowing to make these types of consumption purchases is costly. You'll pay a higher rate of interest than, say, when you are buying a home. And, to add insult to injury, the interest on consumer debt such as credit card and auto loan debt is not tax-deductible.

An important test for making a consumption purchase is whether you have the money on hand to pay in cash. For example, if you want to buy new furniture that will cost $8,000, can you pay cash for it? You don't literally have to pay in cash if you find it more convenient to use your credit card at the store and then promptly pay the credit card bill in full by the due date. The point is that you're not carrying this debt for months on end.

Avoiding the financing of consumption purchases forces you to live within your means. If you're buying new cars and other items by carrying debt month-to-month, you'll have a difficult time saving money in the future. More of your future income will already be claimed and will be gobbled up by debt repayment. And don't forget that these purchases are costing you more the longer you carry the debt.

TIP

Buy what you can afford by saving for it in advance or setting your sights lower.

To simply calculate how much to save per month for a major purchase, first determine the approximate cost of the item in question and over what time period you'd like to save the money. For example, suppose you would like to buy a good-quality used car that goes for about $12,000, and you'd like to complete the purchase in 24 months. Simply dividing $12,000 by 24 yields about $500 per month. If you can't do that, the solution(s) are pretty simple: Cut the expenditure amount and/or save over a longer period.

College cost planning

No doubt, raising a family is a challenge to most budgets. Barring an unlikely fully paid academic, athletic, or other scholarship, paying for a college education is likely to be the largest expenditure you'll make for your children. Here are the current average costs per year for higher education:

>> **Four-year private college:** $56,000

>> **Four-year public college (in-state):** $28,000

>> **Four-year public college (out-of-state):** $45,000

>> **Two-year community college (commuter):** $19,000

Most parents are frightened by such numbers, which are simply averages – the costliest schools can easily run 20 to 30 percent more than these high numbers! So, be sure to explore all your options. What you buy should extend benefits for decades. And unless you're affluent, you're not going to have to shoulder all this financial responsibility yourself.

A variety of loan and grant programs exist, some of which are not based on "financial need." Unless you are wealthy, you're not going to be able to pay for the full cost yourself. Most parents shouldn't even try because they really can't afford it and doing so may cause them other money troubles. Guidebooks, such as my *Paying For College For Dummies* (Wiley), and other information sources for loans, grants, and scholarships can be found in your child's school counseling office, local public libraries, and college financial aid offices. Start your search early — your child's junior year is a good time to think seriously about colleges and aid sources.

Be aware that your best intentions could create financial problems. Wanting to save money to provide for your children's college costs is a good instinct. However, if you do so at the expense of, for example, contributing to retirement accounts, you'll increase your tax bill, both short- and long-term.

Be particularly careful about investing money in your children's names through so-called custodial accounts. Money that is in a custodial account is legally theirs when they reach the age of majority, which varies from 18 to 21 years depending on which state you live in.

The other problem with saving in custodial accounts is that the college financial aid system greatly penalizes you for doing so. Money in your child's name is assumed available and earmarked for college costs. If, on the other hand, you invest the money in your own retirement account(s), the financial aid system generally completely ignores it. (Just keeping it in your own nonretirement accounts is far better than putting it in junior's name.) All other factors being equal, the more money you put in your children's names, the less financial aid they'll qualify for.

Invest in your name, especially your retirement accounts, first and foremost. As detailed in the next section on retirement planning, doing so will minimize your tax burden. And, you will be better positioned to finance your retirement and be able to help your kids financially if you're on stronger financial footing.

Noting the power of tax-deferred retirement accounts

Saving and investing through retirement accounts enables you to compound more of your money over time thanks to tax savings. Take a simple example where someone can save $6,000 total in a retirement account that provides them with an up-front tax benefit and assumes they are in a combined 35 percent federal and state income tax bracket. If this money is not contributed to a retirement account, then $2,100 in taxes is owed. This example further assumes that you invest this money and average an annual pretax return of 8 percent.

After each period in the example, money in the retirement account is withdrawn and taxes are paid at the assumed rate of 35 percent. For the scenario where the money is invested outside a tax-sheltered retirement account, the same tax rate of 35 percent is assumed.

You start with much less to invest when you don't contribute to retirement accounts because money is immediately siphoned off to pay taxes, leaving you with less. The longer the money is invested, the more you profit by investing inside a retirement account.

Year	Using Retirement Account	Not Using Retirement Account
0	$6,000	$3,900
10	$8,420	$6,474
20	$18,178	$10,750
30	$39,244	$17,846
40	$84,726	$29,628

If your employer matches or contributes additional money to your account, you'll be even better off. It's free money, so don't miss out! Some employers, for example, may match your contributions at 25 cents (or more) on the dollar you contribute. Even if you unexpectedly need to withdraw your contribution, you should still come out ahead — the penalties for early withdrawal are only 10 percent federal income tax and whatever nominal amount, if any, your state charges.

Some people are concerned that if their tax rate in retirement is higher than it is during their working and saving years, then funding retirement accounts could lead to higher taxes. While possible, this is unlikely. Because of the tax-deferred compounding, you should come out ahead by funding your retirement accounts. In fact, your retirement tax rate could increase, and you'd still come out ahead.

How high does your retirement tax rate need to be in order to negate the tax-deferred compounding benefits of a retirement account? The following chart shows the same example that we just looked at, with a new twist. You can now see how high a tax rate needs to be applied in retirement so as to eliminate all of the tax-deferred compounding of the retirement account. (Remember that the assumed tax rate of the person contributing to the retirement account was 35 percent.)

Year	Using Retirement Account	Not Using Retirement Account	Retiree Tax Rate to Eliminate Retirement Account Benefits
0	$6,000	$3,900	n/a
10	$8,420	$6,474	50%
20	$18,178	$10,750	61%
30	$39,244	$17,846	70%
40	$84,726	$29,628	77%

As you can see, the longer the money is invested, the higher your tax rate would have to rise to wipe out the tax-deferred compounding benefits.

Retirement accounts that you establish, such as an SEP–IRA (if you're self-employed) and IRAs, can be set up through most major financial institutions, such as mutual fund companies, brokerage firms, and banks. These accounts can be transferred to different firms at your discretion. Simply call the company that you want to move your account into and ask it to send you its account application and transfer forms; with many investment firms, you can complete the forms on their website.

For retirement accounts that your employer maintains, such as a 401(k) plan, you are limited to the investment options that the plan offers. When you leave this employer, you can *roll over* your account balance into an Individual Retirement Account (IRA). Simply contact the investment company that you'd like to use for the IRA and have it send you its account application forms or complete those forms on their website if you're able. Instruct your previous employer where you'd like your money sent — don't take possession of it; otherwise, you'll get hit with 20 percent federal income tax withholding.

If you want to invest more of your money so that it grows without the burden of high taxation, other options do exist. Investments that are more growth oriented, such as stocks and real estate, may make sense for you. See Chapter 10.

Upping Your Income

The focus of this chapter is on managing your spending including during tough times. We can more easily vary and modify many aspects of our expenditures than boost our income.

If you're like most people, you work hard, have interests and commitments outside of your work, and are pretty busy. Your opportunities to boost your employment income, especially in the near term, may be limited.

But there are some things to consider doing to increase your monthly cash flow through increasing your income:

>> **Take charge of your career.** Look around your company or organization, especially at positions a level above yours. Are there openings or likely to be future openings? Can you do the work? Would specific additional experience or training put you in the mix for a promotion? A good boss looks out for those they manage and helps work at developing the skill set and experience of their subordinates. But, there's no reason you can't and shouldn't take a more active interest in doing so, especially if your boss isn't serving this role. Also, if you've reached an apparent dead-end in your job and/or your

employer has bleak prospects, discretely look around at what else is out there for you. Do so on your own time away from work and never on a work computer.

>> **Work more.** In some jobs or organizations, you can make more if you work more. Examine your weekly schedule and identify where you may be wasting time on things that don't improve your life and connections with others you care about.

>> **Go the gig-worker route.** Consider what other ways you could work part-time outside your current job and bring in some needed additional income. Perhaps you could be a youth sports referee or do some tutoring in an academic area of strength. There are all sorts of ways to do some gig work; just be careful that you're able to quickly bring in more than it costs you to do this sort of new work.

Lowering Your Tax Bill

Federal, state, and local income taxes take a large bite out of most peoples' income. So, you must remember to consider taxes in the process of budgeting and planning your financial future.

Knowing your income tax rate

Your taxes are not fixed. There's no reason that you can't utilize some of the simple and legal strategies to reduce your tax burden. First, it helps to know what your current income tax rate is — most people don't.

REMEMBER

Income taxes have a major impact on most major financial decisions such as investing, retirement planning, and real estate purchases. If you make these sorts of financial decisions without understanding and factoring in taxes, you're probably paying a lot more in taxes than you need to be. Understanding the tax implications may also cause you to take a different course of action.

You pay income taxes on what's known as your *taxable income.* This is simply the sum of your income, including that from employment and investments, minus your allowable deductions.

If you pull out your tax return from last year or track your tax payments (check your payroll records and quarterly tax filings with the IRS), you can quickly figure the total income taxes that you paid in a given year. Although it's enlightening to know the total income taxes you paid, this number alone won't help you make better financial decisions.

REMEMBER

A more useful tax number to know, which people are less likely to recognize, is their *marginal income tax rate.* This is the rate of income tax that you are paying on your last dollars of income. Many people don't realize that the income tax system is structured such that you pay a lower rate of tax on your first dollars of income.

As your earnings increase, you pay higher rates of tax on your income but only on your income above certain threshold amounts. These brackets are transparent to you throughout the year because you pay tax at a steady rate based on your total expected income for the year.

Here are the 2021 federal income tax brackets for the two most common filing categories: single people and married couples who file jointly:

Rate	For Single Individuals	For Married Individuals Filing Joint Returns
10%	Up to $9,950	Up to $19,900
12%	$9,951 to $40,525	$19,901 to $81,050
22%	$40,526 to $86,375	$81,051 to $172,750
24%	$86,376 to $164,925	$172,751 to $329,850
32%	$164,926 to $209,425	$329,851 to $418,850
35%	$209,426 to $523,600	$418,851 to $628,300
37%	$523,601 or more	$628,301 or more

In addition to federal income taxes, most states have a state income tax. As you're considering your marginal income tax rate, count both federal and state income taxes. You can find your state's income tax brackets at: taxfoundation.org/state-income-tax-rates-2021/#Structures.

Using your income tax rate

Knowing your marginal income tax rate allows you to assess the tax impact of various financial decisions. You pay income taxes when you earn income from employment or from most investments held outside retirement accounts, and you pay sales tax when you purchase many goods. The simplest and most powerful way to reduce the tax bite in your budget is to spend less (which saves you money on sales taxes) and invest what you save in a tax-advantaged way.

Contribute to lower your income

The single best way for most wage earners to reduce their taxable income is to contribute to retirement accounts, such as 401(k), 403(b), and SEP-IRA accounts. Contributions to these accounts are generally free of federal and state income tax. Thus, in the year of the contribution, you save on federal and state income taxes. Taxes are owed when you withdraw the money, probably in retirement. Therefore, the prime advantage of these accounts is that, over many years, you get to hold onto and invest money that would otherwise have gone to taxes when you originally earned the money.

You may also benefit if, like most people, you are in a lower income bracket in retirement. Even if your tax bracket doesn't decrease in your golden years, retirement accounts should still save you on taxes. (See the section, "Noting the power of tax-deferred retirement accounts" earlier in this chapter.)

Two simple but important prerequisites prevent many people from taking advantage of this terrific tax break. First, you need to spend less than you earn so that you can "afford" to fund your retirement account(s). You certainly don't want to contribute to retirement accounts if you are accumulating debt on a credit card, for example. Plenty of people need to reduce their spending before being able to take advantage of a retirement savings plan.

The second obstacle to funding a retirement account is having access to one. Some employers don't offer retirement savings plans. If yours doesn't, lobby the benefits department and consider other employers who offer this valuable benefit. If you're self-employed, you may establish your own plan — typically an SEP-IRA.

Choose investments wisely

TIP

Whenever you invest money outside a retirement account, you should weigh the potential tax consequences. Income produced from your investments is exposed to income taxation. In matters of financial health, remember that it matters not what you make but what you get to keep after taxes.

Suppose you are considering two investments. The first is a traditional bank savings account that is paying, say, 2 percent. Another alternative you are considering is a tax-free money market fund. Although this investment option pays less — 1.6 percent — this return is federal and state tax-free. Which investment should you choose?

The answer depends on your tax bracket. The savings account pays 2 percent, but this interest is fully taxable. If, between federal and state income taxes, you pay 30 percent, then you don't get to keep the 2 percent interest. After paying taxes, you'll end up with just 1.4 percent.

Now compare this 1.4 percent after-tax rate of interest to the 1.6 percent tax-free money market fund yield. The tax-free money market fund provides you with more to keep. If you were in a low tax bracket, however, the savings account could be a better deal.

In addition to savings and money market accounts, bonds also come in tax-free and taxable interest versions. If you're in a higher tax bracket, tax-free bonds may be preferable.

Consider capital gains

Another issue to consider when investing nonretirement money is capital gains taxes. If you sell an investment held outside a retirement account at a higher price than what you purchased it for, you will owe tax on the profit, known as a *capital gain.* The tax rates for capital gains work a bit differently than on regular income.

Long-term capital gains — that is, for investments held for at least one year — are taxed at a maximum 20 percent by the IRS (high-income earners may be subject to an additional 3.8 investment surtax from Obamacare legislation). Losses from selling securities at a loss may be used to offset gains so long as the offsetting gains and losses are from investments for the long term.

Short-term capital gains (which can be offset by short-term losses) on investments held less than one year are taxed at your ordinary income tax rates.

All things being equal, it's best to avoid investments and trading practices that produce much in capital gains, especially short-term. Among mutual funds, for example, some funds, particularly those that engage in a lot of trading, tend to produce greater capital gains.

Strengthen your deductions

In addition to reducing the amount of your taxable income, maximizing your deductions legally also trims your tax bill. Here are some viable methods to consider:

>> **Check to see whether you can itemize.** If you haven't been itemizing deductions on Schedule A of your tax return, examine the deductions, subject to limitations, that you can claim to itemize. These include state and local income taxes, real estate mortgage interest and property taxes, and charitable contributions (including out-of-pocket expenses and mileage costs). The only way to know if you can take a larger deduction by itemizing is to total them up and compare the total to the so-called standard deduction.

- » **Consider shifting and bunching deductions.** If you have nearly enough deductions in a year, you may consider grouping together, or bunching, more of your deductions into one year. Suppose you expect to have more itemized deductions next year since interest rates are rising and you will be paying greater interest on your adjustable-rate mortgage. Rather than contributing money to your favorite charities in December of this year, you might wait until January in order to qualify for itemizing in the next tax year.

- » **Convert consumer debt into tax-deductible debt.** Interest on debt on credit cards and auto loans is not tax-deductible. Mortgage interest debt for your home, on the other hand, is generally tax-deductible up to $750,000 of indebtedness (the limit is $1 million if your mortgage was originated before December 16, 2017, or for a home you had under a binding contract that was in effect before December 16, 2017, as long as the home purchase closed before April 1, 2018). If you have sufficient equity in your home, you may be able to borrow against that equity and gain a tax deduction to boot. Just be careful not to get into the habit of continually raiding your home's equity — remember, all that debt has to be paid back. Cut up those credit cards after paying off their balances with the home's equity.

- » **Own real estate.** For a home you live in, mortgage interest is largely deductible as explained in the previous bullet. Property taxes are deductible expenses that you may claim on Schedule A up to $10,000 per year when combined with your state income taxes. These deductions serve to effectively lower the long-term cost of owning real estate. Investment real estate has far broader deductions.

- » **Check out Schedule C.** If you're self-employed, make sure to find out about completing Schedule C, "Profit or Loss from Business," and the many legal deductions you may take on that form.

Taxing issues regarding children

You surely have enough challenges raising kids today without the headache of dealing with the IRS. The good news is that dealing with taxes for your children need not be complicated.

REMEMBER

Your first tax encounter with the IRS as a family is securing a Social Security number for your child. Your child must have a Social Security number by age 1 for you to claim the child as a dependent on your tax return. Form SS-5, "Application for a Social Security Card," is available online at www.ssa.gov/forms/ss-5.pdf or by calling the Social Security Administration at 800-772-1213.

The IRS allows you a couple of different ways to defray childcare costs with tax breaks. First, through your employer's benefits plan, you may be able to set aside money on a pretax basis to pay for childcare expenses. This not only saves you on federal income tax, but also on Social Security and Medicare tax and also generally on state income tax. Under current tax laws, you are allowed to set aside up to $10,500 per year, and because of the COVID-19 pandemic, unused amounts can now be carried over to future tax years.

You may come out ahead taking the "dependent care tax credit" instead. Each parent must work at least on a part-time basis (unless a spouse is disabled or a full-time student) in order to be eligible for the credit, and the children must be under the age of 13. (Exceptions are allowed if your child is physically or mentally handicapped.) Complete IRS Form 2441 to claim this credit.

Prior to 2018, children had a unique system of taxation until they reached the age of 18. Until age 18, kids got a bit of a tax break as their first $2,100 of unearned income was taxed at a relatively low rate. Everything above that was taxed at the same rate as the parents' tax rate.

With the Tax Cut and Jobs Act bill that passed in late 2017 and took effect in 2018, investment earnings in excess of $2,100 were taxed at the relatively high tax rates that apply to trusts and estates. Those tax rates for 2021 are as follows:

Income	Tax Rate
Up to $2,650	10%
$2,650 to $9,550	24%
$9,550 to $13,050	35%
Over $13,050	37%

Making quarterly tax filing requirements

When you work for a company, your employer withholds money from your paycheck and sends income tax payments on your behalf to the IRS and your state. If you are self-employed or earn income in retirement or from other investments, you are responsible for paying estimated taxes to the IRS and your state on a quarterly basis.

For making and estimating your quarterly federal income tax payments, you can obtain IRS Form 1040-ES at www.irs.gov/pub/irs-pdf/f1040es.pdf or by calling the IRS (800-829-3676) and asking for it.

If you run your own company, note that you are required to withhold and send in taxes from your employees' paychecks. This may include federal, state, and local taxes, including those for Social Security and unemployment insurance. IRS Forms 940 and 941 provide more details about these rules and regulations. Alternatively, for a modest fee, you can hire one of the numerous payroll processing firms with good reputations.

Ouch! Dealing with Major Medical Bills

Getting sick or injured is no fun. And, to add insult to injury, significant medical problems often result in major medical bills. This section can help you deal with those bills and ensure that you get proper coverage from your health insurance provider and the best deals from medical providers.

Reviewing your billing statements for accuracy

As the bills come rolling in, keep all of them and keep them organized. Be sure that each medical provider has indeed submitted the bill to your health insurance company. Over the years, I've had plenty of episodes where the medical provider and insurance company have "communication" issues, including pointing fingers at each other.

When you first get a medical bill from a medical provider, don't pay it as it likely hasn't been processed through your health insurance plan. Once a provider has processed the bill through your insurance company, you should see that the fees have been "discounted" to the agreed-upon fees that your insurer has in their contracts with the provider. So, for example, a friend recently had to have her appendix removed and the anesthesiologist submitted a $1,300 bill. After an "insurance adjustment" of $960, the final charge was thus $340.

Negotiating with providers or an insurance company

Some billing offices may also offer a prompt pay discount of, for example, 10 to 15 percent. Or they may offer a payment plan over, say, one to two years without a discount.

TAPPING A MEDICAL BILL AUDITOR FOR HELP

Linda Michelson runs The Medical Bill Advocate, which reviews and audits medical bills. Michelson has a good background to do such work — she has nearly three decades of experience on the other side of the table having worked for major healthcare providers in their billing departments. Now, she works with people who are overwhelmed and need help dealing with medical bills.

"I usually charge by the project but can work on a contingency basis as a percentage (25 to 30 percent) of the savings realized," she says. She deals with a range of billing situations including emergency room bills or ongoing bills such as those from cancer treatment. She instructs clients to gather all explanations of benefits and all bills.

Michelson begins her work by perusing bills to look for mistakes and often asks for more itemized bills. "Customers might have been billed for procedures and medications not performed or given. I also look at dates of service to make sure they make sense or are correct," she says.

She also requests copies of medical records if needed, and those can be quite long and extensive. "I compare the itemized bill to the patient's medical records. It helps to have some knowledge of medical terminology," Michelson adds.

The biggest bills are from hospitals, and Michelson explains that you may be able to get those reduced if your income is low enough. "Federal law requires applying for financial help and providing financial details. If your income is below 300 percent of the federal poverty level, a hospital must reduce your charges," she says. (For information on the federal poverty levels, visit www.healthcare.gov/glossary/federal-poverty-level-fpl/).

And you can simply try to negotiate a better rate. Hospitals routinely charge orders of magnitude higher than Medicare. Two sources of fee information to tap include the following:

>> **Healthcare Bluebook** (healthcarebluebook.com): You enter your zip code and medical code to see a range of fees and fair pricing. This service is offered through employers.

>> **Fair Health Consumer** (www.fairhealthconsumer.org): This organization makes information similar to that of Healthcare Bluebook available to healthcare consumers on their website.

Sometimes you may have to pressure an insurance company to pay their share of the bills. "You may get the runaround or encounter incompetent employees," says Linda Michelson (see the sidebar "Tapping a medical bill auditor for help"), who in one case involving a bicycle accident, had to go to the state attorney general for help to press the insurer to do the right thing. You may have to go to the state insurance commissioner if you need help.

One final surprise Michelson warns about is literally just that — surprise medical bills. This occurs when a patient goes to a hospital in the insurance network, but some of the doctors involved in their care may not have been in the insurer's network. These out-of-network providers can "balance bill." Some states have passed laws to address such situations, and Michelson says this topic is being discussed at the national level. Again, in such situations, some providers may be willing to negotiate.

Chapter **10**

Investing Wisely and Securely

More than just about any other aspect of our financial lives, most people equate financial security with their investment portfolios. To manage your investment holdings well, you need to understand various technical details well. You also should have a suitable emotional and psychological approach to deal with and make the most of the inevitable fluctuations that occur in the financial markets.

Checking Out All the Places You Can Invest Your Money

An investment is something you put your money into in the hopes of collecting or withdrawing more in the future. All money, therefore, is in some sort of investment, even what's put in "parking places" – a place to put money until you figure where to ultimately invest it, such as bank accounts or money market funds.

WARNING

Sometimes people make the mistake of feeling as if their money is wasting away or not "invested" if it's in a parking place. They may rush to invest the money elsewhere with the hope of earning a higher return. Later, they may find that these seemingly more attractive investments were also riskier. The risk is that the investment can and sometimes does decline in value. Some investments are riskier — or more volatile — in value.

There's nothing wrong with taking reasonable risks. In fact, an investor needs to accept some risks in order to have the potential for earning a higher return. However, you should try to protect and take little or no risk with some of your money. For example, your "emergency reserve" money should not be in an investment subject to fluctuations in value. This money should be "parked" someplace secure and accessible.

Especially over the longer term, there's also a danger in not taking enough risk. Take investing for retirement. In order to be able to retire, you'll need a certain amount of money saved. If the money you're accumulating is invested too conservatively and grows too slowly, you will need to work more years before you can afford retirement.

So, in addition to understanding the different investments available, you also need to select those investments that meet your particular needs. You've got plenty of time with such longer-term money to wait for a recovery for example if a recession causes a decline in the value of stocks and other growth assets.

Noting how investment types differ from one another

It's helpful to discuss the major dimensions on which investments differ from one another. First, investments may produce *current income,* typically in the form of interest or dividends (which are paid-out profits to corporate stockholders). If, for example, you place your money in a bank certificate of deposit that matures in one year, the bank may pay, for example, 1.5 percent interest. Likewise, if you invest in a Treasury note issued by the federal government, which matures in two years, you may be paid, say, 2 percent interest per year.

Other types of investments, by contrast, may be more growth oriented and not pay much, if any, current income. Investments that are more *growth oriented,* such as real estate or stocks (investments in companies), allow you to share in the success of a specific company or local economy in general. The yield on a good stock from its dividend typically is below the interest rate paid on a decent corporate bond, but some stocks do offer decent dividend yields.

Income-oriented investments, on the other hand, such as Treasury bills, don't allow you to profit when the company or organization profits or does well. When you lend your money to an organization, such as by purchasing bonds, the best that can happen is that the organization will repay your principal with interest.

Some other dimensions on which investments differ from one another include these:

>> **Susceptibility to inflation:** Some investments are more resistant to increases in the cost of living. For example, the purchasing power of money invested in bonds that pay a fixed rate of interest can be eroded by a rise in inflation. By contrast, the value of investments such as real estate and precious metals (such as gold and silver) often benefits from higher inflation. Especially when investing for longer periods of time, it's important to diversify your investments to include those that are inflation resistant.

>> **Taxability:** Apart from investments in tax-sheltered retirement accounts, the interest or dividends produced by investments are generally taxable. The profits (known as *capital gains*) from selling an investment at a higher price than it was purchased for are also taxable.

>> **Sensitivity to currency and local economic issues:** Not all investments move in concert with the health and performance of the U.S. economy. Investments in overseas securities allow you to participate directly in economic growth internationally as well as diversify against the risk of economic problems in the United States. International securities are susceptible, however, to currency value fluctuations relative to the U.S. dollar. Because foreign economies and currency values don't always move in tandem with ours, investing overseas helps to dampen the overall volatility of your portfolio. Investing in U.S. companies that operate worldwide serves a similar purpose.

Financial instruments such as options and futures, also known as *derivatives*, are not investments. Most derivatives represent short-term bets on the price movement of an underlying security, such as a stock, or a commodity (for example, farm products or precious metals).

REMEMBER

Individual investors should stay away from these instruments. Professional investors sometimes use derivatives as a way to speculate or leverage their potential returns. The downside: Derivative holders can lose all of their investment if they guess wrong. Used properly, derivatives are also sometimes used by the pros as a way to hedge investment risk. Proper hedging requires financial sophistication and costs money, so it's best left to the pros. Don't put money in these vehicles unless you treat it as gambling money that you are willing to lose.

Understanding the major investments

Investments are often chosen out of habit, convenience, or inertia. Investing should be a proactive process based on your needs and goals. Only after assessing your personal situation, your concerns, and your desires should you select your investments, which will help you forge your way.

If you read or listen to the financial news, you've probably heard lots of buzzwords and jargon: blue chips, junk bonds, equity-income, hedge funds, municipals, ETFs, and so on. Among all the major securities exchanges where you can purchase stocks and bonds, as well as investment companies that sell a myriad of investment products, there are literally tens of thousands of choices. So, if you are confused and/or overwhelmed, there's good reason.

Forget, for a moment, all the different investment names you have swimming around inside your head. Imagine a simpler world in which you have just two investment options: lending investments and ownership investments.

A *lending investment,* as the name suggests, is an investment where you are lending your money, typically to an organization. For example, when you place your money in a bank account, such as a savings account, you are essentially lending your money to a bank for an agreed-upon interest rate.

Bonds, which are IOUs issued by companies, are another common lending investment. If you purchase, say, a ten-year bond issued by the big retailer Target at 5 percent, you are in essence lending your money to Target for ten years in exchange for 5 percent interest per year. If things go according to plan, you'll get your 5 percent interest annually and your principal (original investment) back when the bond matures in ten years.

With *ownership investments,* by contrast, you own a piece (sometimes all) of an asset that has the ability to produce profits or earnings. Stocks, which are shares of ownership in a company, and real estate are ownership investments.

In a capitalistic economy, individual investors build wealth through being owners, not lenders. For example, if Target doubles in size and profits over the next ten years, as one of their bondholders, you won't share in the growth. As a stockholder, however, you should benefit from a stock price driven higher by greater profits.

Students at the top business schools now pay in excess of $200,000 for a mere 18 months of education. Armies of Ph.D.s and finance professors have spent decades researching the financial markets and returns of different assets and the risks of those assets. The biggest insight from all of this work is that risk and return go hand-in-hand. If you want "safe" — as defined by lack of volatility and low likelihood of the value of the investment declining — you have to settle for relatively low returns. Those who desire more attractive returns and who seek to earn investment returns well ahead of the rate of inflation must seek out investments that provide an ownership stake.

Investors in ownership assets have earned far superior returns over the years and decades than lending investors. Over the past two centuries, U.S. stock market investors have earned an average of about 9 percent per year, whereas longer-term bond investors have earned just 5 percent per year.

The three time-tested ways to build wealth with ownership investments are to invest in stocks, real estate, or small business. I deal with each of these in turn (plus, I offer some safe investment options).

Building wealth with stocks

Stocks, which are shares of ownership in companies, historically, have produced returns averaging about 9 percent per year. To some people, such returns seem like chump change because they expect to double, triple, or quadruple (or more) their money in short order. That's why financial-market programs and blogs that focus on high-flying stocks are so dangerously tempting. Why wait eight years for your investment to double, which is how long it takes with a 9 percent average annual return, when some stocks double or more in less than a year? ("The rule of 72" says that if you take 72 and divide it by your annual return, that will tell you about how many years it takes to double your money.) Well, the reason, quite simply, is that risky investment schemes often crash and burn. Consistently saving a portion of your income and getting moderate returns produces awesome long-term outcomes.

Although some people are able to start their own businesses or achieve high incomes from their work, the best chance for most of us to build the wealth that we desire to accomplish our personal and financial goals is through systematic saving and investing. Consider that through the miracle of compounding, for every $5,000 per year that you can invest in a tax-deferred account returning an average of 9 percent per year, you'll have about $400,000 in 20 years and $1.5 million in 40 years. Wow!

Investing in stocks is one of the most accessible ways for people to invest for long-term growth. When companies go "public," they issue shares of stock that people like you can purchase on the major stock exchanges, such as the New York Stock Exchange or Nasdaq.

TECHNICAL STUFF

As the economy grows and companies grow with it and earn greater profits, stock prices generally follow suit. Stock prices don't move in lockstep with earnings, but over the years, the relationship is pretty close. In fact, the price-earnings ratio or multiple — which measures the level of stock prices relative to (or divided by) company earnings — of U.S. stocks has averaged approximately 15 during the past century. While the ratio has varied and been as high as 30+ and as low as 6, it tends to fluctuate around 15. (It has been slightly higher during periods of low inflation and low interest rates.)

You can choose to invest in stocks through making your own selection of individual stocks or through letting a mutual fund manager do it for you. Researching individual stocks can be more than a full-time job, and if you choose to take this path, remember that you'll be competing against the pros.

Efficiently managed mutual funds offer investors low-cost access to high-quality money managers. Mutual funds span the spectrum of risk and potential returns from nonfluctuating money market funds (which are similar to savings accounts), to bond funds (which generally pay higher yields than money market funds but fluctuate with changes in interest rates), to stock funds (which offer the greatest potential for appreciation but also the greatest short-term volatility).

Even during a successful mountain climb, setbacks occur. And so it is with wealth-building investments such as stocks. The U.S. stock market, as measured by the Dow Jones Industrial Average, has fallen more than 20 percent about once every six years. That's the bad news. The good news is that these declines lasted, on average, less than two years. So, if you can withstand declines over a few years, the stock market is a terrific place to invest for long-term growth.

Investing in stocks or funds

Over the years, increasing numbers of investors have turned to mutual funds and more recently exchanged-traded funds (ETFs) for their stock market investing rather than picking and choosing individual stocks on their own. There's still tremendous debate about the merits of these two quite different approaches, and there are many, many sources pushing investors to individual stocks. Various websites and blogs, financial publications, and television programs advocate for individual stocks. You will rarely see a panel on a major network discussing good funds, but you will frequently see debates for which stocks to buy and sell now.

Numerous private money managers bash mutual funds and ETFs since funds are often their competition. Financial newsletter writers and book authors mislead investors into thinking that picking their own stocks is the best approach to investing in the market.

The principal arguments that stock-picking advocates make for going that route are the following:

>> You will make more money.

>> Most funds fail to beat the broad market averages, so why settle for mediocrity?

>> You can control tax-related issues, such as when you buy and sell securities, and recognize taxable gains or losses.

Here I tackle each of these promises:

>> **The siren song of making more money:** Stock pickers love to point out examples of stocks that, had you only bought them many years ago, would have made you a gazillionaire. Who among us wouldn't have loved to have bought stock in companies such as Amazon, Amgen, Apple, Best Buy, Google, Microsoft, Netflix, and Walmart, which have increased in value thousands of percent in the years and decades since they went public?

The only problem here is that this is investing with a rear-view mirror — 20/20 hindsight! Plenty of companies that issue stock see their stock prices actually go down — in some cases to nothing if the firm goes bankrupt. And among the stocks that do rise, most price increases are far, far less spectacular than these extremely successful examples.

>> **Beating the average by picking for yourself:** If the motivation to pick your own stocks is that you think you can earn higher returns than a money manager running a mutual fund, you should calculate what your actual returns, net of all trading fees and after taxes, have been each year over the past five years. Once you've done that, compare your returns with those of the relevant market averages and those earned by comparable funds. If you can consistently beat the averages and the pros, you're not in the right profession — become a professional money manager!

REMEMBER

Recognize that if you (rather than a fund manager) are picking and choosing stocks and deciding when and what to buy and sell, so much more pressure and stress will be on you during tough times. Will you have the resolve to hold your chosen stocks during an economic downturn or through a personally difficult period? At least with a professional money manager, you have some peace of mind that they have the experience and expertise to know how to better deal with difficult times.

INVESTMENT CLUBS: JOINER BEWARE

In addition to stock-picking advocates, over the years many investment club proponents cite the supposed superior performance of investment clubs. The National Association of Investors Corporation, which published the book *Starting and Running a Profitable Investment Club*, claims that their book will teach you, ". . . a method so successful that 60 percent of investment clubs outperform the market."

If this statistic were true, it would mean that investment clubs perform better on average than professional mutual fund managers! Using trading records from a large discount brokerage firm, Professors Brad Barber and Terrance Odean conducted a thorough review of 166 investment club accounts over a six-year period. They found that the average club actually underperformed the broad stock market average by more than three percent per year. Furthermore, they found that the majority (60 percent to be exact) of the clubs analyzed underperformed the broad stock market index. Also of interest was the fact that they found that the average club turned over a whopping 65 percent of its portfolio annually, which increases trading costs and taxes.

An investment club from Beardstown, Illinois, got a book deal *(The Beardstown Ladies' Common-Sense Investment Guide: How We Beat the Stock Market — And How You Can, Too)* because of its claimed returns averaging nearly 24 percent per year, far ahead of the stock market averages of that period. Not until years after the club penned a best-selling book that claimed to have a system for beating the system did it come out that they only really earned a 9 percent annualized return, which placed its returns far below the market averages! So egregious was this situation that the book's publisher, Hyperion, lost a class action lawsuit brought on behalf of defrauded book buyers.

Now, it is true that most funds fail to beat their relevant market index. There is a simple reason for this — the expenses, which on plenty of funds are more than 1 percent — place a drag on returns. Studies on this topic show that over the long term (10+ years), about seven out of ten funds underperform the relevant market average. However, that's not an argument for picking your own stocks! There's a simple and powerful way to increase your mutual fund returns: Shun costly funds (more on this later when we discuss recommended funds you should consider).

>> **Stock trading is tax friendlier.** You can invest in tax-friendly funds and have lots of control over the realization of taxable gains by holding such funds for the long term.

Picking your own stocks: A cautionary tale

Investing in individual stocks requires extensive research and time if you want to do it well. When taken to an extreme, the time and energy some folks expend watching their investments can negatively impact their emotional and mental well-being, their personal relationships, and, in the cruelest twist of all, the performance of that portfolio they're lavishing so much attention on.

As for control, it's true that you can exercise control over when you decide to buy and sell individual stocks and other securities. This is easier said than done and requires a lot of ongoing vigilance, analysis, and tax expertise, which few people have, and is costly. This is an issue for nonretirement account investing, and there are good solutions with funds that can be chosen with tax considerations in mind. (There are tax-friendly funds.)

REMEMBER

One of the ways that stock-picking advocates seek to damage the reputation of all mutual funds is by claiming that mutual fund fees are outrageously high. Indeed, some funds do have high fees, but avoiding them is easy to do through simple comparison shopping. (See the section "Selecting the Best Mutual Funds and Exchange-Traded Funds" later in this chapter.)

If you're going to buy some individual stocks, be clear as to why you're doing so. Invest no more than, say, 20 percent of your stock holdings in total in individual stocks. You should be stock picking more so for the educational value than because you expect to earn market-beating returns. Be mindful of the common mistake individual stock-picking investors make with being overly optimistic about company's future earnings, which is the single most important stock price determinant in the long term. When investors fall in love with a company and its stock, they tend to lose sight of the harsh realities of competition and economic downturns.

Veteran financial advisor Harold Evensky gives clients who are eager to invest in individual stocks the following "test" when they come to him with their stock ideas:

>> Who is the president of the company, and what is that person's tenure?

>> What is the single largest product or service of the firm, what percentage of the firm's net profit does it contribute, and what share of that market does the firm control?

>> Who is the major competitor in this area, and what has that firm's growth been over the last five years versus the firm you're interested in?

Evensky says, "If they can't answer these questions, I say, 'Don't buy.' No one has ever passed. Almost all fail at 'Who is the president?'"

SPLITTING UP IS HARD TO DO

Companies knowingly take advantage of the human tendency to be drawn toward low prices by using stock splits to entice investors to buy their stock. This was a major mechanism by which grossly overvalued technology and internet stocks continued to attract more investors in the late 1990s. The wildly popular Cisco Systems, for example, split five times in the latter half of the 1990s alone! These decisions enabled the company to keep the stock price well under $100 per share and attractive to far more investors. Had the splits not occurred, the stock would've been trading at nearly $1,500 per share. Investors who snapped up the stock in late 1999 and early 2000 were paying an outrageous price-earnings (PE) multiple of more than 200. (During normal times, the overall stock market sells at a PE of about 15 to 20, whereas fast-growing companies typically sell at about a PE of 30 to 50.) The very next year, 2001, the economy tanked, and Cisco's earnings took a huge hit — dropping by about half. Cisco's stock got hammered, plunging nearly 87 percent in just over a year.

Then internet darling Yahoo! also managed their stock price in similar fashion during frenzied buying of their shares in the late 1990s. At its peak in 2000, Yahoo! reached $125 per share, but it would've been about $1,500 in the absence of its numerous splits in the latter 1990s. At its peak, its PE was an astounding 521! Yahoo's stock plunged nearly 97 percent during the bear market.

WARNING

Another problem that some investors have is getting fixated on a particular price for an investment. Often, this point of stubborn fascination is the original price that they paid for an investment (or it could be the value of an investment when they inherited it). When investors fall into this trap, they can lose their ability to objectively assess the merits or shortcomings of an investment.

The price per share that a stock trades for, in and of itself, is completely and utterly meaningless unless you know the company's earnings per share and other important financial information. A surprising number of investors, however, leap to erroneous assumptions about the attractiveness, or lack thereof, of a company's stock on the basis of the price per share. Some investors shy away from stocks that trade at higher prices per share concerned that they may be overpriced.

Understanding the importance of saving versus market timing

One of the biggest mistakes that investors make is trying to time jumping into and out of the stock market. Market timing is difficult if not impossible to do, even for the best professional investors. But it's tempting to try and time the markets, especially when bad things are happening.

It is far more important and valuable to save regularly and invest than to try to earn a few extra percent per year with market timing. Consider two hypothetical people, Ms. Saver and Mr. Timer, who are each good at one investing strategy. Ms. Saver, as her name suggests, is a consistent saver and is able to save $2,000 per year over the next decade. Mr. Timer, on the other hand, spends dozens of hours following the financial world and is convinced he can beat the markets. Mr. Timer saves just $2,000 in the first year. Ms. Saver stays invested in the stock market and earns an average 10 percent per year return. Suppose Mr. Timer studies and trades in and out of the market and is able to eke out an extra 2 percent per year return (earning 12 percent per year). At the end of the decade, Ms. Saver will have accumulated $31,875, whereas Mr. Timer will have just $6,212.

Please note that in reality, few market timers can beat the market average returns and many actually underperform a "buy and hold" approach. The reason for the underperformance is quite simple. The stock market can move up quickly, and if you're sitting on the sidelines during one of these upward movements, you miss out.

Dimensional Fund Advisors examined what happened if you missed out on some of the best days for stock market returns over the long term. They found that investing just $1,000 in the S&P 500 at the beginning of 1970 would have grown to about $139,000 over the subsequent 50 years. However, if an investor missed out on just the 15 best days over this period, the final investment total would have been just $52,000. Missing the 25 best days would have produced a final investment total of just $33,000.

So, not only does excessive trading lead to your possibly being out of the market on the best days and reduce your returns, but it can also increase your transaction costs and taxes.

Locating money through real estate

Investing in real estate is another time-tested method for building wealth. Over the generations, real estate owners and investors have enjoyed rates of return comparable to the stock market.

Weighing home ownership versus renting

A common place to start with real estate ownership is to buy your own home. The equity (difference between the market value of the home and loan owed on it) in your home that builds over the years can become a significant part of your net worth. Among other things, this equity can be tapped to help accomplish other important financial goals such as retirement, college, and starting or buying a business.

Over your adult life, owning a home should be less expensive than renting a comparable home. The reason: As a renter, your housing costs are fully exposed to inflation (unless you're the beneficiary of a rent-controlled apartment). As a homeowner, the bulk of your housing costs — namely your monthly mortgage — is not exposed to inflation if you finance your home purchase with a fixed-rate mortgage. A homeowner's property taxes, insurance, and maintenance costs do generally grow with overall increases in the cost of living.

Real estate investment decisions are undoubtedly the toughest ones to make. With all those digits in the sticker price, buying a home is rightfully frightening. But it's not only about all that money; it's the actual and implied commitment to establish roots and stay put for a while. Selling a home is no picnic either, especially since most people buy another home after selling. That's two transactions — double the stress and headaches.

Given the ever-present economic uncertainties and other issues in life we face, people often wonder if they should buy a house instead of renting or, if they already own a home, they ask if they should sell before prices drop. The short answer is that it depends upon your local real estate market and your personal situation.

A useful analysis to determine whether buying or renting is advisable is to compare the monthly cost of renting a given home to the monthly (after-tax) cost of owning that same home (mortgage payment + property taxes + insurance + maintenance − tax benefits). You shouldn't be paying a large premium to buy and own. If the monthly (after-tax) ownership costs greatly exceed the monthly rental costs for a given property, renting is a better value and ultimately may attract enough prospective buyers to weaken housing prices.

If you're a renter who has been thinking about buying, you're in a market that's already weak, and you're motivated to buy, you can probably get a decent deal on purchasing a home, especially if the rental costs of a given property are close to the ownership costs. That's not to say that prices won't fall further after your purchase. But you should accept the fact that none of us has a crystal ball and realize that once it's clear that times are getting better, the market will likely have moved higher.

If your local real estate market is just beginning to show signs of weakness, renting is a good value, and you have some personal ambivalence about buying, you should probably wait. Perhaps your job is at risk due to your employer's financial situation or the industry you're in. Maybe you don't want to stay in your current geographic area for much longer.

Purchasing and then ultimately selling a home is a costly proposition. You've got loan fees, real estate agent commissions, title costs, and other expenses that can easily gobble up 15 percent of the home's value between the two transactions. That's why you should plan on holding your home for at least three and preferably five years. Expecting 15 percent appreciation just to cover your transaction costs over shorter time frames is highly risky. That said, sometimes you do get high rates of appreciation in short periods of time as happened in some non-urban parts of the country during the COVID-19 pandemic.

TIP

With regards to selling, if you must sell because you have to move, price your house realistically. If a locally softening economy gets you depressed because your house doesn't net as much as you expected, remember that when you buy, you'll benefit from the lower prices unless you're unlucky enough to be moving from a depressed housing market into a strong one.

Looking into investment real estate

In addition to building wealth through home ownership, you can also consider investing in real estate that you rent out, often referred to as investment property. If you don't desire to be a landlord — one of the biggest drawbacks of investment real estate — consider investing in real estate through *real estate investment trusts* (REITs). REITs are diversified real estate investment companies that purchase and manage rental real estate for investors. You can invest in REITs either through purchasing them directly on the major stock exchanges or through a real estate mutual fund that invests in numerous REITs.

A simple but effective way to invest in REITs is through a diversified mutual fund of REITs such as Vanguard's Real Estate Index fund. Since this fund's inception in 2001, it has produced an annualized average return of 10.1 percent.

If you want to invest directly in real estate, residential housing — such as single-family homes or small, multi-unit buildings — is a straightforward and attractive investment for most people. Before you venture into real estate investing, be sure that you have sufficient time to devote to it. Also, be careful not to sacrifice contributions to tax-deductible retirement accounts in order to own investment real estate. In the early years of rental property ownership, many investors find that their property's expenses exceed its income. This "negative cash flow" can siphon off money that you could otherwise direct into your retirement accounts to earn tax benefits.

WARNING

Novice real estate investors often make the mistake of not thoroughly researching the income and expense realities of particular properties before they buy them. Inexperienced landlords also make mistakes when trying to rent their properties and end up with more vacancies and headaches than they expected. Thus, the early years of rental property ownership can be filled with unexpected losses, which, in the worst cases, have bankrupted owners who already were stretched thin because of the initial purchase price.

TIP

When selecting real estate for investment purposes, remember that local economic growth is the fuel for demand for housing. In addition to a vibrant and diverse job base, a limited supply of both housing and land on which to build is another factor that you should take into consideration. When you identify potential properties in which you might invest, run the numbers to understand the cash demands of owning the property and the likely profitability.

Turning to small business options

A third way many Americans have built substantial wealth is through small business. The most successful small business owners generally earn the highest investment returns. More of the world's wealthiest individuals have built their wealth through their stake in small businesses than through any other vehicle. Small business is the engine that drives much of our economic growth. Most new jobs created are created in smaller firms.

TIP

You can participate in small business in a variety of ways. You can start your own business, buy and operate an existing business, or simply invest in promising small businesses.

If you have the self-discipline and a product or service you can sell, starting your own business can be both profitable and fulfilling. Consider first what skills and expertise you possess that you can use in your business. You don't need a eureka-type experience where a totally new idea comes to you. Millions of people operate successful businesses such as dry cleaners, restaurants, tax preparation firms, and so on that are hardly unique.

Start exploring your idea first by developing a written business plan. Such a plan should detail what your product or service will be, how you will market it, who your customers and competitors are, and what the economics of the business are, including the start-up costs. Small Business Development Center (https://www.sbdcnet.org/) services are an excellent return on your tax dollars if you want to go the small business route.

If you don't have a specific product or service you desire to sell but are skilled at managing and improving the operations of a company, buying a small business may be for you. Finding and buying a good small business takes much time and patience, so be willing to devote at least several months to the search. You will also likely need to enlist the help of financial and legal advisors to help inspect the company and its financial statements and put a deal together.

Check out my book, along with Jim Schell, *Small Business For Dummies* (John Wiley & Sons) for additional information.

Searching for safe money investments

Bonds and savings–type vehicles, such as money market mutual funds, certainly have a place in your portfolio. For money that you expect to use within the next couple of years, bonds and money funds can make great sense. Historically, such investments have produced returns close to the rate of inflation (2 to 3 percent) or a bit more (4 to 5 percent for bonds). The most recent period of ultra-low interest rates is certainly not the historic norm.

While stocks and real estate offer investors attractive long-term returns, they can and do suffer significant declines in value from time to time. Thus, these investments are not suitable for money that you think you may want or need to use within, say, the next five years.

TIP

Money market and bond investments are good places to keep money that you expect to use sooner. Everyone should have a reserve of money that they may access in an emergency. Keeping about three to six months' worth of living expenses in a money market fund is a good start. Shorter-term bonds or bond mutual funds can serve as a greater income-producing, additional, or secondary emergency cushion.

Bonds can also be useful for some longer-term investing for diversification purposes. For example, when investing for retirement, placing a portion of one's money in bonds helps to buffer stock market declines. As I discuss later in the chapter, you may consider deploying some of this money to buy stocks when they are depressed due to an economic downturn. (See the section, "Seizing Investment Opportunities During Tough Times.") When investing for longer-term goals, however, some younger investors may not be interested in a significant stake, or any stake at all, in boring old bonds.

Cultivating Good Investing Habits

Saving money may be a challenge, but investing wisely and sidestepping dangerous temptations and habits poses other major hurdles. The best investing habits can easily translate into hundreds of thousands, if not millions, more dollars in your future. Equally important is the peace of mind that comes from feeling in control and understanding how to properly direct investments.

REMEMBER

The best investors have a simple plan, do their homework, and maintain a long-term perspective. They also understand the vital importance of keeping the fees and taxes that they pay to a minimum.

Investing is clearly more complicated than just setting your goals and choosing solid investments. In addition to considering your goals in a traditional sense before investing (for example, when you want to retire, how much of your kids' college costs you desire to pay, and so on), you should also consider what you want and don't want to get from the process of investing. Is it a hobby or simply another of life's tasks, such as maintaining your home? Do you desire the intellectual challenge of picking your own stocks, or are you content entrusting some of those decisions to others? Deciding how you feel about these considerations will shape your approach to managing your investments. Don't just ponder these questions on your own. Discuss them with family members, too — after all, you're all going to have to live with the investment decisions and results.

This section covers simple, yet powerful, principles that can maximize your chances for the best investment returns and help you sidestep common mistakes that many other investors have suffered through. Misery may love company, but being on the front lines of the school of hard knocks hurts financially. Why not get your education now and make the most of your future investments?

Understanding fees

It stands to reason that if you're earning, say, 1 percent investing in a money market fund, 2 percent in a bond fund, or 9 percent per year in stocks, the fees that you pay can be a huge drain on your returns. Some managed accounts at hotshot investment companies may charge you upwards of 2 percent to have your money managed by investment professionals wearing designer suits and working in mahogany-paneled offices in prestigious locations. Funny thing is, though, your money doesn't care if the people who are managing it are located on New York City's Park Avenue, Flatbush Avenue in Brooklyn, or Omaha, Nebraska. It also doesn't care how well dressed the folks are who are managing it. But even if you earn, say, 9 percent per year in a predominantly stock-managed portfolio, paying 2 percent per year in fees is giving away nearly a quarter of your total returns.

Unfortunately, taxes can gobble a large share of your returns as well. You may find your pretax return of 9 percent knocked down to just 6 percent after taxes. So, a 2 percent management fee is actually sucking away a third of your take-home returns!

Even if you're only paying 1.5 percent, what if you could pay 0.5 percent (or less) instead?

If you think that saving one percent annually in fees doesn't matter, think again! With $10,000 invested over 25 years, you'd end up with $22,000 more by saving just 1 percent in annual fees. So, if you had $100,000 invested over 25 years, that would add up to more than $220,000 more, and with $1 million invested over 25 years, you'd have a whopping $2.2 million more!

Often, high fees go hand-in-hand when you work with salespeople. Some investors assume knowledge, competence, and ethics on the part of hired advisors if the person has an important-sounding title such as vice president; dresses the part; and occupies plush, high-cost office space. But the fact of the matter is that such accessories can just as often be leading indicators of a salesperson earning unnecessarily big commissions and fees siphoned from investors' (your) dollars.

Additionally, placing too much trust in an "expert" can lead to laziness when investors spend too little time monitoring their investments and making decisions without doing independent research. Figuring that Joe Financial Consultant is an expert, some investors blindly follow him straight into bad investments (for the investor, not the commissioned agent) without ever questioning recommendations or analyzing their investments' performance over time.

Mary, an older widow living on a modest fixed income, was drawn to a bank salesperson pitching an annuity with a high initial "teaser" interest rate. She developed anxiety symptoms and sleep problems because of buyer's remorse. She was too proud and ashamed to ask for help with getting out of the annuity, which she felt was a mistake to purchase. Mary didn't need the tax shelter (and the associated high fees) of an annuity, and she would not likely keep her money in the annuity long enough for any small tax benefits to make up for its relatively high fees.

Nick and Joyce had two young children and knew that they needed to buy some life insurance, but they had never gotten around to it. One day, a salesperson, who was a friend of Nick's, called the couple at home and pitched them some costly whole life policies (which combine life insurance with a low-return investment account). Without doing any research or comparison shopping, Nick and Joyce each bought a policy. Due to the high costs, they got far less insurance coverage than they really needed, and they paid nearly triple what they should have for the type of policy because they failed to shop around.

Managing monitoring and trading your investments

One surefire way to increase your fees, taxes, and stress levels is to closely monitor your investments and jump in and out of your holdings based on the current news, short-term price gyrations, and your mood. Investors who are the most anxious about their investments and most likely to make impulsive trading decisions are the ones who watch their holdings closely, especially those who monitor prices daily. The investment world seems so risky and fraught with pitfalls that some people believe that closely watching an investment can help alert them to impending danger. Investors who monitor their holdings closely trade more and, not surprisingly, earn worse returns.

When asked, such investors routinely say that they watch their investments daily because they believe that doing so maximizes their chances of making smart moves. Many people are overconfident in their own abilities and knowledge, especially relative to others'.

In a survey conducted by Robert Shiller of Yale University, consider how individual investors answered the following multiple-choice question:

Q: When trying to pick individual stocks, trying to predict, for example, if and when Ford Motor stock will go up or IBM stock will go up, is

A smart thing to try to do; I can reasonably expect to be a success at it.

Not a smart thing to try to do; I can't.

No opinion.

A whopping 40 percent of investors surveyed chose (A)! Lots of folks believe they can time the markets and know when and what to buy and sell.

In a study entitled "Boys Will Be Boys: Gender, Overconfidence, and Common Stock Investment" (published in the *Quarterly Journal of Economics*), Brad Barber and Terrance Odean found that men tend to be more overconfident, trade more, and earn lower returns than women. Their analysis of tens of thousands of brokerage accounts demonstrated that, ". . . men trade 45 percent more than women and earn annual risk-adjusted net returns that are 1.4 percent less than those earned by women. These differences are more pronounced between single men and single women; single men trade 67 percent more than single women and earn annual risk-adjusted net returns that are 2.3 percent less than those earned by single women."

And, when overconfident investors/traders start losing money, their judgment actually gets even worse. In a landmark study by Dr. William Gehring and Dr. Adrian Willoughby of the University of Michigan, researchers analyzed what happens when people make risky choices in gambling games and lose. Subjects who suffered such losses experienced heightened brain activity symptomatic of distress, which caused them to be more likely to make knee-jerk and irrational decisions to try and quickly win the money back. Unfortunately, the internet, low-cost computers, and smartphones have aggravated the problem by enabling the worst offenders to continually track stock prices and news releases.

To add insult to injury (and give you yet another good reason to trade less), researchers have found a clear link between daily tracking of investments and poor mental health. A study published in the *Journal of Social & Clinical Psychology* reported that those who follow the stock market closely generally had the worst problems with pessimism and depression. Researchers believe that these results are due to the fact that such investors are closely monitoring a situation that they have no control over, and when things go against them, they feel demoralized.

Remember the saying, "Ignorance is bliss." This is not suggesting that you stick your head in the sand and ignore your investments, but if you follow every little up and down, the down times will inevitably wear on you. The stock market goes through some extended down periods, and closely following things during such periods can be especially distressing and depressing.

What these studies didn't highlight is the damage done beyond the investor's poor mental health. Most of us don't have much free time, and if so much time is being devoted to tracking investments, the investors' personal relationships, family members, and friends pay the price too. In their financial planning work, advisors sometimes hear about these broader problems. Typical is the following complaint one woman made: "Every day, my husband spends hours on the internet following his individual stocks. He says we have been doing well, but we never go anywhere or do anything together. This type of investing worries me."

If you consider investing to be your hobby, ask your loved ones and friends to honestly tell you if your perceived hobby has grown into something more problematic. If you're afraid to raise the subject because of what you expect the answer to be, that should tell you something needs addressing.

Consider what it means to be a successful investor: someone who, with a minimal commitment of time, develops an investment plan to accomplish important financial and personal goals and earns returns comparable to the market averages. Some people have control issues with their investments. These folks have great difficulty turning over their money to someone else to manage, which is what you're doing when you invest in a mutual fund. Such investors typically prefer investing in real estate and individual stocks of their own choosing.

Keeping your emotions from following market trends

Investors, and people in general, tend to place too much emphasis on recent events. Before September 11, 2001, most people went about their daily lives and didn't think about terrorism. Post-September 11, 2001, far more people think and worry about the risk of terrorists striking again. The same simplistic thinking occurs with investments. Stocks and sectors that are doing well are usually expected to continue to perform. Likewise, many investors flee falling investments. Investors tend to get more optimistic as prices rise and increasingly pessimistic as prices fall. More often than not, investors make simplistic extrapolations of the past and fail to research and do their homework. This is why many studies have found that the average investor tends to buy high and sell low and actually ends up earning returns lower than the market averages.

REMEMBER

That's why the admittedly rare company investment plans, such as select 401(k)s, that limit people to trading only a few times a year are better for you. (Once per quarter is common.) Instituting a similar restriction for your own personal investment accounts can prevent you from making emotional, impulsive reactions to current bad (or good) news.

Difficult times and market declines will occur. So, be sure to invest new money on a regular basis, such as monthly or quarterly (known as dollar cost averaging), so that you'll benefit from buying during market downswings. Also, consider investing in highly diversified, less volatile mutual funds of mutual funds, such as Vanguard's LifeStrategy funds, that hold several funds investing in stocks worldwide as well as bonds. When investing in funds of funds, be careful to avoid those with extra layers of high fees — those that are recommended later in this chapter don't suffer from that problem.

Dealing with investment setbacks

If you're the type of investor who is unable to mentally and emotionally withstand the volatility of riskier growth-oriented investments (such as stocks) and hold on through market declines, you may be better off not investing in such vehicles. Recognize, though, the "risk" you're taking by placing all of your money in low-return investments like bonds or bank accounts: You'll have to either work more years and save more money to reach your financial goals or accept a lower standard of living.

While some investors realize that they can't withstand losses and sell at the first signs of trouble, other investors find it so painful and unpleasant to sell a losing investment that they'll continue holding a poorly performing investment despite the investment's poor future prospects. The late Amos Tversky, a Stanford psychology professor, and economist and psychology professor Daniel Kahneman of Princeton documented how people find accepting a given loss more than twice as painful when compared with the positive emotion associated with a gain of equal magnitude.

Because most investors find losses more painful to accept compared with the pleasure they get from gains, they often take on more risk holding onto a clear loser to avoid having to actually take a loss. Most investors also prefer to lock in a small gain rather than risk losing it while waiting for a larger gain. These tendencies can cause investors to hold onto their losers and to sell their winners far too early because they don't want the pain that comes with realizing a loss. University of California professor Terrance Odean conducted a study of brokerage accounts and found that the winning stocks that people sell greatly outperformed the losers that they hold onto.

As you research and follow your investments, restrict your diet of financial information and advice. Quality is far more important than quantity. If you invest in diversified mutual funds, you really don't need to examine your fund's performance more than once or twice per year. This recommendation may surprise you, especially if you're an internet-tracking junkie suffering from investment-information overload. An ideal time to review your funds is when you receive their annual or semi-annual reports. Although some investors track their funds on a daily or weekly basis, far fewer bother to read the funds' annual reports. Doing so will help you keep a long-term perspective and gain some understanding as to why your funds are performing as they are and how they're doing in comparison to major market averages.

REMEMBER

When you invest in stocks and bonds, you must accept the fact that there will be short-term declines, and sometimes substantial drops, in your investments' values. This is never enjoyable. For inexperienced or nervous investors, bailing out when it appears that an investment isn't going to be profitable and enjoyable can be tempting. Some investors run to dump falling investments precisely at the times when they should be doing the reverse — buying more.

TIP

Examine your returns over longer periods (months and years, not days and weeks) to help keep the proper perspective. During difficult times, minimize your exposure to financial news coverage. Tuning into the financial cable networks and listening to commentators dwell on the carnage around them on the trading floor won't encourage you to hold onto or add to your investments.

The key to effectively dealing with events that negatively impact your investment portfolio is not to panic. Slow down and pull back from stressful situations and news before making future decisions. As with everything in life, recognize what you can and cannot control. Don't waste your time or energy by closely following things that you have no control over.

Developing a Personal Investing Plan

Before you jump into investing in this mutual fund or that certificate of deposit, you should consider some important personal and financial issues. If you don't, you're putting the cart before the horse. For example, don't begin planning your investments if you have consumer debt and haven't dealt with that or if you haven't developed an overall financial plan.

REMEMBER

A critical issue to weigh before investing is the length of time you have in mind. Most of the better investments are relatively liquid — that's not the concern. The potential problem is that if you invest your money into a risky investment and it drops in value just before you need to sell, you could be forced to take a loss. Thus, you should be concerned about matching the risk or volatility of your investments with the time frame that you have in mind.

Suppose you have some money that you'd like to invest because you plan to use it for a down payment for a home purchase in a few years. With this relatively modest time frame in mind, investments such as stocks or real estate would not be appropriate because they can fluctuate a great deal in value from year to year. These more growth-oriented (and volatile) investments, on the other hand, can be useful in working toward longer-term goals such as retirement that may be a decade or more away.

In addition to the time frame, your need to factor risk into your investment decisions. If the money that you're investing for retirement, for example, grows too slowly, you may not be able to retire when you want or with the lifestyle you desire. To reach your retirement goal, you may need to take more risk.

While your goals may require you to take more risk, that doesn't mean that you necessarily should do so. If you're going to become a nervous wreck and follow the stock market's every move, it may not be worth it for you to take as much risk, and you should consider rethinking your goals. Also, if you're in the fortunate position of not needing to take much risk because you're well on your way toward your savings goal, taking more risk than necessary may cause you to lose what you have.

Taxing situations

A consideration about investing your money is your tax situation. If you invest without paying attention to the tax implications, you may be overlooking simple ways to maximize your returns.

Two simple yet powerful moves will help you to invest in a tax-wise way. First, you should make sure to contribute to your retirement accounts so that less of your money is taxed in the first place. This will reduce your taxes both in the years you make your contributions as well as each year your money is invested.

Second, with money that you invest outside retirement accounts, choose investments that match your tax situation. If you're in a high tax bracket, you should avoid investments that produce significant highly taxed distributions. Thus, you should avoid taxable bonds, certificates of deposit, and other investments that pay taxable interest income and that tend to distribute short-term capital gains (which are taxed at the same high tax rates as ordinary income such as your employment income).

If you are in a high tax bracket and would like to invest in bonds outside a retirement account, you should consider municipal bonds that pay federally tax-free interest. These are also generally free of state income taxes in the state where the bond was issued. Also consider growth-oriented investments, such as stocks, real estate, or investments in your or someone else's small business.

Assessing your current portfolio

Before we leap into how to invest your current money, first cover what to do with your current investments. While it's wise to buy and hold solid investments for the long haul, there are times when selling is appropriate. In fact, if you've been holding investments that seem to be doing poorly over an extended period, closely examine the situation. Try to determine why they've done so poorly. If a given investment is down because similar ones are also in decline, and the long-term perspective still holds, perhaps so should you.

However, if there's something inherently wrong with the investment in question, such as high fees or poor management, take the loss, and make doing so more palatable by remembering two things. First, if it's a nonretirement account investment, losses help reduce your current income taxes. Second, consider the "opportunity cost" of continuing to keep your money in a lousy investment: What future return could that money be providing if you switched into a better investment?

TIP

A useful way to evaluate your portfolio once a year or every few years is to imagine that everything that you currently own is sold. Ask yourself whether you'd choose to go out and buy the same investments today that you were holding. This is an especially good question to ask yourself if you own lots of stock in the company you work for. Are your reasons still valid for holding your investments?

Following are some items to be mindful of when assessing your current holdings:

>> **Don't dump a particular investment just because it's in what will turn out to be a temporary slump.** Even the best investment managers have periods as long as a year or two during which they underperform. (Sometimes this happens when the manager's style of investing is out of favor for the time being.) But remember, a temporary slump can easily last one to two years, not months or days.

>> **Watch attachment issues.** Just as we get attached to people, places, and things, some investors' judgment may be clouded due to attachment to an investment. Even if an investor makes the decision to sell an investment based on a sound and practical assessment, their attachment to it can derail the process, causing them to refuse to part with it at the current fair market value. Attachment can be especially problematic and paralyzing with inherited assets. It is common to have difficulty being objective with and letting go of inherited investments.

>> **Be wary of inertia.** It isn't unusual for some folks to accumulate tens or hundreds of thousands of dollars in checking accounts and continue to leave the money languishing there. Such people are often fearful of selecting an investment that may fall in value. These people know how long and hard they had to work for their money, and they don't want to lose it.

>> **Keep bigger-picture issues in mind.** It's not unusual for some people to have excess cash in a low-interest money market fund or savings account while they carry high-cost debt like auto loans and credit-card balances. If such folks paid down the high-cost debt, they could save or make a good deal of money by doing so.

When purchasing a new investment, many people fail to consider their overall asset allocation. Typically, they read an article somewhere or get a tip from a colleague and then wind up buying a recommended investment. In addition to not having done sufficient homework, investing in this fashion leads to a hodgepodge of a portfolio that's often not properly diversified.

Wanting to be a loyal, team player, other folks fail to consider the big picture and overinvest in employer stock. This strategy is particularly dangerous because a company that falls on hard times can not only lead to the loss of a job, but also the loss of retirement assets when the stock takes a permanent nosedive. Investing more than 10 to 20 percent of your financial assets in your employer's stock may be too risky.

Allocating those assets

When you're just investing money for the short term — for example, for emergency purposes — you simply choose a good money market fund or savings account, and you're on your way. However, when you're investing for longer-term financial goals such as retirement, you'll likely invest in a number of different investments. Those investments may include such things as stock mutual funds, both U.S. and international; bonds; and perhaps real estate.

How you divide up your money among these different types of investments is known as *asset allocation.* Don't be intimidated by this term or the prospect of making such a weighty decision. Asset allocation need not be complicated.

The subject of asset allocation is most often considered for money invested for the longer term — that is, over five years and preferably ten or more years. Before you begin the process, make sure that you have an emergency reserve of three to six months' worth of living expenses tucked away. Estimate even more if your income and job are unstable and you don't have family or friends you could reliably call on financially. Three months is sufficient if your income is safe and stable and/or you have other resources you can easily tap.

REMEMBER

Other investments that you hold outside of retirement accounts, such as stocks, bonds, and mutual funds that invest in stocks and bonds, can quickly be converted into cash. The problem with considering these investments for emergencies is that since they fluctuate in value, the selling price may be much less than what you paid originally.

REMEMBER

While real estate is not a good reserve because it takes time and significant expense to sell, taking out a home equity line against your home can offer convenient, reasonably low-cost access to money. Just be sure to set one up when you're financially healthy. If you wait until you are in a financial pinch to seek out a home equity loan, you may have difficulty getting one. Remember that the easiest time to get a loan from a banker is when you really don't need one!

Worksheet: Figuring your asset allocation for retirement

The following worksheet should be used as a starting point for deciding on your asset allocation for retirement savings. Please read the following descriptions carefully, as they address a number of possibly conflicting factors. For example, in addition to addressing your tolerance for risk, they also raise the issue of how much growth you may need to accomplish specific goals. If you haven't yet done so, complete the retirement planning process (see Chapter 9) so that you have a good sense of where you stand in terms of working toward your goals.

1. Start with your age: _____

2. Subtract one of the following:

- 20 points if you are comfortable investing for growth; can tolerate wide short-term price swings (remember: stocks can drop 10 percent, 20 percent, or more over relatively short periods of time); need to earn higher returns on your investments to reach your retirement goal; or are comfortable accepting the risks inherent with growth investments.

- 10 points if you are willing to take some risk for growth but want more of a balance and less volatility in your investments; or you want or need to earn returns of about 6 to 7 percent per year.

- 0 points if you can't stomach wide price swings that inevitably occur when investing in things such as stocks; or you're well on your way to achieving your savings goal and are more concerned about losing what you have because you can achieve your goal by earning a return of 5 percent or less per year.

If you fall in between one of the preceding descriptions, choose a point total in between the two descriptions.

3. **Subtract Line 2 from Line 1.**

The difference equals the approximate percentage of your investments that you should consider placing in fixed income vehicles (for example, bonds and bond funds).

4. **Subtract the result in Line 3 from 100.**

That's the percentage of your investments to consider placing in growth-oriented instruments such as stocks and real estate.

Allocations for shorter-term goals

Not all of your investments will be made for longer-term purposes. Perhaps you're saving money for a home down payment or for your kid's educational expenses. In these cases, traditional asset allocation does not work because the time horizon is short. Here are some guidelines to consider:

Time Frame for Money Need	Investing Guidelines
Within the next year or two	Money market funds, savings accounts, and treasury bills and CDs with a matched maturity.
3 to 5 years (for example, home down payment)	Shorter-term bond funds and treasury bills and CDs with a matched maturity.
5 to 10 years	Balanced portfolio of stocks and bonds — perhaps no more than 50% to 60% in stocks.
10 to 20 years	Balanced portfolio of stocks and bonds — more skewed toward stocks the longer the time frame and the greater the need to accept risk to make the money grow.

Before you start to invest, make sure that your financial foundation is stable. Have you

» Paid off your high-interest consumer debt, such as credit cards and auto loans?

» Established your emergency cash reserve?

» Funded your available retirement accounts?

» Found out about the different types of investments, risks, and potential returns? (See "Checking Out All the Places You Can Invest Your Money" earlier in this chapter.)

>> Taken the time to understand your current financial status and how much you need to save and what returns you need to earn in order to achieve your financial goals? (See Chapter 9.)

Selecting the Best Mutual Funds and Exchange-Traded Funds (ETFs)

Although there are potential rewards from investing in the stock and bond markets, there can also be significant risks. You can minimize some of those risks by investing in the best professionally managed mutual funds and ETFs. You can maximize your potential investment returns while minimizing risk by screening and selecting "best funds," using the following criteria:

>> **Efficiency (low operating expenses and load fees):** Within a given sector of funds (for example, short-term bonds), funds without *loads* (sales commissions) and with low annual management fees have a greater probability of producing higher total returns. The best funds are those that maintain low operating expenses and no load fees (sales charges).

>> **Historic rate of return versus risk:** Funds that assume higher risk should produce higher rates of return. Thus, in order for a fund to be recommended, it must consistently deliver a favorable rate of return given its risk.

>> **Track record of the fund manager and the mutual fund company within the relevant fund sector**: How has the particular fund manager and their parent company done overall with the particular type of fund you're considering — for example, international stocks, domestic growth stocks, bonds, and so on.

>> **Overall performance and track record of mutual fund family company** (for example, Fidelity, Vanguard, and so on): Does the fund company consistently look out for shareholders' interests? Has the company been involved in scandals?

Selecting the most appropriate funds for you also requires an understanding of your investment goals and your needs and desire to accept risk. If you do not understand what you are investing in and the risks that are entailed, then you should not invest. This is one of the reasons people make mistakes and poor investments when working with commissioned-based investment salespeople. Such salespeople rarely take the time during their sales pitch to understand your needs and overall financial situation and goals. They may also obscure the risks and drawbacks of what they sell.

Selecting funds simply on the basis of the past rate of return is a common mistake made by many investors. As all funds state, "past performance is no guarantee of future results." Analysis of historic mutual fund performance proves that many of yesterday's top performers turn into tomorrow's losers. Many of today's high-return funds achieve their results through taking on high risk. High-risk funds usually decline in price faster in a changing economic environment and during major market declines.

For investments outside of tax-sheltered retirement accounts, you may want to check with a fund to determine when capital gains are distributed. Doing so allows you to avoid making an investment in a fund that is about to make a capital gains distribution (typically in December), as this will increase your current-year tax liability. Low-cost index funds can help minimize taxable distributions too.

Investing in stock and bond funds

In earlier sections, we discuss how to develop an allocation among different types of funds (see the sections "Worksheet: Figuring your asset allocation for retirement" and "Allocations for shorter-term goals"). Having a plan for what percentages to put into different types of investments is a crucial but not final step in the process. Now, it's time to pick some specific funds.

The first step in this process is deciding between actively versus passively managed funds. Most funds are managed by portfolio managers who continually research and trade in an attempt to hold those securities with the best future prospects. Funds that are managed in such a fashion are known as actively managed funds. Some funds' managers trade little, perhaps changing over about 10 percent of their portfolio yearly, whereas others trade heavily, turning over their entire holdings two to three times each year.

In contrast, passively managed funds, also known as index funds, invest in a relatively fixed basket of securities that track a broad market index. For example, the Standard & Poor's 500 Index tracks the performance of 500 larger company stocks in the United States. You can invest in funds that track the S&P 500 index.

The advantages of these index funds are several. First, index funds can be operated at far lower cost since you don't need a portfolio management team researching and monitoring securities. Lower fund expenses translate into higher returns for index-fund shareholders. Second, the majority of actively managed funds lag behind the market rate of return, largely due to their higher fees. Finally, an index fund should be error-free because it mirrors the market and won't perform worse than the market.

If you're considering investing in an actively managed fund, be sure to compare its performance to an appropriate index. Don't be quick to accept the fund's choice of comparison. In an effort to make themselves look better than they really are, many funds compare themselves to others that aren't truly comparable.

A fund's performance should always be compared to a market index that tracks the rate of return of similar securities. For example, a fund that focuses upon investing in larger company U.S. stocks would be compared to the S&P 500 index. When investing outside of retirement accounts, you should also be sure to compare the after-tax returns on a given fund to its relevant index. Over longer investing periods such as a decade, studies have shown that approximately three-quarters of the actively managed funds underperform the comparable market index.

Here are three options to consider for using active versus index funds when investing in stock and bond funds:

>> **Use only index funds.** If you want to place all of your stock and bond market money in broadly diversified index funds, you will do fine over the long term and not be at a disadvantage.

>> **Use a mix of index and actively managed funds.** Jack Bogle, the late founder of low-cost and index-fund pioneer Vanguard, personally used a mix of actively managed and index funds. Index funds can form the core of a portfolio, and you can choose the best actively managed funds to complement the index funds.

>> **Use only actively managed funds.** This is a riskier approach, but advocates argue it offers more upside potential if you select and manage your portfolio of funds well.

For the portion of your portfolio that you're going to index, here are two funds for you to consider:

>> Vanguard Total Bond Market Index

>> Vanguard Total World Stock Index

Each of these funds has a $3,000 minimum initial investment. Also, you will pay a $20 annual account fee for each fund with a balance of less than $10,000. This fee can be waived if you sign up for account access on their website and elect electronic delivery of statements and fund documents or if you have $50,000 or more invested in Vanguard funds.

Minding the ABCs of ETFs

If you're starting out or have smaller amounts to invest, consider using Vanguard's exchange-traded funds (ETFs) or a fund of funds. The first batch of these funds has an estimated retirement date (for example, T. Rowe Price Retirement 2050 would be the fund for a person expected to retire around the year 2050) attached to it, with the logic being that as that date approaches, the fund managers gradually scale back on the risk of the fund (by moving money from stock funds into bond funds). Among the better such funds of funds out there are the following:

>> **Fidelity Freedom funds:** Fidelity's Target Retirement funds' entries by far use the most different funds — typically around two dozen. Their annual operating expense ratios are about 0.75 percent, and they are among the most aggressive.

>> **T. Rowe Price Retirement funds:** These typically invest in about 20 funds at T. Rowe Price, most of which are actively managed. The annual operating expense ratios are about 0.7 percent.

>> **Vanguard Target Retirement funds:** These low-cost funds (operating expense ratios are just 0.15 percent) invest in about five index funds.

If you would rather keep more of a fixed mix of stock and bond funds over time, you could instead use one or two of the Vanguard LifeStrategy funds. Each of these funds of funds uses the same index funds Vanguard uses in their Target Retirement funds.

Because these are funds of funds (the minimum investment is $3,000), you can comfortably use them for one-stop shopping. Their management fees are low — about 0.13 percent. If you seek an asset allocation that is in between two of these funds, simply divide your money between the two closest funds.

Seizing Investment Opportunities During Tough Times

During an economic downturn, the price of stocks generally slides and so does the price of many types of real estate. As stock market investors are forward-looking, the price of stocks usually begins to quickly rebound before the signs are really obvious that the overall economy is greatly improving.

You should also have spare cash for emergency purposes, but if you're good at saving money and trying to build financial security, you may well have more cash than is needed for short-term unexpected events.

Cashing in on reduced stock and real estate prices

In the midst of an economic downturn or crisis, there's usually plenty of bad news. Heading into such a period, stocks usually sell off significantly. And therein lies opportunity for you if, and this is a big if, you have cash to invest in stocks, ideally through diversified mutual funds and exchange-traded funds. The same logic applies to real estate.

Where can you come up with money to invest in growth investments such as stocks and real estate? Here's a short list:

>> **Cash accounts:** This of course includes things like bank accounts, money market funds, and so forth.

>> **Cash value life insurance policies:** If you need life insurance because loved ones are dependent upon your employment income, you're generally much better off with term life insurance. So, if you have money accumulated inside a cash value policy, examine cashing it in after you first secure any needed term life coverage (see Chapter 11).

>> **Bonds and bond funds:** In various accounts, including retirement accounts, you may have some portion of those accounts invested in bonds or bond funds. When stock prices are depressed, you could sell some of those bond holdings to invest in stocks.

If you're earning a modest income, you may qualify for a competitive, no-down-payment housing loan through the U.S. Department of Agriculture's (USDA's) Rural Development program, which is described as follows:

"The Section 502 Guaranteed Loan Program assists approved lenders in providing low- and moderate-income households the opportunity to own adequate, modest, decent, safe, and sanitary dwellings as their primary residence in eligible rural areas. Eligible applicants may purchase, build, rehabilitate, improve, or relocate a dwelling in an eligible rural area with 100 percent financing. The program provides a 90 percent loan note guarantee to approved lenders in order to reduce the risk of extending 100 percent loans to eligible rural homebuyers — so no money down for those who qualify!"

These properties are not limited to what one would typically think of as "rural" areas — think more broadly about non-urban areas. And, while there are income limits, they are pretty generous: Your income can be up to 115 percent of median household income for the particular area. For more information visit the USDA's Single Family Housing Guaranteed Loan Program website at www.rd.usda.gov/programs-services/single-family-housing-guaranteed-loan-program.

Mustering the courage to buy when more people are selling

During an economic downturn, stocks and real estate generally decline in value. This happens as more people lose their jobs and some people remaining in jobs see their income reduced or stagnant.

Think about the fact that fewer people are saving, and less overall money is coming out of people's paychecks and flowing into retirement savings accounts like 401(k) plans during an economic downturn.

The challenge is that the best buying opportunities often occur when things look the bleakest (see the numerous examples I provide in Chapter 2). It takes courage, faith, and optimism to step up and invest during such times.

IN THIS CHAPTER

» **Understanding the purpose of insurance**

» **Looking at health insurance**

» **Protecting your income**

» **Insuring your home and auto**

» **Considering estate planning**

» **Preventing identity theft**

Chapter **11**

Getting and Maintaining Proper Insurance

Although some people worry more than others, most people take precautions, buy insurance, or take other actions to reduce risk. Life is filled with risks. We can't eliminate them all, and most of us realize that reducing or eliminating certain risks takes time, money, and vigilance. Some people hardly ever leave their homes because they worry so much about the bad things that can happen to them in the world. (The COVID-19 pandemic hasn't helped those prone to such thoughts.) Of course, bad things can happen at home too — including developing health problems that are exacerbated by inactivity.

Some risks have major financial consequences, and for those, the purchase of the right kind of insurance can eliminate the financial downside. That's the subject of this chapter. Plenty of risks can be greatly reduced without buying any insurance at all. I address that here as well. I also show you how to secure the best insurance for your situation at the best prices.

Being Prepared: A Quick Lesson on Insurance

Before we dive into the specific types of insurance you may need, it's helpful to discuss some big-picture issues about insurance. For what type of potential losses should you have insurance? And what insurance should you skip buying?

Don't sweat the small losses . . .

Plenty of companies and people will try to sell you insurance for "small stuff." Consider the following appliance service plan pitch. (We've deleted the name of the plan as that's not relevant.)

> Purchasing a Service Plan is one of the smartest consumer decisions you'll ever make. Protect yourself from the future cost of repairing your new product by purchasing a Service Plan!
>
> DESCRIPTION OF SERVICE PLAN AND HOW IT WORKS
>
> This warranty extension goes into effect after your original warranty expires.
>
> It gives you one year of parts and labor coverage on any appliance below $100.
>
> Your appliance warranty completely mirrors the manufacturer's warranty and will be either carry-in or in-home service.
>
> Upon purchasing this extension, we will mail you a registration card, which you must fill out and send back via mail or online.
>
> YOU MUST REGISTER YOUR PRODUCT WITHIN 10 DAYS OF RECEIVING YOUR REGISTRATION CARD.
>
> WHY BUY A SERVICE PLAN?
>
> Q. What is a Service Plan?
>
> A. It is an economical way to extend the terms of your product's manufacturer's parts and labor warranty.
>
> Q. Why should I buy a Service Plan?
>
> A. Even the best products can eventually malfunction, and minor repairs can cost hundreds of dollars. By purchasing a Service Plan, you won't have to hassle with unexpected repair bills.

The pitch goes on to say that the normal price for this service plan is supposedly $30 but is yours today for only $20.

Could the appliance break after the manufacturer's warranty period ends? Of course, it could! In fact, no appliance lasts forever, and you're guaranteed to someday have a problem or two. Please note, however, that this service plan ". . . gives you one year of parts and labor." Just one measly year! Suppose that you buy a blender for $79 on January 10, 2022, and the manufacturer's warranty is good for one year. This extended warranty that you could buy will cover your blender from January 10, 2023, until January 10, 2024.

Now, consider the cost. You're paying $20 to insure a blender that was worth only $79 (brand new)! How absurd is that! Note that in the sales pitch for the service plan, the company has the audacity to say, "Even the best products can eventually malfunction, and minor repairs can cost hundreds of dollars." This is incredibly dishonest given that this extended warranty plan is for an appliance costing less than $100! And, what about the hassle and time involved for you to enroll in the extended warranty plan?

If you can afford to buy a $79 blender, you can afford to get it repaired (or more likely replaced). Even better, do your homework before buying the blender (or any consumer product for that matter) and make sure you get something that has a good track record. Problems do occur, and remember that the manufacturer's warranty may cover those. Reputable manufacturers stand behind their products. Take a few minutes to read the manual that comes with the product so you know how to properly use and care for it.

Define a small loss . . .

What is a small loss for you? Your co-worker, your neighbor, or the person down the block all differ. Suppose for a moment that you're a billionaire like Mark Cuban and you just bought a new $50,000 car. It probably doesn't make sense to pay for and carry collision insurance on your auto policy. If your car were totaled, $50,000 is a lot to lose, but not if you're Mark Cuban and worth billions!

What if you don't have Mark Cuban–like wealth and you own an older car that's worth, say, $5,000? If your assets total, for example, $25,000 or are nonexistent, carrying collision makes good financial sense. Should you carry collision insurance on it if you have $1 million in financial assets? That $5,000 car amounts to just 0.5 percent of your assets. You could go either way: You should consider dropping collision coverage in such a situation, but part of this decision making is one of personal comfort. In the end, you have to decide what losses you'd be willing to accept and which you'd rather not and therefore buy insurance to cover.

And there's the rub. Insurance costs money. The more insurance you buy, the more money you will spend. No one enjoys wasting money on unnecessary insurance.

Buy insurance for the big potential losses, not the small stuff. And remember, if you do insure for the smaller things, you'll have to jump through plenty of hoops to collect.

Insurance not to buy

There are plenty of types of insurance to avoid wasting your money on because such policies ultimately cover small potential losses or cover only certain losses that could be covered through a broader coverage policy.

An example is credit life insurance. This pays off some debt (mortgage or other loan) if you die. The American Council of Life Insurers only tracks such policies that pay off loans due within the next ten years. The amount in force totals about $90 billion, which is about half the amount of a decade earlier, but that's still a lot of wasted money on unnecessary coverage. (If you need life insurance, buy a term policy that will cover these loans — see the life insurance section later in this chapter.)

Another one to bypass is dental insurance if the full cost of the coverage is coming out of your pocket. Dental plans aren't going to cover the really big expenditures, especially if there's a medical need (covered under health insurance) to do corrective work on your mouth, and you certainly don't need to waste money on insurance to pay for periodic teeth cleanings.

When you ship a package through the mail, unless you're sending something really valuable, don't waste money buying insurance. Although the U.S. Postal Service (USPS) does lose or damage things, consider that it will cost you $2.95 on top of the shipping cost to insure sending a gift worth $60. The Postal Service would have to lose one out of every 20 such packages (about 5 percent of packages) for senders to come out ahead buying such coverage! (If it stresses you to ship items without any insurance protection, then use UPS, which includes $100 of protection when you ship with it. Its shipping rates are often lower and its services faster than the U.S. government-run postal service.)

Home warranty plans are another example of wasted insurance dollars on small potential losses. You generally have to pay some of the cost of a service call anyway under these plans, and the costs covered are pretty limited. If someone else such as a real estate agent or house seller offers to pay for the cost of such a plan, you could take it. Alternatively, they could credit you the cost of the plan for you to use toward something for your home.

Insurance worth purchasing

Smart mountain climbers take along gear to make their trip safe and comfortable. What would you do during an extended climbing trip, for example, if temperatures plunged and it started snowing with severe winds? How about if you or one of your hiking companions fell and broke a leg or got sick? What about exposure to an exotic disease like malaria?

Insurance is like appropriate hiking gear and preparation for your outdoor adventure. You hope you won't need it, but if you do, you're glad it's there to protect you against adverse or emergency conditions. On your hiking trip, your "insurance" might include clothing for inclement weather, a first-aid kit, appropriate medications, advance shots (such as for malaria), ropes for steep inclines, and so on.

TIP

You should purchase sufficient insurance to prevent a financial catastrophe. On the other hand, as discussed earlier in this chapter, some small losses aren't worth the money and bother of your time to insure. That's why for all types of insurance that you purchase, you should take the highest deductible you can comfortably accept. The deductible represents the amount of money that you must pay out of your own pocket if you claim a loss. A high deductible helps keep down the cost of your coverage and also eliminates the hassles of filing small claims.

For each of the major types of policies covered in this chapter, I explain who needs it and why and how to get the proper coverage at a competitive price.

Protecting Your Health

Your personal health, of course, matters.

Everyone should have a comprehensive health insurance policy. Even if you're in good health, you never know when an accident or illness can happen. Healthcare is expensive, and when you buy health insurance, you're protecting yourself from getting stuck with large medical bills and having to deplete your savings or going into hock for many years to pay them off.

TIP

To keep the cost to a more reasonable level, buy a health insurance policy with high deductibles (the initial expenses you are required to pay out of your own pocket). You can save on taxes by saving in a tax-advantaged account, such as a flexible spending account or health savings account for out-of-pocket medical expenses (see "Saving tax dollars with health savings accounts" later in this chapter).

Reviewing your current health insurance

Many people get coverage through their employers in a group plan; if you do, request documentation for your plan's benefits and costs. If you're self-employed or otherwise responsible for securing your own health insurance, contact your insurer or agent if you don't have your policy details handy.

When families have more than one plan, sometimes there is duplicate coverage. Unless your employers are paying the full cost of your plans and you couldn't use those benefit dollars in some other way, eliminate overlapping insurance.

As with other financial services and products, be sure to shop for insurance coverage that provides value — a package of benefits that works for your situation at a competitive price. You don't always get what you pay for with health insurance and customer service quality varies by company.

In addition to shopping around for coverage, the single most important action you can take to dramatically cut your health insurance expenses is to enroll in a high-deductible plan (if you can afford the risk of a higher deductible). Not only will this enable you to lower your premiums, but you can also sock money away into a Health Savings Account (HSA) and get a substantial tax break (discussed in the next section).

Be sure to check each plan's list of medical providers. How extensive and good is the list of medical providers? Does it include doctors and hospitals you have used or would like to use?

LOOKING AHEAD TO LONG-TERM CARE

Another form of insurance that some people consider is long-term care (LTC) coverage. The desire to obtain such coverage springs from the concern that an extended nursing home stay or need for extended care in the home has limited coverage under Medicare, the government-provided health plan for those over age 65. Under current rules, Medicare pays for much of the first 100 days of a nursing home stay.

LTC insurance makes the most sense for those folks who fear depleting their assets with an extended illness or incapacity and who would not be satisfied with facilities accepting Medicaid, the state-provided health coverage for those who are financially needy. If you do consider LTC coverage, be sure to get a quality policy that provides truly long-term benefits. Keep the waiting period, which is the policy's deductible, as long as you can tolerate (at least three to six months) since this will help reduce the cost of the coverage.

As you shop among health insurance plans, give preference to those offered by the biggest and longest-standing insurers in the health insurance arena, such as Aetna, Anthem, Blue Cross, Blue Shield, Cigna, Kaiser, and United Healthcare.

WARNING

An insurance agent who specializes in health insurance may be of assistance to you, but beware that agents derive a commission based upon the amount of your premiums, so this presents agents with a conflict of interest. They're not incentivized to advocate lower-cost plans and plan options.

Saving tax dollars with health savings accounts

Health savings accounts (HSAs) hold promise for people to be able to put money away on a tax-advantaged basis to pay for healthcare-related expenses. Money contributed to an HSA is tax-deductible; any investment earnings compound without tax and aren't taxed upon withdrawal so long as funds are used to pay for eligible healthcare costs.

The list of eligible expenses is generally quite broad — pleasantly so, in fact. You can use HSA money to pay for out-of-pocket medical costs not covered by insurance, prescription drugs, dental care (including braces), vision care, vitamins, psychologist fees, and smoking cessation programs, among other expenses. IRS Publication 502 details permissible expenses (www.irs.gov/pub/irs-pdf/p502.pdf).

Most insurance premiums aren't eligible to be paid with HSA money, but some are. According to the IRS, you may ". . . treat premiums for long-term care coverage, healthcare coverage while you receive unemployment benefits, or healthcare continuation coverage required under any federal law as qualified medical expenses for HSAs."

To be eligible to contribute to an HSA, you must participate in a health plan that has a deductible of at least $1,400 for individuals and $2,800 for families. The plan must have a maximum out-of-pocket limit of no more than $7,000 for individuals and $14,000 for families. Ask health insurers which policies they offer are "HSA compatible."

The maximum annual amount that you may contribute to an HSA is $3,600 for singles and $7,200 for families. Those age 55 or older can sock away an additional $1,000. (All of these dollar limits and amounts increase annually with the rate of medical inflation.)

If you work for an employer that offers an HSA and you want to contribute to the account from your paycheck on a pretax basis, you must use the employer's provided HSA. Alternatively, you may find an HSA on your own and contribute after-tax dollars and then get your tax deduction when you file your tax return by filing Form 8889. Anyone (so long as you aren't covered by Medicare) who has an HSA-compatible policy may have an HSA.

Most HSAs require that some amount of money (for example., $1,000) be invested in a safe option like a money fund or savings account, which is accessed with a debit card or checks that enable you to pay for medical expenses. The remainder of your HSAs can be invested, typically in a menu of investments — generally mutual funds. So, when comparing HSAs, you should compare the quality of those offerings.

Also, be sure to examine fees, which can really add up on some HSAs. In addition to the fees of the offered funds, beware of load fees and maintenance fees of about $5 per month (which may be waived for regular automatic investments or once you meet a certain minimum).

So far, mostly banks and brokerages linked with banks are offering HSAs. One worth considering is offered by HSA Administrators (https://healthsavings. com/; 888-354-0697).

Maximizing your personal health

Whipping your finances into shape and saving and investing toward your future goals is pointless if you neglect your health, yourself, and your relationships. In the worst scenarios, you may not even be around to enjoy your retirement account balances.

To keep yourself in good physical and mental health, make the following part of your daily regimen: regular and moderate exercise, maintaining a good body weight (and not being overweight), getting regular and enough sleep, having interests outside of work, interacting with friends, and relaxing regularly. These all play a role in our current and future health.

It's important to acknowledge that addictions — gambling, drinking, smoking, and substance abuse — are a major impediment to accomplishing money goals and touch virtually every family. People with addictions have great difficulty changing their behavior and habits. Plus, the ability to trade investments quickly and easily, especially through the internet, has created a whole new set of problematic, addictive behavior. All of these issues have associated costs and are closely aligned with common financial problems.

Millions of people have successfully conquered costly and deadly addictions. Doing so isn't easy or quick. "Addiction is a chronic disease, like diabetes, asthma, or hypertension. Just like these diseases, one course of treatment is unlikely to result in a complete cure. Ongoing treatment may be required before an addict achieves the final stage of recovery," says the Institute for Research, Education, and Training in Addictions (`ireta.org`).

Consider the following hurdles standing in the way of individuals with addictions getting the treatment that they need:

» **Denial:** Many people with addictions aren't willing or able to admit their problem and the damage it's causing to themselves and their loved ones. Others may understand some of the problems, but they aren't ready to give up their coveted substances and behaviors.

» **Shame:** The enormous humiliation that many people who suffer addictions feel often prevents them from seeking help. To help substance-abuse sufferers combat these feelings, many 12-step programs, such as Alcoholics Anonymous, provide a high level of confidentiality and support.

» **Uncertainty surrounding their options:** Even when people are motivated to finally get help, sorting through treatment options can be time-consuming and intimidating. A general lack of knowledge about and reluctance to offer unsolicited referrals for substance-abuse treatment on the part of many primary care physicians exacerbates this problem. According to a survey conducted by the Partnership to End Addictions (`https://drugfree.org/`), when presented with an adult patient with the early symptoms of alcohol abuse, a whopping 94 percent of primary care doctors failed to include substance abuse among the five possible diagnoses that they offered. Among the reasons, according to the report, explaining why physicians are missing or misdiagnosing patients' substance abuse are lack of adequate medical school training, skepticism about treatment effectiveness, patient resistance, discomfort discussing substance abuse, time constraints, and fear of losing patients.

» **Cost:** While addictions are quite costly, the cost of treatment is perceived to be much higher because its cost is incurred over short periods. Some treatments are covered by insurance so check what is and is not covered by your insurance.

» **Time constraints:** Even if someone locates good treatment options and determines how to pay for the needed help, carving out the necessary time is another significant hurdle. Treatment is time-consuming, and work and family demands can stand in the way.

When you take care of yourself and your health, you set yourself up for success, not only financially, but in all aspects of your life.

Securing Your Income-Earning Ability

Your likely greatest asset, especially if you're under the age of 50, is your future income-earning ability. Even if others are not directly financially dependent on your work income, you are likely dependent upon it. This section explains how to protect that for yourself and dependents.

Long-term disability insurance

During your working years, your future income-earning ability is likely your most valuable asset — far more valuable than a car or even your home. Your ability to produce income should be protected, or insured.

Even if you don't have dependents, you probably need disability coverage. Are you dependent upon your income? Long-term disability (LTD) insurance replaces a portion of your lost income in the event a disability prevents you from working.

Nearly everyone should carry LTD during their working years. One exception: You're already financially independent/wealthy and no longer need to work for the income but do so anyway.

REMEMBER

Except for people working for the largest employers with comprehensive benefit plans, many people lack LTD insurance. According to a recent survey conducted by the U.S. Department of Labor, only 35 percent of all workers are even offered access to a long-term disability plan. Those who work in blue-collar positions, service jobs, or for smaller employers (under 100 employees) have even less access to an LTD plan. Part-time workers rarely have access — typically about 5 percent of such workers have access to LTD insurance.

Even among those in the minority who have access to an LTD, many people don't enroll. One common reason many folks bypass coverage is that they believe the chances of disability are rare. Another perception is that only old people become disabled. Both of these assumptions are false.

According to the Centers for Disease Control and Prevention, National Center for Health Statistics, about 12 percent (one in eight) of Americans suffer from a limitation of activity caused by a chronic condition. Poorer people tend to be hardest hit. See Table 11-1.

You generally can't predict when and what type of disability you may suffer. That's because many disabilities are caused by medical problems (such as arthritis, cerebral palsy, diabetes, glaucoma, multiple sclerosis, muscular dystrophy, stroke, and so on) and accidents (such as head injuries, spinal injury, loss of limb or amputation, and so forth).

TABLE 11-1 **Chronic Conditions Affecting Activity**

Group	Percent Suffering Activity Limitation Due to Chronic Condition
Age 18–24	4.1
Age 25–44	6.6
Age 45–54	13.0
Age 55–64	21.1
Poor*	23.1
Near poor*	17.0
Non-poor*	9.2

* Poor persons are defined as those people having an income below the poverty threshold. Near poor persons have incomes at least equal to the poverty threshold to up to twice the poverty threshold. Non-poor persons are those with incomes above twice the poverty threshold.

Looking at types of disability insurance coverage

Generally speaking, you should have long-term disability insurance that provides a benefit of approximately 60 percent of your gross (pretax) income. Since disability benefit payments are tax-free if you pay the premium, they should replace your current after-tax earnings.

You may be an exception to the guideline if you have significant assets and are close to being financially independent or you earn a high income and spend far less than that. In both such cases, you may want to buy only enough coverage to replace a more modest portion of your current income.

TIP

If you're just getting started in a field (for example, starting a new business or beginning work at an entry level in a professional service field) and you expect your income to be significantly higher in future years, there's another option to consider. You can obtain a policy that enables you to buy a higher level of benefits ("future increase/purchase option") in the future without a health exam, or you can simply shop for a larger policy down the road.

State disability insurance programs and the Social Security Disability Insurance program do not generally provide adequate disability coverage for the long term. State programs typically only pay benefits for up to a maximum of one year, which isn't going to cut it if you truly suffer a long-term disability that can last many years. While one year of coverage is better than none, the premiums for such short-term coverage often are higher per dollar of benefit than those available through the best private insurer programs.

Although the Social Security program pays long-term benefits, you will receive payments only if you are not able to perform any substantial, gainful activity for more than a year or if your disability will result in death. In fact, most applicants for Social Security disability benefits coverage are turned down. Furthermore, Social Security disability payments are only intended to provide for basic subsistence living expenses.

Worker's compensation, if you have coverage through your employer, will not pay benefits at all if you get injured or become sick away from your job. Such narrow coverage that only pays benefits under a limited set of circumstances is not the comprehensive insurance you need.

Reviewing your disability insurance coverage

Features of a disability policy that are worth having include the following:

» **Definition of disability:** Disability should be defined in such a way that the policy guarantees you benefits if you cannot perform your regular occupation. If you work as a teacher, for example, your disability policy shouldn't require you to take a job as a cashier.

» **Noncancelable and guaranteed renewable:** These terms guarantee that your policy cannot be canceled because of poor health conditions. If you purchase a policy that requires periodic physical exams, you could lose your coverage when you are most likely to need it.

» **Insurer's financial health:** The insurance company should have strong financial health with the leading credit rating agencies.

» **Benefit period:** You need a policy that would pay you benefits until an age at which you would become financially self-sufficient. For most people, that would require obtaining a policy that pays benefits to age 65 or 67 (when Social Security retirement benefits begin). If you are close to being financially independent and expect to accomplish that or retire before your mid-60s, seek a policy that pays benefits for five years.

» **Waiting period:** This is the "deductible" on disability insurance, which is the time between your disability and when you begin collecting benefits. As with other types of insurance, take the highest deductible (in other words, the longest waiting period) that your financial circumstances allow. The minimum allowable waiting period on most policies is 30 days and the maximum can be up to one to two years. Most people should consider a waiting period of at least 90 or 180 days.

» **Residual benefits:** This option pays you a partial benefit if you have a disability that prevents you from working full-time.

>> **Cost-of-living adjustments:** This feature automatically increases your benefit payment once you are disabled by a set percentage or in step with inflation.

To get disability insurance proposals, start by considering any professional associations for your occupation or profession. If that's not an option, interview some good agents in your area who specialize in disability insurance.

Life insurance

If you have dependents, you may also need life insurance. Ask yourself and your family how they would fare if you died and they no longer had your income. If your family is dependent upon your income and you would want them to maintain their current standard of living in your absence and they would not be able to do so with your passing, you need life insurance.

Term versus cash value life insurance

Term life insurance, like most other forms of insurance, is pure insurance protection and the best way to go for the vast majority of people.

The other major type of life insurance is cash value coverage (for example, whole life, universal life), which includes a life insurance death benefit (as with a term policy) and a savings and investment feature. You can't generally combine insurance with investing when you buy an auto, disability, or homeowner's policy, so why can you with life insurance? Thanks to an exemption in the tax code.

Those in the insurance business — insurance companies and agents who sell their products and earn commissions — have a bias for cash value life insurance. Cash value life insurance costs a lot more and provides far, far greater profits for insurance companies and commissions to the agents who sell it.

Term life insurance is often called "temporary" life insurance, while cash value life insurance has been pushed as "permanent" life insurance. Since no one lives forever, rather than saying it's permanent insurance, it might better be called "life insurance for as long as you live"!

People who buy term insurance generally hold it as long as they have people financially dependent upon them. The classic situation is where a worker is providing for their family. Eventually, kids grow up and move out (we hope), and we someday retire or have sufficient financial assets to provide for us into our old age.

The cost of life insurance increases with age for the simple reason that the odds of dying increase the older we get. That's why term life insurance costs increase. With some cash value policies, insurers and agents create the illusion that the cost doesn't increase. What really happens is that the increasing cost of coverage is quietly being deducted from a cash balance resulting from such high payments in the early years of the policy.

The other argument that term insurance is for those on a tight budget is also silly. The converse to this is that cash value life insurance is better for the more financially flush. What's fascinating is that the average policy size for term is about $290,000, whereas it's just $85,000 for cash value policies. The main reason for this is that cash value policies are so much more expensive for the level of coverage they provide, which is why most people can't afford to buy enough cash value coverage to properly protect their loved ones.

REMEMBER

Consider that the amount of life insurance you should buy should be determined based upon how many years' worth of your income you seek to replace. For example, if you have young children and desire to replace your income over the next 20 years, you multiply your after-tax annual income by about 15. (See Figure 11-1 for the multipliers to use for varying numbers of years.) So, if your after-tax income is $40,000 yearly, you should buy a $600,000 term life policy.

Cash value life insurance should only be considered by folks with a high enough net worth that they anticipate having an estate planning "problem." When you buy a cash value policy and place it in an irrevocable life insurance trust, the death benefits can pass to your heirs free of federal estate taxes.

Under current tax law, you can leave up to $11.7 million free of federal estate taxes to your heirs (for tax year 2021). If you're married, you can pass on double these amounts through the use of a bypass trust. So, most people don't have an estate planning "problem." Therefore, one might think that the vast majority of people buy term insurance, not cash value policy. Surprisingly, 40 percent of all life insurance policies sold are cash value, and only 60 percent are term policies.

Given the needs and level of affluence of the broad insurance-buying public, 99+ percent of the policies sold should be term! Few people need and would most benefit from cash value policies. The fact that many people are being sold the wrong type of policy is again highlighted in the fact that the average cash value policy sold is for only $85,000 in coverage. Clearly, these policies aren't being bought by wealthy folks but instead are being peddled to many middle-class people.

Figuring your life insurance needs

If you've determined you need some life insurance because you have financial dependents and you're not yet financially independent, remember that your goal here is adequate income protection in the event of the death of an income provider. Life insurance should not be viewed as an investment vehicle!

Use the worksheet in Figure 11-1 to determine how much term life insurance to purchase.

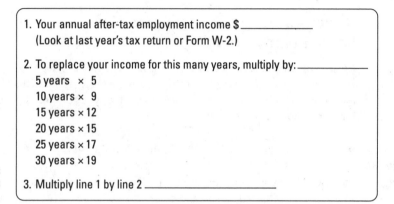

1. Your annual after-tax employment income $_____
   (Look at last year's tax return or Form W-2.)

2. To replace your income for this many years, multiply by: _____
   5 years × 5
   10 years × 9
   15 years × 12
   20 years × 15
   25 years × 17
   30 years × 19

3. Multiply line 1 by line 2 _____

FIGURE 11-1:
Insurance needs worksheet.

This analysis assumes that your beneficiaries invest the life insurance proceeds and earn a modest annual rate of return of about 6 percent, while inflation runs at about 3 percent per year.

TIP

If you bought a term life policy many years ago or you didn't really shop around, get quotes now. You may be able to save a lot on the cost of your coverage by switching carriers.

A good place to obtain term life insurance proposals is a quotation service such as AccuQuote (www.accuquote.com; 800-442-9899) or ReliaQuote (www.reliaquote.com; 800-940-3002). Also check out USAA (www.usaa.com; 800-531-8722).

Insurance on Your Assets

You work hard to earn and save money and buy a home, a car, and similar large purchases. These assets are valuable and would be quite costly to replace.

Also, these assets can be attached in a lawsuit arising from those assets. Insurance can protect you from these potential problems. For example, you should have comprehensive insurance on your home and car(s). This section details what you do and don't need and how to get the best deals.

Insuring your home

If your home burned to the ground, a comprehensive homeowner's insurance policy should pay for the cost of rebuilding the home. This section explains what you need on a home insurance policy and what you don't and how to get the best value for your money.

Understanding the elements of a home insurance policy

I walk you through the elements of a homeowner's insurance policy — get out yours if you own a home. If you're renting, you may want to obtain a renter's policy for two major reasons. First is to protect your personal property. Second is for some liability protection.

Here are the major elements on a homeowner's policy:

>> **Dwelling:** Your home insurer should determine approximately how much it would cost (based on size and cost per square foot) to rebuild your home should it be a total loss. Make sure that your policy comes with "guaranteed replacement cost" coverage. This makes the insurer pay for the full cost to rebuild your home should it cost more than the dwelling coverage portion of your policy. Please note, though, that different insurers define their guarantees differently. Most place some sort of a cap on the coverage — for example, at 20 or 30 percent above the dwelling coverage on your policy.

>> **Other structures:** This covers separate structures such as a shed, fencing, or a freestanding garage. If this coverage is higher than necessary given the actual covered other structures on your land, ask the insurer about options to reduce this coverage amount.

>> **Personal property:** This portion of the policy covers the contents of your home: furniture, clothing, personal possessions, and so on. The coverage amount is typically derived as a portion (for example, three-quarters) of the dwelling portion of your policy. A good policy will cover the full cost to replace damaged items — be sure this is what you're paying for or inquire about the cost of a rider to provide this benefit. Some insurers will allow you to reduce your coverage amount from their standard level if you feel that would adequately insure your personal property.

>> **Loss of use:** This again is standard coverage and often a portion (for example, 20 percent) of the dwelling coverage. If you can't reasonably live in your home after it is damaged, this part of your policy will pay for you to rent and enjoy a similar standard of living.

>> **Personal liability:** If someone sues you for an accident relating to your home, this portion of the policy kicks in. As with your auto insurance, you should have enough liability to protect at least twice your assets. For coverage greater than $500,000, you would typically get excess liability coverage in a separate policy (discussed in the later section "Excess liability insurance").

>> **Medical payments to others:** This is standard on most policies and provides limited coverage for out-of-pocket costs for accidents on your property.

Be sure to get catastrophic coverage as needed in your area. See the next section for details on flood, earthquake, and other such risks and how to reduce your risks of suffering a catastrophe.

Reducing catastrophic risks on your home

You live in your home and spend a lot of time there. You can buy insurance to cover the risks of flooding, hurricanes, earthquakes, and landslides, but do you really want to live through your home being totaled and possibly putting your life at risk?

INVESTIGATE

That's why you should buy a home at low risk for natural disasters. An excellent warning sign for high-risk property is if you have difficulty finding insurance and find only overly expensive coverage from one or two companies.

However, sometimes the location you want or need to live in comes with the added risk of certain disasters happening. Luckily, there's an insurance for that.

The first item to investigate when considering a given home is the risk of flooding. You can start that process at The National Flood Insurance Program's (NFIP) website at www.floodsmart.gov. Among the more sobering statistics from NFIP about floods is that your home has a 26 percent chance of being damaged by a flood during the course of a 30-year mortgage, which is nearly triple the chance (9 percent) of a fire. The site can help you with finding out more about and securing flood insurance quotes.

Hurricanes are another disaster to prepare for, especially if you live in the South and/or along coastal areas. "We're eventually going to get a strong enough storm in a densely populated area to have a major disaster," says former National Hurricane Center Director Max Mayfield, adding, "I know people don't want to hear this, and I'm generally a very positive person, but we're setting ourselves up for this major disaster." Mayfield warns that there could be ten times as many deaths as from Hurricane Katrina and hundreds of thousands and perhaps millions homeless, particularly in the Southeast where Mayfield sees too many homes being built in storm zones. Mayfield argues that two main tactics can mitigate the impact of a devastating hurricane:

>> **Improved building codes:** Housing and other buildings can be constructed to tolerate hurricane-force winds and storm surges. Don't buy and live in properties that don't meet hurricane-proof building codes.

>> **Evacuation and preparedness plan:** Discuss with your loved ones how you plan to remain in touch during an emergency. Also, take the time to understand your evacuation route options and listen for broadcast advice from storm experts as an impending storm approaches.

Earthquakes are another disaster risk you must be smart about. The United States Geologic Survey (USGS) online map clearly highlights the regions of the country at greatest risk (pubs.usgs.gov/fs/fs-131-02/images/CUShazard.jpg).

In addition to buying earthquake coverage if you live in a higher risk area, also be sure to make your house safer through the following measures:

>> Anchor/bolt your home to the foundation.

>> Strengthen cripple walls and pier-and-post foundations.

>> Retrofit masonry foundations and unreinforced masonry walls.

>> Locate gas and water shut-offs and have a wrench handy.

>> Secure a water heater by strapping it to the wall studs and bolting it to the floor.

>> Fasten shelves securely to walls.

>> Place large or heavy objects on lower shelves.

>> Store breakables (for example, bottled foods, china) in low, closed cabinets with latches.

>> Hang heavy items, such as pictures and mirrors, away from beds and couches.

>> Brace overhead light fixtures.

>> Repair fire risks, such as defective electrical wiring and leaky gas connections.

>> Repair deep cracks in ceilings or foundations. Get expert advice if there are signs of structural defects.

>> Store pesticides and flammable products in closed cabinets with latches and on bottom shelves.

>> Identify safe places indoors and out. Inside, that may be under a heavy desk or table; against an inside wall; away from windows, mirrors, pictures, or where heavy bookcases or other heavy furniture could fall over. In the open, stay away from buildings, trees, telephone and electrical lines, overpasses, or elevated expressways.

For more information on earthquake risk assessment and preparation, consult the California Seismic Safety Commission's website (ssc.ca.gov) and the Federal Emergency Management Agency's website (www.fema.gov).

Prospective real estate buyers can research environmental hazards and issues of a specific property they may buy. Environmental Data Resources produces an EDR Neighborhood Environmental Report, which costs $100. You can order a report through an "EDR certified" home inspector, but you need not order a home inspection from that inspector. Call 800-352-0050 or visit EDR's website at www.edrnet.com.

Auto insurance

If your car is involved in an accident, auto insurance helps pay for the damage to the cars and property involved. It can also help pay for associated medical expenses. This section talks about what you should have and probably don't need on your auto insurance policies.

Reviewing the elements of auto insurance policies

Locate a copy of your most recent auto insurance statement. Often called a *declaration*, this statement should detail your coverage types and amounts, and premiums (cost).

The following list goes through each of the elements of your policy:

>> **Liability:** Auto accidents can harm other people and damage property, and for accidents in which you're at fault, you can be sued. The liability portion of your policy provides coverage for these claims and comes in varying amounts; for example, $15,000, $30,000, $50,000, $100,000, $300,000, and so on. This coverage amount is per accident. You should have liability coverage of at least two times the value of your assets. If you have significant assets, you can more cost effectively pick up additional liability protection after $300,000 or $500,000 of liability coverage on your auto policy through an umbrella or excess liability policy (see the later section "Excess liability insurance").

>> **Medical payments:** This optional rider generally provides $5,000 or $10,000 in medical benefits to you or other passengers in your car for medical expenses not covered by their health insurance policy. This coverage is considered nonessential because it is capped at a relatively small amount, and if someone lacks health insurance, $5,000 or $10,000 in benefits won't cover much. If you're at fault and you're sued, your liability coverage will protect you and help pay for the medical expenses of the other party if you're deemed at fault.

>> **Uninsured motorist:** This coverage allows you (and your vehicle's passengers) to be compensated for pain and suffering, lost wages, and out-of-pocket medical expenses when you're in an accident with an uninsured or underinsured motorist. Think of this coverage as buying liability coverage for the other party if they don't have sufficient coverage. Once you have adequate health and disability insurance that would take care of lost wages and medical expenses in an accident, being able to collect for pain and suffering isn't really necessary.

>> **Collision:** This provides reimbursement for damage done to your car in an accident. As with other types of insurance that you purchase, take the highest deductible (such as $500 or $1,000) you can comfortably live with. The deductible represents the amount of money that you must pay out of your own pocket if you have a loss for which you file a claim. A high deductible helps keep down the cost of your coverage and eliminates the hassle of filing small claims.

>> **Other than collision:** Sometimes known as comprehensive coverage, this provides insurance for damage done to your car for things other than accidents. For example, if you're driving down the road and a rock skips off the road and cracks your windshield, or your car parked on the street is damaged by someone driving by or parking near you, this coverage will pay for damage after your deductible. As with collision coverage, to reduce your premiums, choose as high a deductible (such as $500 or $1,000) as you are comfortable with.

>> **Other riders:** Other typical add-ons that insurers and agents may put on your policy include towing, rental car reimbursement, and so forth. Skip these because they ultimately cover small potential dollar items and aren't worth insuring for. Spend your insurance money on protecting against the big potential losses.

Buy a safe car and reduce your driving risks

Without a doubt, the most dangerous thing that you probably do is get behind the wheel of a car or travel as a passenger in someone else's vehicle. Yet, many people give insufficient thought to taking sensible measures to reduce their risk in cars.

For starters, we minimize and trivialize the risk. We say things to ourselves such as, "I drive short distances," or "My large SUV will protect me."

Car buyers often do little if any research on the safety records of cars they ultimately buy. In a survey conducted by Consumer Reports, only 12 percent (about one in eight) of prospective new car buyers said that safety features were the most important consideration in their planned purchases.

Two useful resources for auto safety information are the following:

>> Consumer Reports (www.consumerreports.org)

>> Insurance Institute for Highway Safety (www.iihs.org)

Compounding the fact that many people don't research and buy the safest cars, most people overestimate how good their driving skills are. Consider how drivers responded to the following multiple-choice options in a survey conducted by the Insurance Institute for Highway Safety:

My driving skills are much better or better than average	74%
My driving skills are average	25%
My driving skills are below average	1%

Seventy-four times as many people said their driving skills were above average than said they were below average! And, 99 percent of all respondents rated their skills as average or above! Clearly, that can't possibly be the case in the real world.

To reduce your risk of having to tap into your auto insurance policy and supply any out-of-pocket costs that may come about due to an accident, practice safe driving. Those in the insurance and highway safety realms are well aware of when, why, and how auto accidents tend to happen. That's why the following tips compiled from the AAA Foundation for Safety, Liberty Mutual Insurance Group, and the National Highway Traffic Safety Administration (NHTSA) are so powerful:

>> Don't tailgate.

>> Signal early. Turn on your signal at least five seconds before you turn or change lanes.

>> Adjust and lock adjustable headrests to reduce head or neck injury in accidents.

>> Know how to use your anti-lock brakes. In an emergency, stomp hard and keep your foot firmly on the brake; don't pump anti-lock brakes. Stay calm and ease off the gas while carefully steering in the direction of a skid.

>> Green does mean GO . . . but first make sure the intersection is clear! Many side-impact accidents occur as a result of people not stopping for red lights.

>> Adjust your mirrors to reduce blind spots.

>> Focus. Distractions (such as adjusting music controls, passengers in the car, construction, and aggressive drivers) are factors in half of vehicle crashes.

>> Avoid using your cellphone while driving. If you must make a call while driving, use a hands-free device (which is the law in many states).

>> Avoid solar glare. At sunrise and sunset, you may encounter intense solar glare. Have sunglasses handy so that you are always prepared.

>> Turn on your headlights when you use your wipers. It will help increase your visibility and will help other drivers see you. In many states, it's the law!

>> Keep your car windows clear. Sun or headlights reflecting off a dirty windshield can prevent you from seeing what's in front of you. Clear snow and ice off your car so that it doesn't slide onto your windshield or fly onto someone else's.

>> Don't use cruise control when the roads are wet. An activated cruise control system continually applies power and keeps your wheels spinning.

>> Buckle up every time. Every 11 seconds, someone is injured, and every 12 minutes, someone is killed in a car crash. Seat belts reduce injuries and fatalities.

>> Avoid sudden lane changes and excess speed and be careful on curves with sport utility vehicles (SUVs) because of their higher center of gravity and likelihood of roll-overs.

>> Don't force large trucks to brake or swerve suddenly. Large trucks have many blind spots, so don't linger alongside them. If you can't see the driver in the truck's mirror, he can't see you. When passing a truck, don't pull back in front of it until you see the entire truck in your inside rear-view mirror.

>> Watch your speed. Speeding is one of the most prevalent factors contributing to traffic crashes, according to the NHTSA.

>> Buy a tire gauge and check tire pressure monthly. For suggested tire pressure levels, check the placard located on the inside of your driver's side door. To check tread wear, insert a penny upside down in the groove of the tread on each tire. Look at the distance between the top of Lincoln's image and the edge of the penny. If you can see the top of Lincoln's head, it's time to purchase new tires.

>> Select a designated driver before you and your companions start drinking. Don't wait until you arrive at your destination to decide who will drive home.

>> Watch out for road rage. Be courteous and don't engage in aggressive actions — tailgating, blocking the passing lane, beeping the horn excessively, or using high beams to "punish" other drivers — that could provoke road rage.

Excess liability insurance

If you have assets that total into the hundreds of thousands or millions of dollars, given your current assets and future earnings, which could be garnished in a lawsuit settlement, you have a lot to lose. Excess liability insurance, also known as umbrella liability insurance, which is sold in million-dollar increments, can offer protection against a large lawsuit. (Note that this coverage does not protect against lawsuits arising from your work.)

Many people are surprised at the relatively low cost. The first additional million may cost $200, and up to $5 million should cost about $700 or so.

You generally obtain this insurance through your current home and auto insurers. Be sure to shop around, as prices vary, sometimes significantly.

Will, Trusts, and Estate Planning

Although some of us don't like to admit or think about it, we are all mortal. Because of the way our legal and tax systems work, it's beneficial when people die to have legal documents in place specifying what should be done with assets and other important details.

Starting with a will

A will is the most basic of such documents, and for most people, particularly those who are younger or don't have great assets, the only critical one. Through a will, you can direct to whom your assets will go upon your death, as well as who will serve as guardian for your minor children.

In the absence of a will, state law dictates these important issues. Thus, your friends, less closely related relatives, and charities will likely receive nothing.

TIP

Also, make sure that your named beneficiaries on IRA accounts, for example, reflect your current wishes. Many people mistakenly believe that a will overrides their beneficiary statement or insurance.

Without a will, your heirs are powerless, and the state will appoint an administrator to supervise the distribution of your assets at a fee of around 5 percent of your estate. A bond must also be posted at a cost of hundreds of dollars.

In the event that both you and your spouse die without a will, the state (courts and social service agencies) will decide who will raise your children. Even if you cannot decide at this time who would raise your children, you should at least appoint a trusted guardian who could decide for you.

If you previously completed a will, how many years ago was it prepared, and have any significant changes happened in your life since then (for example, a move, the birth of a child, the passing of a named beneficiary, and so on)? If so, consider updating your will.

Preparing other useful legal documents

Along with your will, prepare a living will (called a healthcare proxy in some states) and medical power of attorney. These documents help your doctor and family members make important decisions regarding your healthcare should you be unable to make them yourself.

Even if you have a will and supporting medical and legal documents, that may not be enough. If you hold significant assets outside tax-sheltered retirement accounts, in most states, those assets must be *probated*, which is the court-administered process for implementing your will.

REMEMBER

Establishing and placing your assets in a living trust can eliminate much of the hassle and cost of probate. Attorney probate fees can run quite high in some states — up to 5 percent of the value of the probated assets.

The federal government levies an estate tax if your net worth (assets minus liabilities) exceeds $11.7 million at your passing. Estate planning can help to minimize the portion of your estate subject to taxation.

One simple but powerful estate planning strategy is to give money to your desired heirs to reduce your taxable estate. If you're in the fortunate position of having great wealth, you may annually give up to $15,000 each to as many recipients as desired.

A relatively simple strategy for a married couple with a large estate to use to double the amount that they can pass on free of federal estate tax is to establish a bypass trust. If you're in that fortunate position, consult a qualified estate planning attorney.

REMEMBER

Wills, living trusts, and estate planning are nothing more than a form of insurance. It takes time and money to do these things, and the benefits may be a long time off.

Considering your preparation options

The simplest and lowest-cost way to prepare a will and living trust is to use one of the high-quality, user-friendly software packages developed by attorneys. You do not need an attorney to prepare a legal will and living trust. Most attorneys, in fact, have their administrative staff prepare wills using a software package! What makes a will valid is that it is witnessed by three people.

Nolo's online will (Nolo Press; store.nolo.com/products) is an excellent program for preparing wills as well as other standard legal documents (such as healthcare directives and durable powers of attorney for finances). Don't use "fill in the blank" will kits, which are prone to errors and challenge.

If doing it all yourself seems overwhelming, by all means hire an attorney. Be sure to retain the services of one who specializes in wills, trusts, and related issues. Also, don't be shy about questioning costs and doing some comparison shopping.

Protecting Yourself from Identity Theft and Fraud

Hucksters and thieves are often several steps ahead of law enforcement. Eventually, some of the bad guys get caught, but many don't, and those who do get nabbed often go back to their unsavory ways after penalties and some jail time.

Crooks may access one of your accounts; in other cases, the criminal activity may develop with someone opening an account (such as a credit card) using your stolen personal information. Victims of identity theft can suffer trashed credit reports, reduced ability to qualify for loans and even jobs (with employers who check credit reports), out-of-pocket costs and losses, and dozens of hours of time to clean up the mess and clear their credit record and name.

Unfortunately, identity theft is hardly the only way to be taken to the cleaners by crooks. All sorts of scamsters hatch schemes to separate you from your money.

Here's what you can do to keep yourself from falling prey to identity theft and unnecessarily losing money:

>> **Beware phone inquiries.** Never give out personal information over the phone, especially when you aren't the one who initiated the call. Suppose you get a call and the person on the other end of the line claims to be with a company you conduct business with (such as your credit-card company or bank). Ask for the caller's name and number and call the company's main number back (which you look up from a recent statement or the company's website). With caller ID on your phone line, you may be able to see what number a call is originating from, but more often than not, calls from business-registered phone numbers come up as "unavailable." Also, crooks use bogus caller ID numbers. A major red flag: calling back the number that comes through on caller ID and discovering that the number is bogus (a nonworking number).

>> **Ignore solicitous emails.** If you're an email user, you may have seen or heard about official-looking emails sent from companies you know of and may do business with asking you to promptly visit their website to correct some sort of billing or account problem. Crooks can generate a return/sender email address that looks like it comes from a known institution but really does not. This unscrupulous practice is known as *phishing,* and if you bite at the bait, visit the site, and provide the requested personal information, your reward is likely to be some sort of future identity-theft problem.

>> **Review your monthly financial statements and account activity.** Although financial institutions such as banks may call you if they notice unusual activity on one of your accounts, some people discover problematic account activity by simply reviewing their monthly credit-card, checking-account, and other statements or reviewing the same online. You don't need to balance bank account statements to the penny. The key is to review the line items on your statement to be sure that all the transactions were yours.

>> **Secure your receipts.** When you make a purchase, be sure to keep track of and secure receipts, especially those that contain your personal financial or account information, and cross-check your receipts against your monthly statements. When you no longer need to retain your receipts, be sure to dispose of them in a way that prevents a thief, who may get into your garbage, from being able to decipher the information on them. Rip up the receipts or, if you feel so inclined, buy a small paper shredder for your home and/or small business.

>> **Close unnecessary credit accounts.** Open your wallet and remove all the pieces of plastic within it that enable you to charge purchases. The more credit cards and credit lines you have, the more likely you are to have problems with identity theft and fraud and the more likely you are to

overspend and carry debt balances. Also, reduce preapproved credit offers by contacting 888-5OPTOUT (888-567-8688) or visiting www.optoutprescreen.com. Unless you maintain a card for small business transactions, you really "need" only one or two pieces of plastic with a Visa or MasterCard logo. Give some preference to accounts you've had open longer as closing accounts you've had open less time won't impact your credit score as much.

>> **Review your credit reports regularly.** You may also be tipped off to shenanigans going on in your name when you review your credit report. Some identity-theft victims have found out about credit accounts opened in their name by reviewing their credit reports. Because you're entitled to a free credit report from each of the three major credit agencies every year, review your reports at least that often. The reports generally contain the same information, so you can request and review one agency report every four months, which enables you to keep a closer eye on your reports and still obtain them without cost. You don't need to spend the $100 or so annually for a so-called credit monitoring service that updates you when something happens on your credit reports. If you're concerned about someone illegally applying for credit in your name, know that another option for you to stay on top of things is to "freeze" your personal credit reports and scores (see the next tip).

>> **Freeze your credit reports.** To address the growing problem of identity theft, you can *freeze* your credit reports, which enables consumers to prevent access to their reports. The individual whose credit report is frozen is the only person who may grant access to the frozen credit report, which can be done anytime you need to apply for credit. Here's the contact information for the three credit reporting agencies to freeze your credit reports:

- Equifax: www.equifax.com/personal/credit-report-services/credit-freeze; 800-685-1111

- Experian: www.experian.com/freeze/center.html; 888-397-3742

- Transunion: www.transunion.com/credit-freeze; 888-909-8872

>> **Don't place personal information on checks.** Information that is useful to identity thieves and that you should not put on your checks includes your credit-card number, driver's license number, Social Security number, and so on. I also encourage you to leave your home address off your preprinted checks when you order them. Otherwise, every Tom, Dick, and Jane whose hands your check passes through knows exactly where you live. When writing a check to a merchant, question the need for adding personal information to the check (in fact, in numerous states, requesting and placing credit-card numbers on checks is against the law). Use a credit card instead for such transactions and remember that your debit card doesn't advertise your home address and other financial account data, so there's no need to publicize it to the world on your checks.

>> **Protect your computer and files.** Especially if you keep personal and financial data on your computer, consider the following safeguards to protect your computer and the confidential information on it: Install a firewall, use virus protection software, and password-protect access to your programs and files.

>> **Protect your snail mail.** Some identity thieves have collected personal information by simply helping themselves to mail in home mailboxes. Stealing mail is easy, especially if your mail is delivered to a curbside box. Consider using a locked mailbox or a post office box to protect your incoming mail from theft. Consider having your investment and other important statements sent to you via email, or simply access them online and eliminate mail delivery of the paper copies. Be careful with your outgoing mail as well, such as bills with checks attached. Minimize your outgoing mail and save yourself hassles by signing up for automatic bill payment for as many bills as possible. Drop the rest of your sensitive outgoing mail in a secure U.S. postal box, such as those you find at the post office.

5

Prepping for Future Armageddon

Know how to deal with fearmongers. It's important to assess the agenda of what other people have to say to find the best route that works for you.

Get ready for the unexpected. Find out what situations may be on the horizon and how to prepare for them.

» Understanding what pundits are selling

» Surveying pundits' predictions and why they are often wrong

Chapter **12**

What Pundits Scare People About

P undits have something to sell. Because most people would rather be rich than poor, teaching you how to amass wealth has long been something pundits have sold.

But fear sells too, and there's plenty to scare people about. For sure, investing includes risks, and as I discuss elsewhere in this book, especially in Chapter 2, economic and other problems adversely affect stocks, real estate, and other investments. So the fearmongering pundits have plenty of fodder to scare you with.

In this chapter, I explain how and why some pouting pundits scare good people like you. I also help you to dissect the common worries being pitched today and the dangers of following pundits' advice.

Fearmongers Have Been Scaring Folks for Generations

TRUE STORY

I've always worked and saved money. I had various jobs as a kid growing up — the most lucrative being a grass cutting and yard care business I ran in high school. As a young adult I had some extra money I wanted to invest. This was back when you got a pretty high level of interest in bank savings accounts and money market funds, but that was largely due to the high level of inflation and overall interest rates.

I kept hearing about concerns of rising inflation and all the problems it was causing and would cause. And in the newspapers, magazines, and financial television programs at that time, plenty of pundits and media folk were touting investing in gold, which had increased in price significantly.

A firm by the name of the International Gold Bullion Exchange was advertising in major publications like the *New York Times* and *Wall Street Journal*. After speaking with some of their representatives, I decided to invest about $2,000 with them.

As I had more interactions with the company after making my small investment with their firm, I became increasingly uncomfortable with them and sought to sell the gold holdings they claimed to have purchased with my money and get my money back. Unfortunately, it was too late as the firm was subsequently raided by law enforcement and a colossal fraud was exposed.

This taught me a powerful lesson at a young age. My mistakes included

>> **Buying into a narrative.** I believed that high inflation would continue and destroy the U.S. dollar and economy and gold would be a safe haven and rise greatly in value.

>> **Failing to research an investment firm.** For sure, there were and still are legitimate firms that sell gold and other precious metals to investors. I erroneously assumed that I had found such a firm because they were advertising in reputable business publications. Unfortunately, those publications hadn't realized they were dealing with a sleazy company — or perhaps they simply weren't interested in doing the necessary due diligence on them. I also failed to check out the firm properly and research competing firms.

>> **Failing to understand my other investment options.** Turns out, stocks were unloved and unappreciated when I bought this fictitious gold. Yes, I "lost" $2,000 on this scam, but the bigger loss was the "opportunity cost" of what I could have invested that money in. With the benefit of hindsight, I should have simply bought some good stock mutual funds and held them. Consider

that the Dow Jones Industrial Average, which has recently been at about 35,000, was at about 1,000 back then! So that index is up 35-fold, but the total return over time was far greater (more like 60-fold) because stocks pay dividends too.

A major reason that I took this career path is that I saw many people I knew and cared about make mistakes similar to or worse than mine.

Case study: Peter Schiff has been scaring investors for generations

Many different people look at the economy and make predictions. The burden to bear is who to listen to and who not to. During the sharp and volatile stock market slide of 2008–2009, Peter Schiff, who heads the brokerage firm Euro Pacific Capital, was frequently on television, especially the cable channels including CNBC. Along with a growing chorus of others making such regular appearances at that time (for example, Nouriel Roubini, Barry Ritholtz, and Gary Shilling), Schiff was one of those guys saying "I told you so" in reference to the 2008 financial crisis, severe recession, and financial-market problems.

Checking how predictions panned out

In an interview with Schiff that appeared in the May 30, 2008, issue of *U.S. News & World Report* magazine, Schiff claimed regarding the supposed accuracy of his predictions over the prior decade, "The reality is I don't think I've been wrong on anything." In that piece, Schiff made a number of predictions I get to in a moment.

Peter Schiff began his career in the financial services world as a stockbroker. In watching and reading his interviews and in speaking with Schiff myself back in early 2009, I was struck by the forcefulness and certainty of his views and predictions. He doesn't hedge, and as he did in the *U.S News* interview, he told me, "Pretty much everything is happening as I scripted it to happen with minor exceptions. . . ."

Before I get to Schiff's predictions made during the 2008 financial crisis, I was able to track down some of his older ones. I always enjoy doing this for prognosticators like Schiff who claim as he did to *U.S. News* that, "The reality is I don't think I've been wrong on anything," in reference to his predictions over the decade prior to the 2008 financial crisis. Let's take a look at that bold claim.

Thanks to the wonders of video technology, we have an accurate record of Schiff's views from a lengthy 2002 television interview. What is notable is that in that 2002 interview, Schiff was saying nearly the same exact things that he did during 2008 and in his early 2009 interview with me.

At the time of his 2002 interview, the U.S. stock market had already suffered steep losses and the economy was in recession. The highlights of Schiff's predictions: He saw substantial downside over the next couple of years for the stock market. He predicted that the Dow, which was around 10,000 at the time, would plummet to between 2,000 and 4,000 and he even went so far as to say that the Dow might fall below 2,000. He expected the Nasdaq to drop to 500 from its then level of 1,700. He also said that the dollar was going to fall sharply, and interest rates were going to go through the roof accompanied by dramatic inflation.

On all of these counts, Schiff wasn't simply wrong but ended up being hugely wrong. Now, fast forward to the May 30, 2008, U.S. News article titled, "Perma-bear Peter Schiff's Worst-Case Scenario." Let's review some of the key predictions he made in that piece. As for his investing predictions, he said, "I'm getting my clients' money outside of the United States as fast as they can send it to me . . . You've got to own resources and energy . . . I've been buying gold, silver, industrial metals, and all kinds of stocks. My main theme is the global economy will survive, and the U.S. economy is a disaster. Everything is about how you benefit from the increased purchasing power and rising standard of living in the rest of the world."

This was wrong, as commodity prices plunged tremendously after Schiff did this interview. Foreign stocks actually declined more in 2008 than did U.S. stocks, so Schiff was wrong on that count too. And in the years following, U.S. stocks greatly outperformed foreign stocks. Resource and energy stocks did quite poorly in the following years.

When asked, "Why don't you think soaring oil, grains, or commodities prices are the next bubble?" Schiff replied:

"These prices do not constitute bubbles. They simply constitute the repricing of goods to reflect the diminished value of our money. The way you can tell there's not a bubble is that these markets are clearing. People are buying food and eating it. They're buying gasoline and using it. Speculators aren't buying gasoline and warehousing it in big facilities because they think the price is going to go up." Schiff went on to say:

>> "Gold is going to be $1,200 to $1,500 by the end of the year."

>> "Oil prices had a pretty big run and might not make more headway by the end of the year. But we could see $150 to $200 next year."

>> "At a minimum, the dollar will lose another 40 to 50 percent of its value."

Well, Schiff was wrong on these 2008 predictions on gold, and wrong on oil, which plunged with the commodity bubble bursting. And he was wrong about the U.S. dollar, which gained strength in subsequent years.

When asked, "So how bad do you think this economy will get?" Schiff said, "We're going through a very rough period in our history. In many ways, it's going to be worse than the Depression." That's what prompted my call to Schiff in early 2009 for him to explain this stunning statement. "During the Depression, the U.S. economy was actually still fundamentally sound. The U.S. government created the Great Depression . . . Japan's government made the same mistakes in the 1990s and made the downturn worse and longer lasting," he said. He went on to explain, "We allowed our economy to move from producing goods to a service economy. Our economy now is completely phony."

In his 2002 television interview I discussed earlier, Schiff similarly argued that the U.S. economy would crater because of the decline of our manufacturing base. Perhaps if Schiff had studied some basic economics, he would have learned that economies change and that's not a bad thing. If Schiff had lived 100 years ago, he would have been screaming over the decline of our farming industry.

Jeremy Siegel's classic book, *Stocks for the Long Run*, documents the changing composition of our industry base over the decades and generations and the fact that these changes are not in and of itself concerning in our global economy. We actually have a highly diverse economy. In my 2009 interview of Schiff, sounding a lot like he did back in 2002, he said, "The government is trying to fix the economy through intervention and will make the situation worse. We can't afford all of this government. The dollar is still rising, and the world is still giving us more rope to hang ourselves. The dollar will plunge and that will cause rapid inflation and high interest rates." As for being wrong on commodity prices after his 2008 *U.S. News* interview, Schiff maintained in 2009 that prices would make new highs and claimed that the only reason that hadn't happened yet was because the dollar hadn't yet collapsed.

Why hadn't this yet happened and why did commodity prices collapse in late 2008 while investors worldwide bought U.S. Treasury bonds and bills? "I overestimated the intelligence of the world to see the coming inflation," Schiff told me.

Following the money trail

To really see how and why pundits such as Schiff make their predictions, it's a good idea to find out what may be persuading them.

Schiff appears to have built himself a profitable brokerage business by harping on the simple message that the United States is going down the tubes and you've got to get your money overseas and into commodities. It's a schtick – a way to get attention, scare people and appear to be a knowledgeable investment advisor. Maybe he believes it, but it doesn't really matter because it's been a terrible investment approach and strategy. His clients' performance (apparently following his risky and flawed predictions) has been sub-par as has been documented in numerous sources, including in the *Wall Street Journal* (www.wsj.com/articles/SB123327685671031439).

As I've long argued, stock market investors should hold modest portions of overseas stocks for diversification purposes and to benefit from foreign economies that, like the United States, are growing over time. However, buying individual stocks as Schiff advocates is costly (although profitable for his brokerage firm). Commodity investments are a high-risk, dangerous game for novice investors and the only long-term winner there is usually the broker getting a piece of the trades and investments. Over the very long term, commodity prices and gold have barely kept investors up with the rate of inflation. Over brief periods of unexpectedly higher inflation, such investments tend to do well, but timing such moves is quite difficult to do.

Questioning qualifications

Whenever you are considering the predictions and recommendations of someone being held up as a prognosticator or pundit, you should examine their qualifications and background. This would include looking into their educational and work experiences and examining their past predictions if forecasting is something they do.

When I asked Schiff what training and experience he had to form his economic views and opinions, I asked if he was an economist or had any economics training. "I think I know more about economics than anyone with the title, and I know more than anyone in government," he boasted, adding, "These other guys are witch doctors, and I'm the real doctor."

As for when he developed his economic genius, Schiff told me, "I've always known this much — ever since I was a kid and my dad wrote a book called *The Biggest Con: How the Government Is Fleecing You*, I've understood capitalism and how it works. I read Ayn Rand and I read some of the Keynesian economics stuff and could see why those economists were all wrong."

Understanding what pundits are trying to sell you

It's rarely obvious what a particular pundit, especially those that I've observed as among the most successful, is actually selling. Increasingly so, you may find yourself hopping onto a phone call to engage with someone who is ultimately a salesperson to discover what a particular pundit's firm is selling. But I explain some simple ways to ferret out what a pundit and their company is actually selling and whether their advice is worth considering.

INVESTIGATE

The first time that you come across a particular pundit, if you find yourself drawn to them and their perspectives, make careful note of what they are saying and how it comports with your views of the world. Typically, we are drawn to people who make arguments that at least incorporate some of our personal views and concerns. Of course, if a pundit is well spoken and comes across as intelligent and informed, that can help their appeal.

TIP

Since the fundamental premise of nearly every one of these pundits is that they make investment recommendations based upon what they see happening in the future economy, you should investigate what their past predictions were and how that compares with what actually happened. You can begin this process if you're interested in doing so for a pundit by simply doing an online search using their name. You will typically find old articles about their predictions as well as videos on services like YouTube. Something that is independently produced has far greater credibility than something that the pundit has chosen to leave up regarding their past forecasts.

Examine how the pundits' prior recommendations turned out. For example, if ten years ago they said to buy gold and avoid stocks, compare the stock market's returns to gold's returns over the years following their advice. This simple analysis alone will turn you against continuing to follow nearly all such pundits.

If you're still enamored of a given pundit after doing my recommended basic research, you may want to investigate what they are selling and how they make money from people like you. You should always take this step if you're considering subscribing to or buying anything the pundit is selling. You can begin this part of your investigative work by visiting the pundit's or their firm's website and looking around there. If the pundit is affiliated with or running a company with a separate name, check out that website thoroughly as well.

While on a company website, be sure to check out tabs with labels such as "About Us" and "Services." Many firms engage in money management, and you can generally read about those services and fees charged through their websites. Also, some companies operate mutual funds, which are a great vehicle to review since their track records are public and can't be fudged. I rarely if ever see mutual funds worthy of investing in from pundit-driven firms.

WARNING

Don't fill out forms requesting a call back or providing personal information such as your home address, phone number, net worth, investable assets, and so forth. These inevitably lead to sales contacts and calls.

Seeing why fearmongers' predictions are often wrong

I don't know of a single pundit who is routinely in the media or busily promoting themselves whose predictions and investing track record is better than the actual track record of the best professionally managed funds, including index funds. Sure, sometimes pundits are right on a call here or there. But over the long term, they are often wrong in terms of the specific investments they are recommending or shunning and/or the timing of their calls. The premise of many pundits' predictions is that they can time the markets — in other words, they can adeptly tell you when and what to buy and sell.

This makes sense intuitively. For starters, those who are really good at investment management can make oodles of money doing that. Second is the fact that many of the best investment managers will tell you that market timing is nearly impossible to do and not something they are necessarily skilled at.

Why, then, do the predicting pundits continue to get media coverage and attract attention for their promotionally oriented content and advertising? Here are some important reasons:

>> **Making provocative predictions is entertaining and gains attention.** Always remember that the media is largely about attracting viewers, readers, and listeners. Sensational predictions attract curious and concerned people to pay attention. The more folks are tuning in or clicking on their content, the more money can generally be collected from advertisers.

>> **Media and others rarely hold anyone accountable.** In addition to making outrageous predictions, plenty of pundits also make outrageous, false, and unsubstantiated claims about the accuracy of their past predictions. It's disappointing how the media lazily won't bother to check pundits' past predictions or claims related to those predictions.

>> **Many investors want to believe that pundits know more than they do.** When someone appears in the media and seems confident and authoritative, they get attention. The world of finance and investing is intimidating and often confusing, so it may provide some hope and comfort to believe that certain pundits can help us sidestep problems and better tap opportunities.

Surveying the Leading Worries Being Pitched Today

The most common fears and predictions being pedaled these days actually don't differ as much as you'd think compared to what was being hyped 30 or 40 years ago. In this section, I discuss what the biggest fears and associated predictions are now, and for each one, I provide my take and thinking.

(The things that are concerning the smartest people I know are discussed in Chapter 13.)

Excessive government debts

If you follow politics and government at all, you know that politicians generally like to spend money. Especially during difficult times, there are all sorts of government programs and reasons for government to spend more money. During such times, government revenue (taxes collected) tends to drop. Annual deficits (the difference between taxes collected and government spending) typically balloons as does the total debt outstanding.

So, almost every time we go through a recession, renewed talk and worries spring up about governments taking on too much debt and soon going bankrupt. The worse the recession and the larger the deficits accumulated during the recession and aftermath, the more concern I hear about too much government debt and looming future bankruptcies.

The severe financial crisis of 2008 and into 2009 provoked years of concern on this dimension.

On the February 26, 2009, *O'Reilly Factor* television show, popular host Bill O'Reilly focused on President Barack Obama's then proposed budget, it's large deficit (about $1.75 trillion), and how it was projected to balloon the total federal debt outstanding to $13 trillion. After citing these numbers, O'Reilly stated:

> "We can't ever pay that off. The Feds simply cannot tax folks enough to raise the money. That means the country could go bankrupt just like the state of California is tottering on bankruptcy. The U.S. dollar will collapse, and we'll all be in big, big trouble."

O'Reilly then introduced guest Dick Morris, former political advisor to President Bill Clinton. O'Reilly asked Morris if because of all of this debt he thought that the country would be bankrupt in about five to seven years. Morris responded that he thought we'd end up in a depression and with a Republican Congress in 2010 (he got one thing correct). They also discussed the state of California, which they agreed was in a "desperate situation" and on the "verge of toppling."

Joining O'Reilly and Morris was Glenn Beck, who has long had an affinity for the doom-and-gloom folks advocating that you buy gold, firearms, and extra food for the economic Armageddon. While I enjoyed reading Beck's irreverent book, *An Inconvenient Book: Real Solutions to the World's Biggest Problems* (Threshold), I find him unduly pessimistic on the economy. He thinks folks like Peter Schiff are economic prognosticators worth following. (Disclosure: I dislike most politicians and find myself watching and listening to a range of discourse. I praised O'Reilly's comments on the financial markets in the fall of 2008 when he urged folks to remain calm and not panic when the stock market plummeted.)

I spoke with Beck at this time about his views on the federal debt and he said, "Imagine the day when our children get out of college and they have to pay the enormous taxes for all debt. It's not just the debt but all of the services that we are promising. If economists are right and the economy doesn't take too long to improve, then we'll be okay. If not, our debt would spiral out of control."

Putting the amount of debt in perspective

So, how big a problem was the federal debt outstanding and likely to be outstanding in the future? The total federal debt in early 2009 was about $11 trillion. That did indeed sound like a large number because it is a large number to the average person. (Post-pandemic, this debt number has now surpassed $22 trillion as of late 2021).

What would you think of a person's debt burden if I told you they had total debts outstanding of $33 million? Would that number on its own tell you she was financially irresponsible? Of course it wouldn't because you have no context for it. I know someone in Congress who had $33 million in debt (mostly through mortgages on various real estate investment properties her family owns), while her assets totaled $96 million. So, now her debt doesn't seem so bad, does it?

The same phenomenon holds true for the federal government. The total federal debt in early 2009 was about $11 trillion, and the average interest rate on that debt was 3.8 percent (which was down from just over 5 percent in mid-2007). The fact that the federal government was able to borrow $11 trillion at an average interest rate of just 3.8 percent clearly tells us that the marketplace of investors around the globe thought that lending Uncle Sam money was pretty darn low risk! (This same analysis holds true post-pandemic with the U.S. federal government debt now exceeding $22 trillion in late 2021 at an average interest rate of just 1.7 percent.)

Now, consider this important and revealing fact about the federal debt and the burden of that debt. The portion of federal tax receipts (the revenue coming into the government) needed to pay the annual interest on the debt was just under 14 percent back in 1998 and was just 10 percent in early 2009! (Post-pandemic, the portion of federal tax receipts needed to pay the annual interest on the debt is now even lower at about 9 percent as of late 2021.)

To put this in perspective, consider a person who is earning $50,000 per year and has a mortgage that costs $5,000 per year in interest (10 percent of their income). Would we consider that person to be in severe financial trouble and on the verge of bankruptcy? Of course we wouldn't! (In the early years of a mortgage, nearly all of the payments go to interest, and those mortgage costs can easily take up to 25 to 30 percent of a person's income).

When I pointed out to Beck that the interest on the federal debt was consuming just 10 percent of federal tax revenue, he said, "But how long before the rest of the world won't loan us money or will the rate increase if our debt starts to spiral . . . we're behaving like we are 70 years old and nearing the end of our earnings' cycle. We are a country that no longer values production . . . we value consumption." Beck points to medicine being the only field in which the United States is a leader, but I pointed out to him that we're a leader in technology, which is clearly a growing and emerging industry.

Flipping the coin to surpluses

It's hard to believe, but back in 2001, then Federal Reserve Board Chairman Alan Greenspan was actually concerned about budget surpluses — yes, you read that right. In his testimony before the U.S. Senate Committee on the Budget, Greenspan said the following:

> "The most recent projections from the OMB indicate that, if current policies remain in place, the total unified surplus will reach $800 billion in fiscal year 2011, including an on-budget surplus of $500 billion. The CBO reportedly will be showing even larger surpluses . . . The most recent projections, granted their tentativeness, nonetheless make clear that the highly desirable goal of paying off the federal debt is in reach before the end of the decade. But continuing to run surpluses beyond the point at which we reach zero or near-zero federal debt brings to center stage the critical longer-term fiscal policy issue of whether the federal government should accumulate large quantities of private (more technically nonfederal) assets. At zero debt, the continuing unified budget surpluses currently projected imply a major accumulation of private assets by the federal government. This development should factor materially into the policies you and the Administration choose to pursue."

It's hard to believe that these comments came from Chairman Greenspan in 2001. He was expecting that the annual budget surpluses would be so large during the 2000s that the federal debt would be paid off by the end of that decade! And, he was concerned about the federal government having to buy private assets with continuing surpluses once the debt was paid off!

REMEMBER

The 2009 angst over ballooning budget deficits and Greenspan's 2001 comments about never-ending surpluses show how often pundits, economists, and others make the mistake of extrapolating from current experiences. Just as spring follows winter and day follows night, economic expansion will follow recessions, and shrinking budget deficits will follow growing budget deficits.

If you are concerned about the federal debt growing for a long time and becoming a problem, that's actually another reason to be diversified in stocks globally, as I have long advocated. If you're thinking about gold, remember it has mediocre long-term returns — averaging just 0.5 percent annually above the rate of inflation. Don't make the mistake of panicking and dumping your retirement investments because of media folks venturing outside of their areas of expertise.

Is government spending a problem?

Interestingly, when I've written articles about the size of the federal debt and tried to put it into perspective, some folks branded me as supporting big-spending liberalism! Consider these missives in my email box:

> "I find little in your article . . . to be accurate and truly represent the current state of the U.S. economy. It is this apparent 'media bias to support a liberal legislation agenda' that will result in the bankruptcy of this country."

> "I usually don't respond to such pathetic displays of idiocy . . . but I just couldn't help myself today after I read your column. The financial system that just presided over the largest loss of household wealth in the past 60 years is your answer to our government spending well beyond its means? What sage advice!"

Well, these folks were off base in their criticism. The point of my writings on the federal debt has been to examine the federal debt in relation to tax revenue. I am not saying and did not say that proposed government spending was fine. In fact, I do believe that U.S. federal government spending has at times been a problem. According to Brian Wesbury, Chief Economist with First Trust, federal tax revenue as a share of GDP has varied around 18 percent over the decades. Meanwhile, federal spending as a share of GDP increased from 18.4 percent in 2000 to 20.7 percent in 2008 and spiked over 30 percent during the COVID-19 pandemic.

"Every percent increase in federal spending decreases GDP by about 0.25 percent per year as it is taken from the private sector and means you have less resources to do other things with," says Wesbury, who adds, "Every dollar spent must be either coming from tax or debt."

Each year, The Council for Citizens Against Government Waste (CCAGW) tabulates its congressional ratings, evaluating how each member of congress measures up on key tax and spending votes. CCAGW is a private, nonpartisan, nonprofit organization founded in 1984 by the late industrialist J. Peter Grace and syndicated columnist Jack Anderson.

To see where politicians stand on the issue of government spending, I encourage you to visit the "Congressional Ratings" section of their website (https://www.ccagw.org/). CAGW rates them on a 100 percent scale with 100 percent being the top "lifetime" possible score (lifetime scores track all of their votes over their years in Congress).

High inflation and worthless currencies

Worries about high inflation and worthless currencies are much quicker and easier to cover because the discussion builds upon concerns about excessive government spending and debt that I cover in the preceding section.

WHAT ABOUT FUTURE GOVERNMENT ENTITLEMENTS?

Regarding the federal debt outstanding, there are some who worry about future federal liabilities. For example, the Peter G. Peterson Foundation (www.pgpf.org/) has been trying to raise awareness of the "large and national debt that endangers the viability of Social Security, Medicare, and our economy itself."

The Peterson Foundation has highlighted concerns about the tens of trillions of dollars in total federal government obligations. However, it is important to recognize in thinking about this large number that this is largely future benefits owed to ourselves (for example, Social Security and Medicare).

This foundation fails to do an apples-to-apples comparison and compare these estimated future liabilities to future expected economic activity or tax revenue. Also, these estimated total future obligations are not debt, and the number could easily change and be reduced as needed by future legislation.

When a government engages in excessive spending and debt, that can lead to its currency falling in value and prices rising (inflation). Some economists refer to this cycle as too much money chasing too few goods.

In the aftermath of the COVID-19 pandemic, we've seen this phenomenon play out as more sectors of the economy have reopened and consumers have been ready to make deferred purchases and spend, including using stimulus money distributed by the government. Too much money chasing too few goods led to faster rising prices in many sectors of the economy in 2021. And this came on top of all the extra government spending, reduced tax revenue collections, and increased debt that governments ran up due to the COVID-19 pandemic.

Pundits pushing this pessimistic view urge their followers to load up on things that do well during times of high inflation and falling currency values. That could include gold and silver and commodities more broadly; more recently, some argue for cryptocurrencies. Ironically, the number of cryptocurrencies continues to explode and grow, so the argument that, like gold and other precious metals, cryptocurrencies may provide a hedge against inflation is counterintuitive and not something I buy into.

In most developed and developing markets, inflation ebbs and flows and is generally not a big problem. The pundits who continually scare people about supposedly imminent inflation and currency devaluations have caused many investors to leave good investments like stocks and put their money into long-term mediocre performing investments like precious metals. Gold's returns historically have barely kept investors up with the rate of inflation.

Another reason to not stress excessively about future inflation fears is that in the classic book *Stocks for the Long Run* (McGraw-Hill Education), author Jeremy Siegel documents how stocks are actually a good long-term inflation hedge although they typically aren't in the short term. I have also observed that before numerous recessions, many pundits fret about rising inflation and then when a deepening recession hits, those fears turn to deflation concerns.

Anarchy and the breakdown of society

This concern has been floated for plenty of years and has gained more traction online thanks to the increasing usage of the internet in recent decades. The websites and pundits trafficking in this worry typically highlight and focus upon all the negative things they see happening in the world around them.

I can't tell — and perhaps it doesn't really matter — if these purveyors of calamity really believe the end is fast approaching or they engage in this narrative to get their followers in the right mood to buy the things they're selling and profiting from. These pundits typically recommend things like the following:

>> **Loading up on guns and ammo:** As government and society break down, you will need to rely on yourself for personal safety.

>> **Keeping long-term supplies of freeze-dried food:** Supply chains and the economy overall will break down and cease functioning as we know it.

>> **Having physical gold and silver (and now cryptocurrencies) with which to buy things and trade:** Government-backed paper currencies won't be valued, so you should have other sources of funds that are accepted and valued.

The pundits and their websites make money from such things by selling these things themselves and/or taking advertising from companies selling these things.

Making emergency preparations is a personal matter and choice in terms of what you elect to do. If you're going to feel a little more confident and protected by doing some things, especially if it doesn't take too much of your time and money, consider those steps and always obey the law!

Chapter **13**

Preparing Yourself for Unexpected Future Crises

Think back to 2019, especially late in 2019.

You may have specific memories of where you were working, people you spent time with as well as times you traveled. Perhaps you remember gatherings for major holidays like Thanksgiving or Christmas near the end of 2019.

For the Thanksgiving holiday that year in late November, I remember picking up my son out of state and driving home with him. He had been sick the week prior and seemed to be getting better. Not long after we arrived home, I got sick, and I was sick for about the first half of December. I had a fever, was achy, and was at times low on energy and required more sleep. I had a dry cough and was frustrated with how long it was taking for me to get over it. It had been many years since I had been this sick. It felt like the flu, and I finally went to the doctor to have my lungs checked to make sure I wasn't developing something more concerning like bronchitis, which thankfully I was not. When I was almost fully recovered, I remember attending a crowded holiday party. I had difficulty talking for any length of time and doing so made me cough.

My life returned to normal by the end of the year and into early 2020. In early 2020, we began to hear some reports about a new coronavirus causing respiratory problems, pneumonia, and death in some people in and around Wuhan, China. Over the two prior decades, two other coronaviruses — SARS (severe acute respiratory syndrome) and MERS (Middle East respiratory syndrome) — caused pandemics. Numerous "experts" reassured the public that there was no reason to have great concern over this new coronavirus, and the experience of the other two prior coronavirus pandemics was generally reassuring as well.

Stock prices experienced a modest correction in mid-January 2020, but that was neither surprising nor worrisome since the market was due for a correction after longer-term strength. Another downturn unfolded about a month later, and that one gradually gained steam and turned into a major downturn of about 35 percent in just six weeks through the end of March 2020. Government-mandated economic shutdowns and regular press conferences about the dangers of the virus raised many people's anxieties, deepened the economic pain and layoffs, and created great uncertainty.

Why am I talking about what has come to be known as the COVID-19 pandemic here? Because it's an excellent recent example of something that few predicted that caused some significant problems. (In Chapter 2, I discuss the COVID-19 pandemic and its economic and financial-market fallout more fully).

REMEMBER

More than anything else, the financial markets and the world at large are moved by surprises. The "thing" that many people are talking about and worried about rarely ends up causing the multitude of problems that people fear. When COVID-19 became the "thing" that everyone was talking about, as I discuss in Chapter 2, the financial markets and economy were already looking ahead and on the mend. Vaccines and other treatments were being developed. And that explains why numerous people were surprised and disappointed, for example, with having sold stocks in the spring of 2020 and regretted not having stayed the course.

What Possible Future Crises Should You Be Prepared For?

Honestly, I can't tell you with any degree of certainty what specific future crises we're likely to encounter.

In this section, I discuss those that are more likely to cause problems and warrant your consideration. For any of these, I'm not suggesting that you make significant changes in your overall financial or personal lives. But there are some simple and potentially powerful things you can do, which I cover later in this chapter.

Dangers of excessive dependence upon technology and internet

Technology continues to seep into more and more areas of our society and culture, and the COVID-19 pandemic and associated government-mandated economic closures accelerated that process. For sure, technology has produced a number of improvements to our lives such as convenience, quick access, and the ability to more easily comparison shop.

But when taken to an extreme, many of the benefits of technology have downsides. For example, as an employee or small business owner, this can mean that those trying to contact you expect you to be available more hours and quicker.

As technology becomes more fully integrated into our society, business world, and ways of life, problems caused by technology or disruptions to technology upon which we depend could cause widespread disruptions and breakdowns.

The more we depend upon and allow technology to oversee and control everything, the more we will potentially be at its mercy, including if unsavory actors can hack it and terrorize through it. That's concerning. On the flip side, intelligent cybersecurity measures keep the bad guys from firmly gaining the upper hand for any length of time.

I wouldn't lose sleep over this concern. As it relates to your personal life, I like the idea of having backups in place if the technology you use fails you.

Hazards of faster and inaccurate "news" flow

With the growth and spread of the internet and the explosion of "news" and blogs online, assisted by social media, just about anything happening anywhere in the world can be known about and the news coverage spread quickly. While there are benefits to this, there's an obvious downside in the lack of editors who are fact checking and seeking accuracy instead of throwing things out there and not caring about whether it's accurate or assuming it is.

Misinformation and outright lies can spread and metastasize quickly and easily online. Even more concerning is the fact that such falsehoods can be further amplified and spread by media and other outlets that are partisan or simply interested in hyped stories that get clicks, viewers, and listeners.

Another problem is that free speech and counter viewpoints are being suppressed in numerous venues. More specifically, censorship is at work to stop others from combatting a desired or provocative narrative. Allow me to illustrate with an example from the recent COVID-19 pandemic.

Early on in the pandemic, in the spring of 2020, a number of people including some scientists as well as laypeople who simply are thoughtful and analytic, challenged the prevailing narratives about the COVID-19 virus and government-mandated economic shutdowns and other restrictions. During 2020 and into 2021, I frequently found the following alternative viewpoints were regularly censored and suppressed:

>> The fatality rate is comparable to a bad flu season. The media continually reported the number of deaths supposedly caused by COVID-19 and then would mindlessly divide that number by the number of positive cases documented. Many media people and partisan politicians then falsely claimed that the death rate from COVID-19 was on the order of 3 to 6 percent. Common sense would suggest that there were many people who had mild cases who were never tested and documented as having had the virus. In fact, early on, numerous antibody studies found that about 20 to 40 times as many people in specific geographic areas showed antibodies in their tested blood for the COVID-19 virus. This meant that the actual fatality rate from the virus was more on the order of a bad flu season — less than 0.3 percent.

>> Broad lockdowns failed to protect the most vulnerable and caused excessive and unnecessary economic and personal harm. Keeping young people, including healthy working-age people locked up at home failed to protect the most vulnerable, including sick people in nursing homes and hospitals. Lockdowns caused a multitude of mental health and other health problems for otherwise healthy people. And subsequent studies have found that COVID-19 spread more within homes subject to long-term lockdowns as sick family members were more likely to infect other family members spending so much time at home.

>> Getting vaccinated is a personal choice and less beneficial for young, healthy people. All medicines have a profile of possible benefits and drawbacks. With COVID-19, the vaccines that have been approved under an emergency use authorization by the FDA statistically offer the greatest potential benefit to those who are older and who suffer from notable health problems. Younger, healthy people statistically are at extremely low risk of suffering due to COVID-19 yet may suffer from problems caused by the vaccine itself. Just as not everyone gets the flu vaccine each winter and can make a personal choice, plenty of people felt similarly about the COVID-19 vaccines, especially since these new vaccines had no longer-term track record.

For sure, folks can have different perspectives on these topics. But it's concerning that these counter point-of-view ideas about COVID-19 were censored. Our society is built upon personal freedoms and choice, and free speech. Ideas, facts, and differing viewpoints should be shared, discussed, and debated.

Spreading socialism

Spreading socialism is one of the greatest threats to the economic bounty and associated financial security that the engine of capitalism has provided in America and other countries that embrace it. My biggest concern is the growing popularity of socialism in the United States in general and especially among young adults. (In Chapter 2, I discuss and compare capitalism with socialism and also present some concerning data.)

According to the respected polling company Gallup, since 2010, about half of all young U.S. adults give positive ratings to socialism, and their ratings of capitalism have continued to deteriorate. These trends are due to a number of factors including what is and is not being taught to young people in our educational institutions, and portrayal of the economy and capitalists in the media and by partisan politicians, especially those who embrace socialist policies.

If these trends were to continue, eventually they would have deleterious effects on the broader economy and economic opportunities in this country. Socialism is antithetical to financial security. Socialism leads to too much government and too little economic growth, development, and opportunities.

TIP

Your best protection against spreading socialism is to invest in stocks globally, not just in the United States. And get involved in current affairs and politics, at least as an educated and regular voter.

Climate change (also known as global warming)

My educational and professional employment background includes extensive training and work in the sciences and in analysis. I enjoy reading and gathering facts and data. And I'm open to changing my mind as I find out more about a topic.

I've done quite a bit of reading on the topic of climate change/global warming and have also engaged numerous people I know and interact with. I do believe that we should take care of the environment. That said, I find a good deal of the hand wringing and worrying about what used to be called global warming and now is more typically referred to as climate change to be unwarranted. Even if you choose to disagree with what I'm sharing with you in this section, I very much doubt that the climate is going to change in a significant way in time frames that are meaningful to our collective existence.

There is no conclusive evidence for global warming, which is why some of its advocates fudged data and changed the name of the movement to climate change in recent years. With the new name, every seemingly extreme weather event (for example, large snowstorms, big rainstorms, hurricanes hitting populated coastal areas, and so forth) can be pointed to as evidence that something is wrong.

As I like to do for folks making economic and financial-market predictions, it is instructive to go back and see how prior climate change predictions made in past decades have turned out. You can find an eye opening and revealing compilation entitled "Wrong Again: 50 Years of Failed Eco-pocalyptic Predictions" on the Competitive Enterprise Institute (CEI) website (cei.org/blog/wrong-again-50-years-failed-eco-pocalyptic-predictions). Here's the introduction to their trove of 50 plus years' worth of erroneous climate predictions:

> "Modern doomsayers have been predicting climate and environmental disaster since the 1960s. They continue to do so today. None of the apocalyptic predictions with due dates as of today have come true . . . More than merely spotlighting the failed predictions, this collection shows that the makers of failed apocalyptic predictions often are individuals holding respected positions in government and science. While such predictions have been and continue to be enthusiastically reported by a media eager for sensational headlines, the failures are typically not revisited."

What's fascinating in this history tour is to see the many predictions for global cooling that were prevalent just decades ago. Also, the Malthusian arguments for population growth leading to catastrophe have been around for generations, and the older predictions have been universally wrong. Paul Erhlich's writing popularized this back in the 1960s, and his predictions, which you can see in CEI's compilation of prior climate predictions, were 100 percent wrong. Far left (socialist) politicians subscribe to this point of view, and they want government to regulate many things. Such thinkers believe and say that people should stop having babies. This overlooks and ignores the fact that, like Japan, our country's population is at risk of declining in the future.

I also encourage you to visit the Global Warming Petition Project website (petitionproject.org/). There you can read about the 31,487 American scientists who have signed a petition stating their opposition to the notion that global warming is occurring, is man-made, and can and should be stopped through human intervention. The site's purpose is as follows:

The purpose of the Petition Project is to demonstrate that the claim of settled science and an overwhelming consensus in favor of the hypothesis of human-caused global warming and consequent climatological damage is wrong. No such consensus or settled science exists. As indicated by the petition text and signatory list, a very large number of American scientists reject this hypothesis . . . Moreover, from the clear and strong petition statement that they have signed, it is evident that these 31,487 American scientists are not skeptics. These scientists are instead convinced that the human-caused global warming hypothesis is without scientific validity and that government action on the basis of this hypothesis would unnecessarily and counterproductively damage both human prosperity and the natural environment of the Earth.

Also on that same website, you can read the informative "Summary of Peer-Reviewed Research" (`petitionproject.org/review_article.php`). Finally, if you're worried about climate change, I encourage you to read *The Politically Incorrect Guide to Climate Change* by Marc Morano (Regnery Publishing).

Power grid failures and resource shortages

Utility failures have gotten lots of media coverage, especially when it's caused by more extreme weather events. In early 2021, portions of Texas and surrounding southern states were hit hard by unusually cold and snowy weather and associated power failures. The news media showed people shivering in unheated homes and burst pipes that flooded some unheated homes.

Other states have had rolling blackouts during the worst heat waves. The state of California did the same out of concern that sparking power lines could ignite dry conditions and lead to massive wildfires. There's also the water shortage that's a perennial problem in the West.

With these and related concerns, my strong suggestion is that first you examine the risks you are possibly exposed to given where you live, and then develop your personal backup and emergency plans. For example, regarding the early 2021 unusually cold and snowy weather in and around Texas, such bad weather weeks have happened before and should have been anticipated even though they are not common. As a homeowner in such an area, you can make sure that your home is well insulated and consider getting a backup home generator in the event of an extended power outage.

Alternatively, you can pre-arrange to stay with a relative or friend you can safely travel to be with who has such a system. In that case, you should also know where the master water shut-off line is for your home in the event that you want to shut it off if your heat is off during a cold period and power outage.

I also point out these risks and concerns are well known and generally well planned for, so it's highly unlikely that there would be such a geographically widespread and prolonged outage that it would be harmful to the broader economy.

Solvency of Social Security

Some people, but by no means all folks, understand that the federally administered Social Security system is projected to run short of money in the not-too-distant future. Some pundits are warning of a full-fledged crisis that could lead to greatly reduced benefits. Others warn that it will touch off more money printing and massive inflation, which will greatly devalue your earned benefits.

According to surveys, about half of American adults under the age of 35 and more than a third of those between the ages of 35 and 49 think that Social Security benefits will not be available by the time they retire.

Contrary to widespread skepticism, Social Security should be available when you retire, no matter how old you are today. In fact, Social Security is one of the sacred cow political programs. Imagine what would happen to the group of politicians who voted to greatly curtail benefits!

Social Security is intended to provide you with a subsistence level of retirement income for the basic necessities: food, shelter, and clothing. Social Security is not intended to be your sole source of income. Some of the elderly are quite dependent upon Social Security: It's the only source of income for about two in ten of the elderly, and about two out of three Social Security recipients derive at least half of their total retirement income from their Social Security retirement check. Few working people can maintain their current lifestyles into retirement without supplementing Social Security with personal savings and company retirement plans.

Here are some likely future changes that will shore up the solvency of Social Security benefits:

>> Reduced benefits and/or higher tax rates on high-income earner benefits

>> Pushing the age out further for full retirement benefits (it was last increased from age 65 to age 67).

>> Higher tax rates and/or more employment wages subject to Social Security taxation.

>> Usage of a different cost-of-living adjustment that shows a lower overall inflation rate.

Preparing Financially and Otherwise for New Future Crises

I can't predict the future. And neither can anyone else, including you.

If you read this entire book and take to heart what I'm saying, you can do better with your money and achieve more of your personal and financial goals. But you have to expect problems along the way — such as economic downturns and negative personal events — that are well outside your explicit control.

Here's my advice on how to best prepare for and handle unpredictable future crises:

>> **Take the time now to optimize your finances.** Read, consider, and implement the advice that works for you in this book. Be sure to maintain a decent-size emergency reserve of cash to weather tough times and for investing opportunities during such periods.

>> **Live your life now and don't postpone things you enjoy.** Personal and global problems can change your life as you know it. Take time every day and week to do things you enjoy, including spending time with those you care most about. Call a friend you haven't spoken with in a while and catch up. Don't wait. Go exercise today, start reading a book you've been wanting to read, and so forth. Your current life likely has plenty of obligations and demands, but that doesn't mean you shouldn't regularly do things you choose and enjoy.

>> **Stay optimistic.** Tough times can weigh on you, especially if they drag on and morph into other problems. Be sure to minimize your consumption of media and remind yourself that they hype things to keep you tuned in and worried. Yes, you should be informed, but choose your sources wisely and limit your intake of media that dwells upon the negative.

>> **Expect the best but be prepared for the worst.** This theme runs throughout this book, and insurance is an excellent example of it. It's why you carry insurance on your home but with a high deductible. This protects you against an unlikely big potential loss but doesn't waste your insurance money on smaller potential losses.

>> **Have contingency and backup plans.** Consider, for example, what you would do if your power were out for several weeks or even months. Does it make sense to spend money on having a backup home generator? Would a good friend or relative be able to put you up for that length of time?

And one final point here about unexpected crises. There are entities, both public and private, that have solutions and responses ready to deal with nearly all the types of problems that are thrown at us. With every crisis, solutions arise. You can, and I think should, choose to be a glass-half-full kind of person with regard to the unknowns that could cause future problems.

6

The Part of Tens

IN THIS PART . . .

Understand that financial security is tied to personal safety. Find ways to keep yourself safe.

Is saving too much a bad thing? It can be. Find a balance between saving and spending.

Chapter **14**

Tens Ways to Improve Your Personal Safety

T his book is about your financial security and money. But we all know that our personal safety is an important part of our overall security.

And for some good insights on that topic, I turn to noted crime prevention expert Jeff McKissack. In his book *Power Proverbs for Personal Defense*, McKissack teaches his "golden rules" for avoiding dangerous people and situations.

Combine Your Instincts with Proven Strategies

McKissack notes that while many times we can trust our instincts to alert us when a potentially treacherous situation is near, we also must draw upon the effective strategies of our predecessors that have withstood the test of time. His recommendations highlighted in this chapter capture those valuable approaches.

Of course, no system or approach to personal safety can guarantee 100 percent protection, but McKissack's strategies can and should greatly decrease your risk of being a victim of crime or violence.

What You Don't Know Can Hurt You

McKissack begins with the idea that "what you don't know can hurt you," more specifically zeroing in on the dangerous implications of getting into a verbal or physical altercation with a complete stranger. The author recounts the slaying of a man outside Dallas who was beaten to death by a group of teenage boys whom he had yelled at earlier that day for drag racing down the street in front of his house. The inclusion of this anecdote is meant to illustrate the fact that you have no idea whether the seemingly harmless stranger that you may encounter is, in reality, capable of violence or not.

Sadly, if you follow the daily news, you will hear stories similar to this one. As I write this book, there was a recent case in southern California where a mother was driving with her six-year-old son, and the son was fatally shot in a road rage incident that escalated when the mom flipped off the driver of another car.

In McKissack's words, you have to be careful not to "[throw] fuel on an open flame."

Do Unto Others As You Would Have Others Do Unto You

It is also important to remember to do unto others as you would have others do unto you. There is no sense in giving someone a reason to target you for an attack.

For example, if you're dealing with a difficult customer, employee, or person, don't publicly humiliate or embarrass them. Treat them the way in which you would want to be treated.

Don't use the fact that you would never have committed the offending behavior in the first place as justification for your response. That's irrelevant and not the point.

Err on the Side of Caution

As a general rule of thumb, McKissack encourages us to err on the side of caution, explaining that it is always "better to be safe than sorry." He uses the common example of how to react upon seeing a car broken down on the side of the road, and notes that while our first instinct may be to pull over and offer personal assistance, it is far more prudent to call a professional for help rather than put ourselves at risk by offering direct assistance to a stranger.

He urges us to take heed of the fact that many criminals are inherently desperate and will in turn be quite resourceful in their scams. We need to ask ourselves: "Can I verify this stranger's identity?" And more importantly, "Am I in a position of vulnerability by agreeing to assist or cooperate with this person?"

There's (Some) Safety in Numbers, But There May be a Weak Link

McKissack qualifies another old saying, highlighting the fact that while "there's safety in numbers," ultimately and ideally the people you are with must be fully aware and prepared to defend themselves in order to successfully do so.

While it is fairly common for an American citizen to own a gun for self-defense, the author points out the fact that many of these people do not even know how to use a gun and, moreover, have never been trained to use one under the pressure of an unexpected attack. (Of course, there are other ways to defend oneself such as through the use of mace or a taser.) Whether or not you have the ability to handle yourself in a fight is often beside the point, due to the fact that violent encounters can come in the form of sudden attacks and not fair fights.

If It Looks Too Good to Be True, It Probably Is

Due to the rise of the internet, the inclusion of the axiom "if it looks too good to be true, it probably is" is particularly relevant, mainly due to the fact that there really is "no such thing as a free lunch." McKissack recognizes the fact that it is only human nature to look for a solution to a problem or a good deal, and this can many times be our downfall.

While the internet does afford us the potentially positive benefits of connecting with other people, it also provides criminals with the ability to remain anonymous. Countless stories are out there about men and women who agreed to meet up with an internet acquaintance for a date, appointment, or exchange only to be attacked and killed upon finding out that their internet "friend" was not who they said they were.

Before meeting someone offline that you met online, the author tells us that we need to ask ourselves:

>> See if anyone can vouch for the stranger's true identity.

>> Make sure someone knows where you are and have them check in with you.

>> Plan to meet in a public place and opt to bring a companion.

Don't Assume "Lightning Never Strikes Twice"

McKissack goes on to note that just because an unfortunate and unusual situation has happened to you once, you should not assume that it cannot happen again just because "lightning never strikes twice." Instead, he encourages you to consider the reasons why perhaps you may have been considered a favorable target for such an occurrence.

McKissack uses the example of his experience owning a Honda Accord, a car that he had stolen from him a whopping four times. He later discovered that Accord was a model that was extremely popular amongst car thieves and subsequently bought a different car.

Thus, if you are routinely falling prey to wrongdoing, ask yourself: What behaviors do I need to change? Am I putting myself at unnecessary risk? Am I allowing myself to be put in dangerous situations? McKissack notes, "an ounce of prevention is worth a pound of cure."

Don't Judge a Book by Its Cover

McKissack touches upon how our perception of things around us determines our safety. He urges not relying upon stereotyping strangers based on appearances. In other words, "Don't judge a book by its cover. Instead, be appropriately concerned with behaviors."

It's important to understand that the most dangerous people may often appear harmless. Thus, you may need to reevaluate your childhood stereotype of a "stranger" who dons a ski mask and a black sweatshirt.

Trust Your Instincts

Above all, McKissack urges us to trust our instincts. He advises us that if we ever feel unsure of ourselves, there is probably a reason why and that we should not ignore this feeling.

He reminds us that oftentimes, the best way to respond to a situation is with the intuition of a child combined with the intellect of an adult, and that we should exercise extreme caution before giving our trust to anyone. As a whole, McKissack lays out a logical, succinct blueprint we should heed to avoid dangerous situations and people.

Share Your Concerns with Someone You Trust

If you're involved in a situation that is playing out over time, you may well be able to reach out to someone you know well and trust. Use them as a sounding board for your concerns.

Sometimes, the simple act of having to verbalize the situation that you find yourself in will lead you to a clearer sense. Those who care about you can raise issues you may not have considered or suggest a safe way to gather more information before proceeding.

Chapter **15**

Ten Ways to Address Over-Saving

Yes, it's true: Over-saving is possible. Some people, in fact often the best savers, get hooked on amassing more and more money and have trouble enjoying and using their money. Super savers and money amassers generally equate more money with more financial security.

If you don't have this problem of over-saving, and you think that this is like hearing about someone complaining that they have too much caviar, please consider reading on — you may have loved ones, friends, or other contacts who suffer from this problematic issue!

This chapter can help you address and temper this mindset.

Understanding the Over-Saver Mindset

Just as some people think that their financial problems would be solved if only they could earn a higher income, over-savers typically believe that if they could reach a greater level of assets, they'd be more relaxed and could do what they really want with their lives. The bar, however, continually gets raised, and the level of "enough" is rarely attained. For this reason, some of the best savers and money accumulators also have the most difficulty spending money, even in retirement.

Some super savers have insecurities relating to money. Specifically, they view amassing financial assets as providing them with safety and security that extend far beyond the financial realm. While having more financial assets, in theory, provides greater financial peace of mind, these riches don't necessarily provide more of the other types of security — friendships, for example, for which hoarders are searching.

When money hoarders marry people with significantly different money personalities, fireworks ensue, and divorce may be the result. Financial security doesn't translate into emotional security and contentment.

Achieving a certain level of affluence can provide for greater access to quality healthcare. However, once one reaches the point at which quality healthcare is the norm, the incessant pursuit of more money can have a negative impact on an individual's long-term health and quality of life. For example, super savers often believe that they will be better protected as seniors and better able to enjoy their retirement years with hefty account balances. But the pursuit of more money, which typically entails longer work hours and greater stress, can lead to more health problems before and in retirement.

Many super savers, who also tend to be obsessed with work, come from homes and families where they felt on the edge economically and emotionally. Although there are so many things that we can't control in the world, money amassers typically derive a sense of both economic and emotional security from saving a lot of money.

Super savers have an amazing ability to selectively hear particular stories that reinforce rather than question their tendencies and beliefs. For example, stories periodically surface about how the legions of baby boomers retiring will bankrupt Social Security and cause a stock market collapse. Super savers batten down the hatches, save more, and invest even more conservatively when such stories worry them. News stories about stock market declines, corporate layoffs, budget deficits, terrorism risks, rising energy prices, and conflicts in the Middle East and elsewhere cause super savers to close their wallets, clutch their investments, and worry and save more.

Balancing Spending and Saving

Most people don't want to work their entire adulthood. And, even if they do enjoy working for pay that much, who wants to live on the edge economically, always dependent upon the next paycheck to be able to pay the monthly bills?

That's why you should avoid the extremes of overspending and over-saving. Consider the analogy to eating food: Eat too little or not enough of the right kinds of foods, and you go hungry and possibly suffer deficiencies of energy and nutrition; too much eating, on the other hand, leads to obesity and other health problems.

Overspending and its companion, under-saving, hamper your ability to accomplish future personal and financial goals and in the worst cases, can lead to bankruptcy. Over-saving can lead to not living in the moment and constantly postponing for tomorrows that we may not live to enjoy.

Remember Goldilocks and her quest at the bear's home for the bowl of porridge that was not too hot and not too cold and a bed to rest in that was not too hard and not too soft. Everyone should save money as a cushion and to accomplish important personal and financial goals.

Keeping Money Accumulation in Proper Perspective

As with any good habit, you can get too much of a good thing. Washing your hands and maintaining proper hygiene is worthwhile, but it becomes problematic when you obsess over cleanliness and it interferes with your life and personal relationships.

Conquering over-saving and an obsession with money typically requires a mix of education and specific incremental behavioral changes. Substantive change typically comes over months and years, not days and weeks.

The vast majority of super savers work many hours and may neglect their loved ones and themselves. They typically need to work less and lead more balanced lives. That may involve changing jobs or careers or simply coming up with a "stop-doing list," the opposite of a "to-do list."

Giving Yourself Permission to Spend More

Money amassers usually need to discover how to loosen the purse strings. Figuring out how to spend more and save less is a problem more folks wish they had, so consider yourself lucky in that regard! Give yourself permission to spend knowing that the money you've saved will continue to grow and be available to you as you need it.

Doing Some Retirement Analysis

Understand the standard of living that can be provided by the assets you've already accumulated. There are numerous useful retirement planning analytic tools you can use to assess where you currently stand in terms of saving for retirement.

Among the various mass market website retirement tools, I really like T. Rowe Price's (www.troweprice.com/usis/advice/tools/retirement-income-calculator) and Vanguard's (investor.vanguard.com/calculator-tools/retirement-income-calculator/).

Getting Smart about Investing Your Money

While super savers love watching their money grow, some have trouble with investing in volatile wealth-building investments like stocks because they generally abhor losing money. Even bonds can be a turn-off because they, too, can fluctuate in value.

So, part of the challenge with getting comfortable with spending more of your money is to get wiser about investing. Please see Chapter 10.

Going On a News Diet

Super savers often benefit from minimizing and even avoiding news programs that dwell on the negative, which only reinforces your fears about never having enough money. One justification that super savers use for their actions that constantly resurfaces in the news is the litany of fears surrounding the tens of millions of baby boomers hitting retirement age around the same time. The story goes that retiring boomers will cause a mammoth collapse of the stock market as they sell out to finance their golden years. Real estate prices are supposed to plummet as well, as everyone sells their larger homes and retires to small condominiums in the Sun Belt.

Such doomsaying about the future of financial and real estate markets is unfounded. The fear that boomers will suddenly sell everything when they hit retirement is bogus. Nobody sells off their entire nest egg the day after they stop working; retirement can last up to 30+ years, and assets are depleted quite gradually. On top of that, boomers vary in age by up to 16 years and, thus, will be retiring at different times. The wealthiest (who hold the bulk of real estate and stocks) won't even sell most of their holdings but will, like the wealthy of previous generations, pass on many of their assets.

Treating Yourself to Something Special

Regularly buy something that you historically have viewed as frivolous but which you can truly afford. Once a week or once a month, treat yourself!

By all means, spend the money on something that brings you the most joy, whether it's eating out occasionally at a pricey restaurant or taking an extra vacation during the year. How about tickets to your favorite sporting events or other performances?

Buying More Gifts for the People You Love

Money hoarders actually tend to be more generous with loved ones than they are with themselves. However, over-savers still tend to squelch their desires to buy gifts or help out those they care about.

Think about those you care most about and what would bring joy to their lives. Try hard to think about what they really value and enjoy.

Going Easy When It Comes to Everyday Expenses

How would you like it if a family member or close friend followed you around all day and totaled up the number of calories that you consumed? Well, then, why would you expect your family to happily accept your daily, weekly, and monthly tracking of their expenditures? In some families, super savers who habitually track their spending drive others crazy with their perpetual money monitoring. Personal finances become a constant source of unnecessary stress and anxiety.

Especially if you're automatically saving money from each paycheck or saving on a monthly basis, does it really matter where the rest of it goes? (Of course, none of us wants family members to engage in illegal or harmful behaviors. But other than that, enjoy life.)

Work at establishing guidelines and a culture of spending money that everyone can agree and live with. Some couples, for example, only discuss larger purchases, which are defined as exceeding a certain dollar limit such as $100 or $200. Parents who teach their children about spending wisely pass along far more valuable financial lessons than do elders who nag and complain about specific purchases.

Index

A

AAA Foundation for Safety, 215

AccuQuote (website), 209

actuarial value, 60

addictions, 202–203

Adjusted Gross Income (AGI), 62

ADP National Employment Report, 84

advisors

  attorneys, 80

  benefits of hiring, 72

  financial advisors and planners, 72–74

  insurance agents, 80

  interviewing, 72

  investment managers, 76–77

  overview, 71

  real estate agents, 77–79

  tax preparers and advisors, 79

Aetna, 201

Affordable Care Act (ACA), 59

age, 62

Agnew, Spiro, 30

Alcoholics Anonymous, 203

American Council of Life Insurers, 198

American Home Mortgage, 32

American Rescue Plan Act (ARP) of 2021, 59

ammos, 238

anarchy, 238–239

Anderson, Jack, 237

annualized numbers, 91

Anthem, 201

The Anxiety Toolkit (Boyes), 73

appliance service plans, 196–197

appliance warranty, 196–197

Arab oil embargo, 29–30

asset allocation

  defined, 185

  overview, 185–186

  for retirement, 186–187

  for shorter-goals, 187–188

Associated Press, 85–86

assumptions, 2

Athens Stock Exchange General Index, 19

attachment to investments, 184

attorneys, 80

auto insurance

  car buying and, 214–215

  collision coverage, 214

  comprehensive coverage, 214

  elements of policies, 213–214

  ensuring adequate coverage, 59

  liability coverage, 213

  medical payments coverage, 214

  other riders coverage, 214

  other than collision coverage, 214

  overview, 213

  reducing driving risks, 215

  uninsured motorist coverage, 214

auto lease, 140

auto loans, 140, 185

auto theft, 256

B

baby boomers, 260

backup plans, 250

Bank of America, 32

bank savings account, 154

Barber, Brad, 168, 179

The Beardstown Ladies' Common-Sense Investment Guide, 168

bear markets, 27, 31, 68

Bear Stearns, 32

Beck, Glenn, 116–117, 234

benefit period, disability insurance, 206

Bennett, Paul, 113

government spending, 236–237

Grace, J. Peter, 237

Great Depression, 27–29, 83–84

great San Francisco earthquake, 27

Greece, 19

Greenspan, Alan, 128, 235–236

Gregory, David, 105, 106

gross domestic product (GDP), 23–25, 91, 93, 95–96, 104–105

growth oriented investments, 162

guidance, 98

guns, 238

gurus. *See* experts

H

Hassett, Kevin, 31

Healthcare Bluebook (website), 159

healthcare proxy, 218

health insurance
  checking coverage, 43
  employer's coverage, 63
  ensuring adequate coverage, 58
  long-term care, 200
  overview, 199
  reviewing, 200

health insurance subsidies
  calculator, 61–63
  cost-sharing subsidies, 61
  levels of plans, 60
  Medicare eligibility effects on, 63
  overview, 59–60
  premium tax credit subsidies, 61
  understanding, 60–61

health savings accounts (HSAs), 201–202

The Healthy Mind Toolkit (Boyes), 73

high-frequency data, 98

home
  assessing, 10
  new and existing home sales, 101
  ownership, 171–173

home insurance
  catastrophic coverage, 211–213
  dwelling, 219
  dwelling coverage, 210
  earthquake insurance, 212–213
  elements on homeowner's policy, 210–211
  ensuring adequate coverage, 59
  flood insurance, 211
  loss of use coverage, 210
  medical payments coverage, 211
  other structures coverage, 210
  overview, 210
  personal liability coverage, 211
  personal property coverage, 210

home warranty plans, 198

housing assistance, 65–66

Housing Choice Voucher Program, 66

HSA Administrators (website), 202

Huffington Post, 85

Hulbert, Mark, 118

Hurricane Katrina, 211

hurricanes, 211–212

I

icons, used in this book, 2–3

identity theft prevention
  computer and files, protecting, 222
  freezing credit reports, 221
  monthly financial statements, reviewing, 220
  overview, 219
  personal information on checks, avoiding, 221
  phishing, 220
  phone inquiries, 220
  receipts, securing', 220
  reviewing credit reports, 221
  snail mail, protecting, 222
  solicitous emails, ignoring, 220
  unnecessary account closure, 220

About the Author

Eric Tyson is an internationally acclaimed and best-selling personal finance author, lecturer, speaker, and former advisor. Through his work, he is dedicated to teaching people to manage their money better and to successfully direct their own investments.

Eric is a former management consultant to businesses for which he helped improve operations and profitability. Before, during, and after this time of working crazy hours and traveling too much, he had the good sense to focus on financial matters.

He has been involved in the investing markets in many capacities for more than three decades. Eric first invested in mutual funds when he opened a mutual fund account at Fidelity in high school. With the assistance of Dr. Martin Zweig, a famous investment market analyst, Eric won his high school's science fair with a project on what influences the stock market. In addition to investing in securities over the decades, Eric has successfully invested in real estate and started and managed his own business. He has counseled thousands of clients on a variety of investment quandaries and questions.

He earned a bachelor's degree in economics at Yale and an MBA at the Stanford Graduate School of Business. Despite these impediments to lucid reasoning, he came to his senses and decided that life was too short to spend it working long hours and waiting in airports for the benefit of larger companies.

An accomplished freelance personal finance writer, Eric is the author of numerous best-selling books, including *For Dummies* books on personal finance, investing, mutual funds, and home buying (co-author), and is a syndicated columnist. His work has been featured and quoted in hundreds of national and local publications, including *Kiplinger's Personal Finance magazine,* the *Los Angeles Times,* the *Chicago Tribune, The Wall Street Journal,* and *Bottom Line Personal,* and on NBC's *Today Show,* ABC, CNBC, FOX, FOX Business, PBS's *Nightly Business Report,* CNN, CBS News Radio, Bloomberg Radio, National Public Radio, and Business Radio Network. He's also been a featured speaker at a White House conference on retirement planning.

You can visit him on the web at www.erictyson.com.

Dedication

Numerous people at Wiley helped to make this book possible. They include acquisitions editor Tracy Boggier and development editor Linda Brandon and copy editor Christine Pingleton! Thanks also to everyone else at Wiley who contributed to getting this book done and done right.

Thank you also to our brilliant technical reviewer, Dr. Mary Ann Campbell, who helped improve both the accuracy and insights of this book!

Publisher's Acknowledgments

Senior Acquisitions Editor: Tracy Boggier

Development Editor: Linda Brandon

Copy Editor: Christine Pingleton

Technical Editor: Dr. Mary Ann Campbell, CFP

Production Editor: Mohammed Zafar Ali

Cover Image: ©jgroup/iStock/Getty Images

Dummies is the global leader in the reference category and one of the most trusted and highly regarded brands in the world. No longer just focused on books, customers now have access to the dummies content they need in the format they want. Together we'll craft a solution that engages your customers, stands out from the competition, and helps you meet your goals.

Advertising & Sponsorships

Connect with an engaged audience on a powerful multimedia site, and position your message alongside expert how-to content. Dummies.com is a one-stop shop for free, online information and know-how curated by a team of experts.

- Targeted ads
- Video
- Email Marketing

- Microsites
- Sweepstakes sponsorship

20 MILLION PAGE VIEWS EVERY SINGLE MONTH

15 MILLION UNIQUE VISITORS PER MONTH

43% OF ALL VISITORS ACCESS THE SITE VIA THEIR MOBILE DEVICES

700,000 NEWSLETTER SUBSCRIPTIONS TO THE INBOXES OF

300,000 UNIQUE INDIVIDUALS EVERY WEEK

# of dummies

Custom Publishing

Reach a global audience in any language by creating a solution that will differentiate you from competitors, amplify your message, and encourage customers to make a buying decision.

- Apps
- Books
- eBooks
- Video
- Audio
- Webinars

Brand Licensing & Content

Leverage the strength of the world's most popular reference brand to reach new audiences and channels of distribution.

For more information, visit dummies.com/biz

PERSONAL ENRICHMENT

Staying Sharp

9781119187790
USA $26.00
CAN $31.99
UK £19.99

Facebook

Carolyn Abram

9781119179030
USA $21.99
CAN $25.99
UK £16.99

Guitar

Mark Phillips
Jon Chappell

9781119293354
USA $24.99
CAN $29.99
UK £17.99

Investing

Eric Tyson, MBA

9781119293347
USA $22.99
CAN $27.99
UK £16.99

Beekeeping

Howland Blackiston

9781119310068
USA $22.99
CAN $27.99
UK £16.99

Digital Photography

Julie Adair King

9781119235606
USA $24.99
CAN $29.99
UK £17.99

Meditation

Stephan Bodian

9781119251163
USA $24.99
CAN $29.99
UK £17.99

Pregnancy
ALL-IN-ONE
6 Books

9781119235491
USA $26.99
CAN $31.99
UK £19.99

Samsung Galaxy S7

Bill Hughes

9781119279952
USA $24.99
CAN $29.99
UK £17.99

iPhone

Edward C. Baig
Bob "Dr. Mac" LeVitus

9781119283133
USA $24.99
CAN $29.99
UK £17.99

Crocheting

Karen Manthey
Susan Brittain

9781119287117
USA $24.99
CAN $29.99
UK £16.99

Nutrition

Carol Ann Rinzler

9781119130246
USA $22.99
CAN $27.99
UK £16.99

PROFESSIONAL DEVELOPMENT

Windows 10

Andy Rathbone

9781119311041
USA $24.99
CAN $29.99
UK £17.99

AutoCAD

Bill Fane

9781119255796
USA $39.99
CAN $47.99
UK £27.99

Excel 2016

Greg Harvey, PhD

9781119293439
USA $26.99
CAN $31.99
UK £19.99

QuickBooks 2017

Stephen L. Nelson, MBA, CPA, MS in Taxation

9781119281467
USA $26.99
CAN $31.99
UK £19.99

macOS Sierra

Bob "Dr. Mac" LeVitus

9781119280651
USA $29.99
CAN $35.99
UK £21.99

LinkedIn

Joel Elad, MBAs

9781119251132
USA $24.99
CAN $29.99
UK £17.99

Windows 10
ALL-IN-ONE
10 Books in one!

Woody Leonhard

9781119310563
USA $34.00
CAN $41.99
UK £24.99

SharePoint 2016

Rosemarie Withee
Ken Withee

9781119181705
USA $29.99
CAN $35.99
UK £21.99

Fundamental Analysis

Matt Krantz

9781119263593
USA $26.99
CAN $31.99
UK £19.99

Networking

Doug Lowe

9781119257769
USA $29.99
CAN $35.99
UK £21.99

Office 2016

Wallace Wang

9781119293477
USA $26.99
CAN $31.99
UK £19.99

Office 365

Rosemarie Withee
Ken Withee
Jennifer Reed

9781119265313
USA $24.99
CAN $29.99
UK £17.99

Salesforce.com

Liz Kao
Jon Paz

9781119239314
USA $29.99
CAN $35.99
UK £21.99

Coding

Nikhil Abraham

9781119293323
USA $29.99
CAN $35.99
UK £21.99

dummies.com

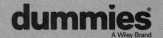
dummies
A Wiley Brand

Learning Made Easy

ACADEMIC

9781119293576
USA $19.99
CAN $23.99
UK £15.99

9781119293637
USA $19.99
CAN $23.99
UK £15.99

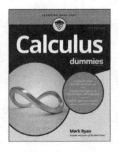

9781119293491
USA $19.99
CAN $23.99
UK £15.99

9781119293460
USA $19.99
CAN $23.99
UK £15.99

9781119293590
USA $19.99
CAN $23.99
UK £15.99

9781119215844
USA $26.99
CAN $31.99
UK £19.99

9781119293378
USA $22.99
CAN $27.99
UK £16.99

9781119293521
USA $19.99
CAN $23.99
UK £15.99

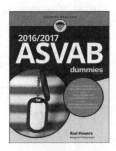

9781119239178
USA $18.99
CAN $22.99
UK £14.99

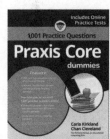

9781119263883
USA $26.99
CAN $31.99
UK £19.99

Available Everywhere Books Are Sold

dummies.com

A Wiley Brand

Small books for big imaginations

GETTING STARTED WITH Coding
Get Creative with Code!
Camille McCue, PhD

9781119177173
USA $9.99
CAN $9.99
UK £8.99

MODDING Minecraft™
Build Your Own Minecraft Mods!
Sarah Guthals, PhD
Stephen Foster, PhD
Lindsay Handley, PhD

9781119177272
USA $9.99
CAN $9.99
UK £8.99

MAKING YouTube® VIDEOS
Star in Your Own Video!
Nick Willoughby

9781119177241
USA $9.99
CAN $9.99
UK £8.99

DESIGNING Digital Games
Create Games with Scratch™!
Derek Breen

9781119177210
USA $9.99
CAN $9.99
UK £8.99

GETTING STARTED WITH Raspberry Pi™
Program Your Raspberry Pi!
Richard Wentk

9781119262657
USA $9.99
CAN $9.99
UK £6.99

EXPERIMENTING WITH Science
Think, Test, and Learn!
Chris J. Mullins, PhD

9781119291336
USA $9.99
CAN $9.99
UK £6.99

CREATING Digital Animations
Animate Stories with Scratch™!
Derek Breen

9781119233527
USA $9.99
CAN $9.99
UK £6.99

GETTING STARTED WITH Engineering
Think Like an Engineer!
Camille McCue, PhD

9781119291220
USA $9.99
CAN $9.99
UK £6.99

WRITING Computer Code
Learn the Language of Computers!
Chris Minnick and Eva Holland

9781119177302
USA $9.99
CAN $9.99
UK £8.99

Unleash Their Creativity

dummies.com

dummies®
A Wiley Brand